To my family, for their love and support,
and in memory of my godfather, Captain Frank Lynch,
and my friend, John Joseph Cahill

Chris Burke and Jo Beth McDaniel

★ ★ ★ ★ ★ ★ ★ ★ ★ ★ ★ ★ ★ ★ ★

A Special
Kind of Hero

★ ★ ★ ★ ★ ★ ★ ★ ★ ★ ★ ★ ★ ★ ★

Chris Burke's
Own Story

DOUBLEDAY
NEW YORK LONDON TORONTO SYDNEY AUCKLAND

PUBLISHED BY DOUBLEDAY
a division of Bantam Doubleday Dell Publishing Group, Inc.
666 Fifth Avenue, New York, New York 10103

DOUBLEDAY and the portrayal of an anchor
with a dolphin are trademarks of Doubleday,
a division of Bantam Doubleday Dell
Publishing Group, Inc.

Library of Congress Cataloging-in-Publication Data

Burke, Chris, 1965–
A special kind of hero: Chris Burke's own story/by Chris Burke
and Jo Beth McDaniel.—1st ed.
p. cm.
1. Burke, Chris, 1965–   . 2. Life goes on (Television program)
3. Handicapped in television. 4. Television actors and actresses—
United States—Biography. I. McDaniel, Jo Beth.
PN2287.B79A3 1991
791.45′028′092—dc20
[B] 91-3536
CIP

ISBN 0-385-41645-8
Printed in the United States of America
October 1991
First Edition

1 3 5 7 9 10 8 6 4 2

INTRODUCTION

★ ★ ★ ★ ★ ★ ★ ★ ★ ★ ★ ★ ★ ★ ★

MY NAME is Christopher Joseph Burke. I was born August 26, 1965, in New York City. My parents, Marian and Frank Burke, were upset when they first found out I had Down syndrome. The doctor said it wasn't easy raising a child with Down syndrome, and told them to put me in an institution. But they fell in love with me and took me home. I am very thankful they took me home and didn't put me in an institution like people did back then. I don't think I would have liked it there.

I loved growing up in New York City. When I was born, my brother J.R. was twelve, my sister Anne was fourteen, and my sister Ellen was sixteen. They love me a lot and we had lots of fun together. They took me to the playground with them, and they taught me how to read and swim and play basketball and ride a bike. Me and J.R. are real good buddies. I wanted to grow up to be just like him.

Some people treat me differently because I have Down syndrome, but I just want to be treated like anyone else. And some people think that just because I have Down syndrome, I'm stupid or handicapped. I don't feel that way. My Down syndrome never kept me from doing anything I wanted to do. Everybody is born in different ways. I just happened to be born with an extra chromosome, but it doesn't make me feel any different. I don't like it when people say I am a victim, or when they say I suffer from it. It's not a disease. I don't like it when they show the pictures of the little chromosomes, because it's personal to me. But I think it's great to have an extra chromosome and I like talking about it. It doesn't make me feel "down." Actually, I call it "Up syndrome" because I am happy and excited about my life.

All my life, I've wanted to be an actor. When I was growing up, I loved to watch movies and television. I always wished that I could be on the screen, too. I thought I could help the handicapped by showing people that we're not so different after all. I liked to write stories for my favorite television shows with a handicapped actor. I wanted to play those parts myself. And I dreamed that someday I could do that.

My family was always there to help me. They are wonderful. I feel lucky that they are my family. I owe everything to them. My parents raised me to be strong and independent. They taught me all through my life to work hard and focus on my abilities, not my disabilities. And my family believed in me. They didn't think I could be an actor, but once it happened, they stuck with me and helped me make my dream come true.

So this is my story, but it is also the story of Frank and Marian Burke, Ellen and Anne and J.R., and my friends and teachers and coworkers who helped make all this possible. I love them all so very, very much. They helped me do what I wanted to do with my life. What I wanted to do ever since I was a little tyke, was to let people know that the inside of me is just like everyone else.

ONE

★ ★ ★ ★ ★ ★ ★ ★ ★ ★ ★ ★ ★

AMERICA WAS AT WAR. The Japanese had bombed Pearl Harbor, the Nazis were marching through Europe, and Frank Burke, a gangly Irish kid from the Upper West Side of Manhattan, was eager to jump in the fray. The week he turned eighteen, Frank joined thousands of other young men in New York's Grand Central Palace, where he volunteered for service in the newly formed Army Air Corps.

A year and a half later, Frank was a left-waist gunner on the B-17 bomber plane *Maggie's Drawers.* In the four months since he arrived in Bury St. Edmunds, England, he had flown eight missions, six deep into Germany, including the first bombing of Berlin. That flight had almost ended tragically over the English Channel when the bomber ran low on fuel. The crew hastily threw guns and equipment overboard to lighten the load, making it back to the base with only fumes in the gas tank. The close brush with tragedy had done little to sway Frank's enthusiasm for his duty. In his innocence, he still felt invincible in combat. He was the youngest of his crew, with a flaming head of red hair, a sharp, dry wit, and a new promotion to sergeant in the Army Air Corps 94th Bomb Group.

On Easter Saturday, April 8, 1944, Frank awoke to a beautiful sunrise, then prepared for his ninth mission. He visited the base chaplain to receive general absolution, then tucked his rosary beads into the pocket of his flight suit. *Maggie's Drawers* would fly second lead in a formation of six hundred other bombers, traveling deep into Germany. Allied strategy at the time was to hit air depots, flight schools, and aircraft factories to achieve air superiority over the invasion area and weaken the forces for a ground assault.

Frank checked his oxygen mask and the heating wires of his flight suit, which would keep him warm and breathing in the thin air and subzero temperatures at twenty-five thousand feet. As the bomber taxied down the airstrip, he wondered what would be served for dinner when he returned. He had no way of knowing that this mission on April 8, 1944, would change his life forever.

The flight was five hours of boring routine, except for the chilling sight of Nazi Germany stretching out below. The crew tensed as they neared the target in Handorf and heard, through the roar of the plane's engines, the thunder of German guns below. Intelligence had estimated eleven antiaircraft guns, called "Famous 88s," at the target. To Frank, it seemed as if they were all pointed straight at the metal sides of *Maggie's Drawers*.

Frank was aiming at a German fighter plane when suddenly an explosion of shrapnel ripped through the B-17, knocking him to the deck. He forced himself up, but his knee buckled in pain.

The intercom crackled: "Ground fire hit one engine. We're still going on in. Everyone okay?"

Frank pulled himself up with a groan. "I'm okay," he radioed back, leaning against his gun. A few minutes later, when *Maggie's Drawers* reached the Handorf air depot, the bombardier released hundreds of bombs.

As the plane was turning back toward England, the men breathed deeply with relief. Suddenly, another German barrage peppered its right side. The plane again shook violently with the explosion. But this time, a thin plume of smoke fanned back from the right wing, flames licking up toward the gas tanks.

"Second engine's on fire!" the pilot screamed over the intercom. *"Bail out! Bail out now!"*

Frank's mind jangled with raw fear. Below lay Nazi Germany, and the town near the air depot they had just bombed. He choked on the acrid smoke pouring through the cabin and stumbled for balance as the plane began its sickening descent. Blood sloshed in his boot, a troubling sign that his knee, now numb, was more badly wounded than it felt. He ripped away from his station, groping for his chute pack. As he strapped it onto his chest, he noticed a charred hole where a piece of shrapnel had burned through it.

He jerked the red handles of the escape door. No give. Try again. Stuck.

Frank stepped back on his wounded leg to kick the door out into the gray. He froze for a moment: the plane was in a deep dive, about twenty-one thousand feet above the ground. Flak still spat in the air, its puffs of black smoke crackling with explosion. He curled into a fetal position and rolled clear of the plane.

It was his first jump from an airplane. The Army didn't train the men for parachuting because it knew more men would die practicing than would ever be forced to bail out in combat.

On earlier missions, Frank would have known only to pull the cord after he jumped, an action that could be fatal if a soldier didn't clear the plane. But just three weeks before, the man who packed his chute had given him a few survival tips.

Now, as he fell two hundred feet a second through the sky, Frank recalled the advice. He stretched out his arms and legs, making a stiff X with his body. A swirling gray mist blinded him as his ears were filled with the shrill hiss of air.

He delayed pulling the rip cord until he had reached a lower altitude. When he yanked it, his body was jerked from its fall, suspended in an eerie quietness.

Looking up, he was relieved to see a full, billowing white mushroom. But in each panel, blue sky shone through a softball-sized hole where the shrapnel had burned. Frank murmured a quick Hail Mary, adding a plea for his crewmates. He scanned the skies, but saw no other parachutes. As his eyes began to focus on the ground below, he realized he was being pulled backward by the wind. Then he remembered to pull hard on one strap to spin around toward the direction he was blowing. He sent up another prayer, this one thanking the man who had taught him the parachuting lesson that may have saved his life.

Suddenly, high above him, *Maggie's Drawers* exploded. Fire rained down—twisting, burning chunks of metal all too close to his chute.

Behind him, a buzzing noise grew into a roar. An FW 190 fighter plane was circling him so closely he could see the grim German face in the cockpit. Each time the plane drew near, Frank's parachute ruffled, then flattened slightly in the backdraft. The ground seemed to be rushing up to meet him—fast, too fast.

Looking down, he could now see green forests and tiny farms growing larger each second. As his feet swept above the trees, Frank aimed for a small clearing to avoid the branches. He landed not too roughly, pulling back on his straps in the last few seconds.

Shaking, Frank unstrapped his chute, buried it beneath a pile of leaves, and walked away. Or tried to. His legs buckled. He sat down to inspect the large rip in the left knee of his flight suit.

A fresh wave of fear hit him when he saw his blood-soaked leg. "I'm wounded, I'm in Germany, and I can't escape," he thought miserably. In his innocence and bravado, he had never dreamed of this experience: bad things only happened to "the other guy," the careless ones. It was a rude awakening for Frank to realize that within the span of a few minutes, he had become "the other guy."

Then he heard shouts. A ragtag group of about twenty German peasants, mostly elderly and children, ran over and surrounded him. They waved rifles, sticks, and pitchforks, cursing him in angry German.

Frank had no weapon: none of the Americans carried handguns when flying over Germany. If they had the bad luck to go down in the Third Reich, well, it was better to hide out or surrender with as few complications as possible. A gun would only give the Germans more reason to shoot.

Frank pointed to the jagged tear in his flight suit, miming to them that he needed to check his wound. The crowd only moved closer, jabbing at him with increasing bravado. An elderly woman was knocking him soundly over the head when a German soldier appeared, gun raised. He motioned the group away, then turned to Frank and said, in well-practiced English, "For you, the war is over."

The soldier half-carried him through the forest to the prisoner truck. A few miles down the road, Frank was reunited with his crew. Of the ten men who began the day in *Maggie's Drawers,* two didn't make it: the pilot, Lieutenant James Burnette, and copilot, Lieutenant Gilbert Leverance, were killed in the explosion.

The eight survivors were herded into a train for the journey to Dulag Luft, the Nazi interrogation center near Frankfurt. At each station, they were led out and paraded before townsfolk, who laughed and spit at them. Even the children in the crowds taunted the men, swooping pointed hands downward with the sound effects of a crashing plane. But the worst times were when the train would stop suddenly, and the German soldiers would rush off to their bomb shelters. Minutes later, the prisoners would listen uneasily as British air squadrons dropped bombs around them.

At Dulag Luft, a Nazi officer offered to send in a doctor to tend to Frank's knee, provided Frank tell them about his missions. Frank declined the help. By then, the thumb-sized piece of shrapnel lodged against the bone had swelled his leg to an ugly purple mass.

A few days later, the prisoners were sent to Stalag 17-B, the camp near Krems, Austria, that held forty-three hundred captured American airmen. In its three other sections, Stalag 17 held another thirty thousand prisoners from European countries, who were forced to work in factories and fields. The camp was a dreary, muddy place, its rough-hewn wooden barracks surrounded by layers of barbed wire fences separating it from a small forest and a vast, open field. Armed guards with dogs policed the perimeter, while others watched closely from towers at each corner.

Frank entered the compound on a stretcher, a temporary bandage on his leg. Like all new arrivals, he was greeted with a raucous gauntlet of Americans eager for any news from home.

"Anybody from Omaha?"

"Who plays softball?"

"Are the Dodgers winning?"

"What's the latest on the hit parade?"

Frank laughed at that question. "You won't believe it," he yelled. "It's a song called 'Don't Fence Me In'!" The group roared with laughter.

The levity stopped when the newcomers were led inside the barracks to have their heads shaved. They were stripped, sent into a huge room with showers, and sprayed with a delousing solution.

Frank was now prisoner number 106161 of the Third Reich.

As a noncommissioned officer, he was protected from forced labor by the Geneva Convention. Ironically, that same status put him low on the list for medical care. The Germans wouldn't waste scarce medicine on anyone who was not helping the cause.

American doctors in the camp switched his bandages frequently, but they had no tools to remove the festering metal deep in his knee. They warned that his leg would have to be amputated if it was left untreated much longer. It was no surprise to Frank: his entire left leg was swollen and throbbing with pain. Weeks passed with Frank in agony before he was sent to the prison hospital for surgery to save his leg.

The operation left a crude six-inch scar that would flame with arthritis even forty years later. But Frank was healing. Within weeks, he was hobbling, then walking, then jogging around the compound, building up strength.

He returned from the hospital to bunk with his best friend Mickey Daly, the radio operator from *Maggie's Drawers*. At thirty-seven, Daly was one of the oldest men in the camp, and he coached the young Frank on the art of survival. The two formed a "combine" with another two bunkmates to scavenge for extra food and supplies, and they traded their allotted cigarettes with fellow POWs for food.

Mickey, who called his friend "Red" for his full head of auburn hair, remembers that Frank was well liked by the other prisoners. "Red had a good attitude," he says. "I thought the world of him. He kept his sense of humor, though there wasn't much fun there."

It was a harsh life, and some guards seemed to relish making it worse. They tormented the prisoners in little ways, withholding letters and packages from home and insulting them at every chance, calling them "Luftgangsters." At sunrise, they strode through the barracks with shouts of *"Rausch! Rausch!"* as they herded the POWs into the yard for a head count. The prisoners kept clean by turning up the bathroom faucets and running naked underneath the chilling spray. Every three months, the guards shaved the prisoners' heads, then led them into the shower room for a warm spray of delousing solution. The men hated this degrading routine, and a few conspired to end it by rubbing oleo and sand through their hair to jam the German hair clippers. The trick worked, but it backfired: the group was sent to the "boob," rough solitary confinement sheds, for several weeks. The perpetrators were barely fed while confined, so each barracks saved the Red Cross food parcels due to the men during that time, and they had a feast of canned goods when they were released.

To prevent the prisoners from stockpiling food for use in an escape, the guards pierced holes in rationed cans so that the food inside would quickly spoil. Mickey taught Frank how to seal the holes with oleo, not for escape, but in case the food supply dwindled. The guards collected the empty cans and tossed them outside the fences to make a noisy carpet for anyone who dared break out. A few men dug tunnels out to the forest area and crawled to an uncertain freedom, but most of the men considered escape attempts too dangerous.

Mostly, the POWs faced an irritating, stifling boredom. "There's nothing worse than having nothing to do," Frank remembers. Stalag 17-B had a few surreptitious freedoms. Some men had devised stills for bootleg whiskey and put together crude radios to catch news from the outside. There were softball games and basketball games pitting prisoners from, for example, Pennsylvania against those from New York. Church was held each Sunday, including mass said by a priest who had been captured. Sometimes a few POWs dressed like women, put on some music, and staged a show, at which the men would howl and scream as if Betty Grable herself was singing to them. It was mystifying to Frank at first, but before long, he joined the choir and the basketball team, worked as intelligence supervisor in his barracks, and was helping the priest by serving mass.

Occasionally, one of many letters from home would make its way through to Frank. He especially enjoyed hearing from his girlfriend, Marian Brady, a freshman in college back in New York. Frank had met Marian in August of 1942, when she was sixteen and working part-time wrapping gifts at Macy's on 34th Street in New York City. She was one of a legion of high school girls called "Saturday Onlys," a misnomer because the girls worked both Thursday nights and Saturdays, for wages of about $3.50 a week. Marian had taken the job, as well as babysitting jobs, just for spending money. Frank, then seventeen, was out of high school and held a full-time job delivering packages between departments. He was taken with the petite, blond, blue-eyed Marian at first glance. "I kept making more trips to her department than was necessary," he says. Within the week, he had wangled a proper introduction from a co-worker, then waited a few days to ask her out. Marian remembers him walking over to her that day, his head up and a big smile on his face. "I just knew, 'Oh, he's going to ask me out,' " she says. He was a tall, handsome young man, with a full head of thick auburn hair and deep dimples in his cheeks. But Frank was an Irish lad from a tenement neighborhood in West Harlem. Marian was more accustomed to dating boys she had known since childhood, in her middle-class Bronx neighborhood of Kingsbridge, yet Frank's quick wit and easygoing manner soon disarmed her, and she accepted his request for a date.

That Saturday evening, Frank took the long subway ride from Manhattan up to Kingsbridge. When he arrived at the Brady apartment, Marian's mother Helen took one look at him and said to herself, "This is the man my daughter's going to marry." She told Marian, who thought her mother had lost her mind. But Marian enjoyed the evening. She and Frank walked down the Grand Concourse of the Bronx to the elegant Loew's Paradise, to see the movie *Mrs. Miniver,* a wartime drama starring Greer Garson and Walter Pidgeon. Afterward, they stopped for ice cream cones, then ambled down the concourse. "Back then, you could walk all over the Bronx with no fears," says Marian. By the time they had returned to the tree-lined streets of Marian's neighborhood, Frank had asked Marian to go roller skating the next week at the nearby Fordham Roller Rink.

Within a few weeks, they were spending a great deal of time together. Marian met Frank's parents at a veterans' dance, and he got to know her family better at church activities. She liked Frank's dry humor and the way every situation held a joke or a challenge that he always seemed ready to meet. Frank was infatuated with Marian's cheerfulness and delicate beauty.

Like most girls her age, Marian dreamed of settling down and getting married, though it seemed far away. She knew from her babysitting jobs that she loved children, and she knew she wanted a family, though she didn't stop to think about the particulars. At sixteen, her relationship with Frank didn't cause many more thoughts on the subject. "Going steady" was not encouraged by Marian's friends or family. "We all played the field," says Marian. "I made a habit of dating others."

Yet the two shared much in common. Like Marian, Frank was a full-blooded Irish American, a reasonably devout Catholic from a stable family. His father, Henry Burke, had been a barge operator, a coal company engineer, a longshoreman, then an elevator operator, moving from job to job with every layoff during the Great Depression. His mother Catherine had lost two sons and a husband in the flu epidemic of 1917 before marrying Henry and having three more sons: Henry, John, and Frank. She also had a daughter, Mary, from her first marriage, who kept an eagle eye on her half brothers to make sure they stayed away from trouble in the streets.

Frank's neighborhood, Manhattanville, was tight-knit, with very little crime. In the heat of the summer, people kept their doors and windows open with no fear. Police patrolled the area and knew the families by name. Once, when nine-year-old Frank hitched a free ride aboard a trolley, a police officer collared him and whisked him home. Upon the news of his son's crime, Frank's father bellowed, "Take him away!" as the officer pulled Frank toward the door to take him to jail. "I was crying, holding onto my sister, and she was holding tight to the kitchen sink," recalls Frank. "I didn't realize until years later that it was just a big act. But I never hitched a ride again."

The Depression years that began when Frank was five years old were tough on the large family, but they always managed to have food on the table. Frank remembers an exchange over dinner one night, when his brother complained that the bread was too hard. His father retorted brusquely, "It's harder when there isn't any."

Frank was a teenager before he felt paper money: when he ran to the store for his mother, he carried a pad of paper on which the grocer would write down the credit he was extending. The Burkes got free rent by supervising and cleaning the buildings where they lived. Through the years they moved up from cold-water flats, heated only by stoves in the kitchen and parlor, to an apartment with the luxury of radiators. The boys took care of the building furnace and the tenants' garbage, sweeping and mopping each of the five floors.

From an early age, Frank and his brothers also delivered newspapers, shined shoes, and sold firewood to help out. "We were always hustling. We were poor and everybody else was poor, but nobody told us we were poor, so we didn't know it."

The only time Frank felt self-conscious about his lot in life was in public high school, where he worked mornings and afternoons for the federally funded National Youth Administration to earn free lunch coupons. "It embarrassed me," he says. "I tried to hand my lunch coupon over as discreetly as possible." In class, he enjoyed poetry and Spanish, but maybe because he was so busy working, Frank never applied himself much in school. His senior year, he worked from 1 P.M. to 7 P.M., delivering telegrams for Western Union, to pay for his class ring and senior dues.

By the time Frank met Marian, he was pleased at the way he was moving up in the world, with his sixteen-dollar-a-week job at Macy's. He even splurged on a membership in the neighborhood pool, a step up from his boyhood swimming spot at the docks on the Hudson River.

In contrast, Marian Brady's family had weathered the Depression years in style. Her father, Joe Brady, like his father before him, was a New York City policeman, a cherished civil service job that afforded the family a few luxuries. At the height of the Depression, the Brady family took an ocean cruise on the *Belgianland* to Bermuda and Halifax, and another across the Great Lakes to Chicago's World's Fair in 1933. "We were middle class, but to have a city job at that time was almost like being in the upper class," Marian explains. "At the time, I didn't realize the difference between my family and those of many friends, whose parents were struggling very hard."

Joe Brady was an affable man who took great interest in his children's schooling and activities. Neither he nor his family considered police work dangerous, since Joe's father had enjoyed a long police career. Joe was shot once while apprehending a robber, but Marian was only three, and she remembers the incident only from the yellowed newspaper reports she read much later. Another time, Marian, then eleven, was walking home from school when she saw her father being chased by a crazy woman with a pitchfork.

Both Joe and his wife Helen grew up in Manhattan; Helen's parents were illiterate Irish immigrants who scraped and saved to make a better life for their children. They were proud of Helen's middle-class lifestyle and her business school education. Even after Helen was married, she still brought her wash to her mother Bridget. But when a nosy neighbor criticized Bridget for babying Helen, she responded in her imperious Irish brogue, "I raised my daughter to be a secretary, not a washer-woman!"

Like Bridget, Helen Brady wanted only the best for her children. She enrolled her daughters in tap-dancing lessons and sent Marian, her older sister Eileen, and her younger brother Bud to the small but strict Sisters of Charity grammar school, with twenty-five students in each grade. Upon graduation, Marian joined her older sister at the renowned Cathedral High School, a large girls' school in Manhattan. There, Marian was active in the drama club, starring as Amy in a production of *Little Women*. After school, she often joined the "bobby-soxers" at Frank Sinatra and Tommy Dorsey concerts in the Paramount Theatre. Marian had free entry to the shows because she babysat the theatre manager's children.

Several times a year, Helen took Marian and her friends to Manhattan for a fifty-cent Chinese lunch and a fifteen-cent matinee at the elegant Roxy Theatre. Other Saturdays, Marian spent the day at the local Kingsbridge movie theatre, where she gazed at the silver screen and dreamed of being an actress like her favorites, Shirley Temple and Judy Garland.

Mostly, the Brady family life centered on the local Catholic church and the parish, where basketball games and big-band dances were held at different churches each Friday night. The crowd danced "The Lindy," "The Big Apple," and "The Shag," and joined up for conga lines that stretched across the floor.

Living in a safe haven in the midst of the horrors of the Great Depression gave Marian a narrow view of life's tragedies. "Looking back on it, I realize that I led a sheltered life. I remember thinking as a child that nothing bad would ever happen to us. I was so confident of life. I thought people should be around us because then nothing bad would happen to them, either."

Frank and Marian had dated only a few months when he told her of his plans to enlist in the Army Air Corps. He wanted to enter the Air Cadet program that could train him to be a pilot, navigator, or bombardier on a bomber plane. Volunteering would give him that choice more than if he was drafted later. Frank's older brother Henry was already serving in the Aleutian Islands after enlisting in the National Guard in 1940, and his brother John would soon serve with the amphibious combat engineers in Europe. Just days after Frank turned eighteen in September 1942, he entered the Grand Central Palace, a midtown New York exposition hall the Army had taken over as a recruiting office. Upon the physical examination, doctors found that his tonsils were infected, and the Army wouldn't accept him until he had them removed. Frank immediately scheduled the surgery, then returned to his job at Macy's, anxiously waiting for the call that would jettison him into the excitement of training and combat.

It didn't take long. In January of 1943, Frank was called up for basic training in Atlantic City. "I wasn't surprised when he enlisted, but I was surprised he was called up so quickly," says Marian. Before he left, Frank and Marian shared a New Year's Eve celebration, ending in an embrace in Marian's living room. Frank kissed her and gazed for a long time into her blue eyes. "I never thought I would say this to any girl," he started shyly. "I love you, Marian." It was the first time he had uttered the words. Marian told Frank she loved him too, but it was a response with a fraction of the intensity. "I was touched. But I loved lots of boys back then," she says.

For the next year, Frank zigzagged across the United States, from schooling in Syracuse University to bombardier training in San Antonio, Texas. Then, when the Air Corps decided it didn't need more bombardiers, he volunteered for gunnery school in Las Vegas. Marian and Frank wrote letters frequently, enjoying this new phase of their courtship. Still, Marian's social life was in full swing. She was a pretty, outgoing teenager, not the type to sit around and pine for someone far away, no matter how much she loved him.

Frank was more serious in his affection. He had not dated anyone else since he met Marian, and he missed her terribly. One snowy evening in Dyersburg, Tennessee, he and two friends slipped away from the air base, evading military police to catch a train bound for New York City. When Frank arrived at the Brady apartment the next day, Marian was out with friends, but her mother tracked her down. She came rushing back home to see Frank. "He was so handsome in his uniform," she said. "We spent a wonderful evening together." There were no more chances to visit: in January of 1944, Frank was assigned to the 94th Bomb Group in Bury St. Edmunds, England.

By then, Marian was caught up in the whirl of collegiate life. That fall, she had entered the College of Mount St. Vincent, a prestigious Catholic women's school in Riverdale, New York. Just a year before, further education had seemed out of reach, especially for a female in a family where no one had gone to college before. But her close friend and cousin, Pat Egan, was planning to attend, so Marian's parents decided they would send her there, too. "I remember walking onto campus the first day, feeling like the world was my oyster," Marian recalls. "It was such a beautiful place, overlooking the Hudson." For the next four years, Marian left her family home each day for the forty-minute ride to the campus. She took liberal arts and business courses, working toward a business degree. She planned to be a corporate secretary, a prestigious, well-paying job.

Marian continued to write Frank, and she was proud to know someone involved in the war. "It was very popular for a girl to go visit the family of her boyfriend in the service," says Marian. "So I did it too. It gave me the chance to get to know the Burkes. We talked about the letters we had received, to see if we could give each other some sort of news the other didn't have."

Then in April, the Burkes called Marian with the grim news: they had just received an Army telegram informing them that Frank's plane had been shot down. It devastated Marian. In her sheltered life, she couldn't visualize anything that serious happening to someone she knew. Six anxious weeks passed before a second telegram reassured them that Frank was alive, but imprisoned in Stalag 17-B.

Even with this latest news, Marian could not imagine the hardships of Frank's life as a war prisoner. "We didn't know how bad it was. I could tell from his letters that he wasn't happy there, but beyond that, I didn't know. We never heard much about the prison camps." Unlike press reports on modern-day war, news during World War II focused more on the positive, morale-building stories; negative aspects such as hostages were censored or treated lightly. Some stories portrayed the camps as pleasant country clubs, with POWs busily playing table tennis and ice hockey.

The conflicts that raged all over the world seemed far removed from the busy schedule of Marian's campus life. "It was not like having a war in your own country, or like today, when you see everything right as it is happening," says Marian. "A boy from my neighborhood was killed, and I had a cousin in the war. But unless you were married to a soldier, or had a brother fighting, it was hard to know what they were going through. The knowledge disseminated was so slight, and so censored. I bought war bonds and sent care packages to Frank. But mostly, I went on with my silly little life."

That life held a full schedule of collegiate social events. Marian was a cheerleader for an intramural basketball team and entered singing contests with her college class. She had lost interest in acting, but she joined friends for campus horse shows and horseback riding in New Rochelle. On weekends, they traveled into Manhattan to shop or visit theatres and museums. Always, there were brunches and lunches, dinners and dances to attend. "We did mostly girl things because so many of the boys were away in the war," she says. Still, Marian managed to date frequently, seeing either the boys left behind or soldiers home on leave.

Afternoon tea dances were the rage that year, and Marian wrote about them to Frank with enthusiasm. She described in detail the band that would be playing, the new hat, dress, and gloves she would be wearing, and the elegant tea, cookies, and petit fours that would be served on china. She often added, "I wish you were here to go with me." These letters thoroughly amused Frank and his bunkmates, who read them while sitting on the thin straw mattresses of Stalag 17. A big dining event for them was to get something other than weak soup and canned rations for supper.

Frank's letters, when they made it back, were hard to read. Censors chopped out so much that the paper looked like Swiss cheese; what remained looked like a shopping list. He asked Marian to send coffee, canned food, cocoa, chocolate, chewing gum, toothpaste, and cigarettes for bartering. By Geneva Convention rules, the prisoners were fed basic meals, but they were far from tasty or nourishing. Frank dreamed of his favorite foods: the chocolate éclairs in the bakeries of Manhattan, the fresh lobsters from the coast, the huge dinners his mother would be cooking back home.

And always, he prayed. The fear—of hunger, death, and disease—was ever present. As a prisoner, he knew his conditions could easily take a turn for the worse. Just before he arrived, some POWs had tried to escape the camp through a tunnel. The Germans shot them, then fired into their barracks, killing some of their friends as well. Another time an American soldier lost his mind and started scaling the fences just a few feet from the guard tower. Frank ran after him, calling to the guard, "Crank! Crank! He's sick, crazy! It's okay!" The guard, who could have easily reached from his tower and plucked the crazed man off the fence, instead shot him dead.

At night, Frank lay awake, thinking about the horror around him and the life he wanted to live if given the chance. He made a vow: if he lived to see his twentieth birthday, he would appreciate every minute he was given and never be upset at anything that happened to him again.

Frank's birthday, September 9, came while he was still in camp, a place where such days usually meant little to the jaded prisoners. But Frank was overjoyed that his prayers for his life had been answered. And Mickey Daly surprised him with a crude birthday cake made of C-ration biscuits, baking soda, and chocolate. That night, Frank repeated his vow in his prayers, bargaining with God that if he lived through this, his would be an honest and fruitful life. "Being held prisoner gave me a sense of what was important," he says. "It separated the wheat from the chaff."

A few months after Frank was shot down, the camp celebrated the news that Allied forces had invaded Western Europe on D day. Even the most cynical believed that by September, they would be headed back home. But September came, and they were still imprisoned. Fall dragged past, and by Christmas, the grim news of the Nazi campaign at the Battle of the Bulge filtered through. Morale was low; the prisoners realized that Allied forces were in peril. Their freedom, which had seemed only weeks away, was now in jeopardy.

The arrival of the Christmas Red Cross shipment raised the men's spirits again until the boxcars were unloaded. Inside were no new blankets, no warm clothes, no good food for a holiday dinner. Instead there were, inexplicably, hockey sticks, thousands of table-tennis balls, and rolls of toilet paper. There was only use for the last. "That just sank us in a deeper despair," says Frank. "It was a terrible Christmas, a terrible winter."

Then springtime came to Austria, and with it the news that the Allied forces were closing in on the Third Reich. British and American planes, flying in from Italy, buzzed over the camp all day and night, dropping bombs on nearby military targets. The American P-38s were the most beautiful sight to the prisoners, who rushed outside to cheer when they heard the whir of engines overhead. "I remember the P-38s doing these slow rolls over the camp, to let us know, 'Hey, fellows, we're winning this war. We're right here on top of you,'" says Frank. One night, an Allied plane lit the darkened camp with flares; the Germans cowered, waiting for bombs to hit their guardhouses, but the planes were just marking the camp so they wouldn't inadvertently bomb it.

As the prisoners celebrated each new wave of Allied planes, their captors grew harsh with anxiety. The Nazis saw that the end of the war was near, and they feared their fate in the hands of the advancing Russians, who were rumored to be torturing and killing the Nazis they captured. The Nazi central command decided to approach the Americans for a peaceful surrender, using the thousands of Allied prisoners as a bargaining chip. In April, all stalags in the Third Reich were ordered to move Allied prisoners to Berchtesgaden, a city southeast of Munich in Germany and the site of Hitler's mountain home.

One cold spring morning, the Germans hurried all able-bodied prisoners outside the Stalag 17 compound. The POWs weren't aware of the reasons, but they knew they were marching west, through Austria, toward Germany.

From dawn to dusk, the guards brutally pushed the four thousand prisoners onward, while Nazi SS troops patrolled them on motorcycles. The POWs would be shot if caught straying beyond the tight perimeter. Few of the men would have dared: their Allied intelligence officers had heard on the radio that the end of the war was near, and they urged everyone to stick close together on the march for safety. Deserters from the German Army filled the hills along the roads, and they might, in fear, shoot at any POWs who wandered their way.

The group trudged through the hills and valleys surrounding the Alps, always wondering what awaited them ahead. In their haste, the guards rarely stopped to dole out water or food. Frank does not know how many prisoners died or fell ill during the march: when prisoners could not keep up, they were taken away in a truck to an unknown fate. Frank and his friends took matters into their own hands. They traded their cigarettes and soap secretly with townsfolk along the way, sometimes netting a few potatoes or a loaf of bread. At night they would split up, one to search for shelter, the others for food, water, and firewood to keep them warm.

Frank went hunting for food, carrying a chocolate bar which he could sometimes trade for something more substantial that would feed four men. Once he came upon a house, and he asked the woman who lived there for a trade. She declined, but her little girl inside heard him say "chocolate," and she began crying for the candy. Frank was torn. He knew that if he didn't find anything, the chocolate would be the night's meal for the four men in his combine. When Mickey Daly returned from hunting for firewood, he found Frank crying, upset that he was in such a state in his world that he could not give a piece of chocolate to a child who cried for it.

Another night, Frank returned from foraging with a huge grin on his face. "You're not going to believe this," he said, and he opened his jacket.

"My God, Red, you stole a chicken!" said Mickey in surprise. They carefully sneaked away to a remote area to cook the bird, then the four men of the combine shared their only nourishing meal in the long weeks. "The only thing we didn't eat on that chicken was the feathers," recalls Mickey.

The secrecy was important: there was no way of knowing how severely the guards would have dealt with the theft. But the men were desperate. They knew they were quickly starving to death. In eighteen days, they had marched nearly 120 miles. In that time, Frank had lost 30 pounds; he had just 135 pounds left on his six-foot frame.

Frank and his friends considered themselves lucky to find a shelter, such as a barn or shed, within the guards' perimeter. More often, they slept on the cold ground with only their overcoats for warmth.

Even in his misery, Frank was awed by the beauty of the Alpine region. He swore that someday he would return to enjoy it as a free man. But now, the whole country was under siege, and there was danger at every turn. Outside Linz, Austria, Frank's group passed the bombed remains of a railroad bridge. They bedded down in a nearby hayloft, looking up at the moon and stars through the open roof, which had also been raked with bombs. A few hours later, more explosions lit the sky. The prisoners awakened from an already restless sleep, praying silently as bombs whistled down. The next morning, they were amazed to hear that none of the large group had been injured.

Nights were usually passed in such rural areas, far away from towns. But in the small village of Klam, Austria, the guards formed a circle around the outskirts, and the prisoners were on their own within it. Many Austrians despised their Nazi occupiers; a few of them treated the Allied prisoners with some respect and understanding. Frank was able to trade his shirt for a small knife, which he could use for cutting any food he might scrounge. An Austrian gentleman approached him on the street and said, in halting English, "That is too bad your president died." Frank, hardened by the guards' constant torments, answered sarcastically, "Yeah, and that's too bad Hitler died." The man shook his head sadly. "No, no, I listen to BBC [British Broadcasting Company radio reports]. Your President Roosevelt died." It was a shock: President Franklin D. Roosevelt had steered the United States through the Depression and the war for more than twelve years. The soldiers grieved deeply at the sobering news and wondered what could happen next.

That Sunday, Frank and Mickey attended mass in Klam's small Catholic church. "It was odd, sitting and listening to the familiar Latin phrases, as prisoners among our bitter enemies. People were looking at us strangely. We were on different teams but, in the big picture, on the same team."

On May 2, 1945, the ragtag group met advancing American forces, who promptly arrested the Nazi guards, then marched onward. Frank's freedom came, ironically, in Braunau, Austria, the birthplace of Adolf Hitler, only two days after the Nazi leader committed suicide in his bunker. Five days later, Germany surrendered to allied forces.

The Army didn't know quite what to do with the released American POWs. Frank and his friends waited several days in an abandoned Braunau aluminum factory, then were sent by truck and train back through France. Within a few weeks, Frank crossed the Atlantic Ocean on a troop ship headed back home.

The ship's tables of food were a shock to his eyes and stomach. Frank had to fight his instincts to keep from grabbing everything and hoarding it for later. He knew he would never forget the nights of hunger, fear, and exhaustion, and the attitude of survival his experience had fostered. Though just twenty, he was now a serious, reflective man, fully aware of the fragility of life.

From then on, he would remember his vow to God, the nights he had begged to reach his twentieth birthday. He would take life as it was offered, no questions asked. "My life had been spared, when so many were lost," he says. "I realized that you must be thankful for life and play the hand you were dealt."

TWO

★ ★ ★ ★ ★ ★ ★ ★ ★ ★ ★ ★ ★ ★

AS MUCH as Frank now valued his life, he returned to New York confused. In the safety of his parents' home, he was somber and shaken, and in no mood for a celebration. But his parents threw a small dinner party, inviting Marian and some friends from the neighborhood, including a German couple Frank had known since his childhood. The Germans arrived bearing flowers and candy for Frank, and they tried to apologize to him for what their countrymen had done. Frank couldn't bear to listen to them. He and Marian left the apartment to walk around the neighborhood.

Marian was happy that Frank was home, but she grew uneasy talking with him. This gaunt man who returned from the war was a total stranger to her, not at all like the easygoing, jovial boy for whom she had waited all these years. "He was so thin, and so serious, almost sullen," recalls Marian. "He wasn't himself. He wasn't willing to relax much yet." Though he was just twenty years old, he seemed more like fifty to her.

In the two and a half years Frank had been away, Marian had blossomed into a beautiful woman, with a self-assured collegiate style. In contrast, Frank was shy about his appearance: his old clothes hung loose on his skeletal frame, and the short, choppy haircut from his prison days seemed to take forever to grow out.

In the weeks that followed, Frank also struggled to cope with a life that suddenly included basic comforts and freedoms. After a year under armed guard, behind rows of fences, Manhattan stretched out before him, but he didn't know what he wanted to do. "Some days I'd be walking down the street and suddenly stop and say, 'What am I doing here? Why am I here?' I was so used to the regimentation of camp, with someone always telling me where to be and where to go. This new freedom confused me."

Frank slept fitfully, tortured by nightmares that he was still in camp, trying to avoid a German guard or a bomb falling through the sky. After a sixty-day furlough, he was to report back to duty in Atlantic City. While he didn't think he would be shipped out to combat again, he had no guarantees. "I didn't know what would happen to me," Frank recalls. "I kept thinking, 'What are they going to do with me?'"

The uncertainty about his future added to Frank's discomfort, which would today be called "post-traumatic stress disorder," or "hostage syndrome," or a variety of other psychological names. In 1945, he was expected to simply jump back into his old life. He was barraged with questions about the year he had spent as a prisoner, but he brushed them off with a stony silence. He could not and would not talk about it: not with his parents, not with his friends, and especially not with Marian.

The war still raged in the Pacific, but to Frank, Americans didn't seem to care. He anguished over the soldiers still in combat, including his two brothers. "Life was going on as usual," recalls Frank. "There didn't seem to be much concern that soldiers were still getting killed. It bothered me to hear people griping about having to have ration coupons for meat, or complaining about not being able to get good cigarettes because of the war. Women thought it was a real coup to acquire a pair of nylon stockings. It seemed to me that everyone was wasting a lot of worry about insignificant things."

Nylons seemed very important to Marian. She was just a year younger than Frank, but she was unblemished by the war fought abroad. Her life was centered firmly on her college activities, which, in Frank's eyes, seemed the ultimate in frivolity. When Marian asked him to her beloved afternoon tea dances, Frank turned her down cold. "I was sorry the boys were away at war, but I was still having a good time," says Marian.

Frank also smarted at the way Marian had continued to date other men while he was pining for her in Stalag 17. "I was heartbroken when he was shot down, and when I learned that he was a POW, but I still kept on with my life," says Marian. "That was hard for him to understand when he came home. He had changed, but I hadn't. He wanted me to catch up with him, but I couldn't." Little arguments blew up into large ones, and before long, the two parted company.

In retrospect, Marian is glad the relationship crumbled. "We both needed to go our own ways. We were still very young," she says.

After his sixty-day furlough, Frank was assigned to duty at an Army Air

Corps base in upstate New York. Then a few months later, the Army enacted a policy releasing former prisoners of war from further military obligations. Frank returned to New York City with an honorable discharge, moving into his parents' apartment. Within a month, he went back to work at Macy's selling men's underwear. That job was a different type of combat: America was suffering a wartime shortage of underwear, so shoppers lined up outside, then crowded through at opening time, grabbing everything on the shelves.

Frank was renewing his friendships in the old neighborhood, but he still made trips to Kingsbridge. Marian's mother Helen continued to invite him over for dinner when Marian was away. Helen still believed her first instinct about Frank and felt that, given time, Frank and her daughter would mend their broken romance. She and her husband both liked this mature, mannerly young man. When he was able to relax, his sense of humor seemed as strong as before.

In time, Frank adjusted to life back in the States. Like many who grew up in the hardship of the Depression, he wanted a secure job that would weather economic changes. He recalled the Depression-era affluence of families, like Marian's, whose fathers held civil service jobs. So he entered a school that prepared students for the grueling New York City civil service exams. Frank had regained his health and stamina, and he performed well on both the fire and police department tests, passing the difficult written exams plus a physical endurance test of distance running, lifting weights, and climbing fences. He chose police work, because he felt most comfortable in its semimilitary environment. "It was similar to the Army," says Frank. "Maybe I worried a little about the danger involved in police work, but I was young and still felt somewhat invincible."

That summer of 1946, Frank ran into Marian at Rockaway Beach. Frank could see that Marian had matured. Marian was glad to see him, and she could tell that he was more relaxed and happy again. He surprised her with the news that he had passed the police exam and would soon be entering police academy as a probationary patrolman. "He seemed very determined to get his life back in order," she remembers. "But he wouldn't walk me home that night, and he waited several months before he asked me out. He didn't want to seem too easy."

That fall, when Frank called and asked her out, Marian accepted with enthusiasm. "Everything was wonderful. That evening, we just knew we were meant to be together," she recalls. There was one minor setback, when Frank refused to go to a college dance with Marian. But by the spring, they became engaged during festivities surrounding Marian's college graduation. For the following year, Marian planned the wedding while working as a corporate secretary. She enjoyed her job, but she waited anxiously for the day she would be married and have a family to raise. "It was just the normal thing to want," she says. "I never really thought of having a career, except as a wife and mother. We were fortunate that Frank made a good salary, so I could make that my career. I think a mother at home is very important, but I realize many people don't have that choice."

Frank and Marian were married on October 2, 1948, in St. John's Church in Kingsbridge. Their reception was held in Manhattan's McAlpin Hotel, diagonally across from the Macy's store where they had first met.

The couple spent their wedding night at New York's Waldorf-Astoria Hotel, then took a train down to the King and Prince Hotel on St. Simons, a serene little island getaway on the Georgia coast. They made friends with other honeymooning couples, rode bikes around the millionaires' mansions on adjacent Jekyll Island, and dined at night in the elegance of The Cloister on nearby Sea Island.

After two romantic weeks, they returned to New York to live in an apartment in Stuyvesant Town, a high-rise community that the Metropolitan Life Insurance Company had just opened in downtown Manhattan. Though most young couples in New York were still desperately seeking anywhere to live due to a severe postwar housing shortage, Frank's veteran status put him high on the list for this luxurious new rental complex with a projected population of thirty thousand. "It was the new thing," says Marian. "You had to be a veteran in order to get an apartment there. It was a marvelous place to go as a newlywed, because everyone was young and fun and ambitious. It was really like a small town within a city." The apartments had beautiful wood parquet floors, walk-in closets, and big windows. Marian loved the small working kitchen with an adjacent eating nook. "Growing up, we had always eaten on a table in the kitchen. It was all so modern."

Soon after they had settled into the new apartment, Marian found out she was pregnant. "My mother was so thrilled and so proud of me," she recalls, laughing. "She thought I was a genius. It had taken her eight years to get pregnant." When they went together to buy a layette, her mother embarrassed Marian by boasting to the sales clerks, "She's only been married seven months and she's already having a baby!" That summer, nine months after the honeymoon, Marian gave birth to a blond-haired, blue-eyed baby girl, whom they named Ellen.

Frank was working as a policeman in Highbridge, a peaceful Jewish and Irish neighborhood in the Bronx, just north of Yankee Stadium. He remembers the job fondly. Back then, few criminals carried guns and fewer still would have dared shoot at a policeman. Frank served at school crossings and patrolled the tree-lined streets, stopping to chat and drink coffee with shopkeepers along the way. Marian helped him study for promotion tests and frequently timed him in shooting practice.

Since Frank's pay was good, and the family's expenses were low, there were never times of hardship. In their second year of marriage, the Burkes bought a new two-door Plymouth, though Marian did not learn to drive it until years later. Twenty-seven months after Ellen was born, Marian gave birth to Anne, a red-haired sprite. Another twenty-seven months passed, and they welcomed the birth of Francis Dewey Burke, Jr., whom they promptly dubbed "J.R."

Motherhood was all Marian had expected it to be. "There were moments when I wished I was out having a good time rather than washing diapers, but overall I enjoyed it. Frank was a big help with the children, and that made it much easier for me. And I always had my mom to help me." Frank and Marian were also able to take vacations by themselves, while Marian's mother watched the children.

The Burkes' circle of friends grew quickly, made up of neighbors and many of Marian's high school and college friends who had moved to the complex. Most of the neighbors were, like them, young couples with small children. Parks and playgrounds filled the courtyards; shops and restaurants lined the nearby streets. The children could walk to nearby schools, yet beyond them lay the broad world of all the city could offer. It was, Marian and Frank thought, the perfect place to raise a big family.

Sometime in the first few years of their marriage, Frank finally began to open up and share his war experiences with Marian. She was shocked to hear about the conditions of the camp, and the brutal march he had endured. "It took him such a long time to be able to discuss it," says Marian. Still, when the movie *Stalag 17* came out in 1953, Frank preferred to go watch it by himself. But his internal wounds were healing. Before long, he jokingly referred to Stalag 17 as "Krems University" (Krems was the closest town to the camp), because he had learned so much about life while he was there. And Marian learned to defuse his occasional bouts of stress by asking, "Is it life-threatening?"

One night, Marian playfully asked Frank what he thought about most during his time as a POW. Frank replied without hesitation: chocolate éclairs. Marian was miffed at first, then found it funny. A few months later, on April 8, the anniversary of the day Frank was shot down, she prepared an elaborate steak and lobster dinner, topped off with the biggest, richest chocolate éclairs she could find. The children were too young to understand the significance of the dinner until years later, when April 8 had become a regular holiday in the Burke household. On those nights, the Burkes talked of answered prayers, of the importance of family, friends, and freedom. But most of all, they celebrated survival, and the way life's problems can rebound in wonderful and mysterious ways.

The tradition spread to other setbacks the family encountered. After Frank lost a special assignment that had allowed him to work regular weekday hours, he and Marian went out for a fun night on the town. "If anything didn't go the way we wanted, the first chance we had, we would go out and celebrate," says Marian. "It was our way of saying, 'We'll work it out. We'll make the best of it.' It helped us get back on track and feel better about it."

Marian had yet to suffer any setbacks or tragedies. Her parents were both in relatively good health, and her children were breezing through their early years with few problems. Then one morning, her mother Helen went into the hospital because she had not been feeling well. While she waited for the doctors to treat her, her gallbladder burst. Helen died almost immediately, at the age of sixty-three.

The anger and shock of the loss consumed twenty-eight-year-old Marian. "It was terrible, terrible," says Marian. "I've never gotten over it. She was so important to me." She and her mother had always been close, but Marian's early years of motherhood had drawn them into a tight, steady friendship. They frequently shopped together, lunched together, and talked on the phone every day. Her mother had helped her raise all three children, babysitting them so that she and Frank could go out for special occasions. And once a week, Joe and Helen had joined the Burkes for a big family dinner.

Three months after her mother died, Marian noticed that Anne, just three, had a slight fever. She put her to bed for a few days, but the fever persisted. Marian called her pediatrician, a woman with whom Marian had become close friends during her children's early years. The doctor made a house call to examine Anne, then held a light at the foot of the bed. "Look at the light, Anne."

Anne struggled to sit up. "I can't. My legs hurt," she replied. The doctor gave her medicine, telling Marian to check her temperature and call her a few hours later. That afternoon, Anne seemed to feel better, but Marian was surprised to see that the fever had not broken. When she called, the doctor told her, "Marian, wrap her in a blanket and get her to the hospital immediately. I'll meet you there." Marian called a neighbor to come watch the other two children, then rushed Anne by cab to the hospital. There the pediatrician examined her again and gave a grim diagnosis: Anne had either poliomyelitis or spinal meningitis. Only a spinal tap would determine which. The husband of the neighbor who was watching the other Burke children had met Marian at the hospital and tried to console her. Frank had gone into work not thinking anything was seriously wrong with his daughter. "How's everything?" he said cheerfully when Marian called him at the precinct. Marian, in a daze, could barely get the words out, and it didn't help that Frank, on duty, couldn't come join them at the hospital for hours.

The tests came back positive for polio, the dreaded viral infection that attacks nerve cells in the brain and spinal cord, causing paralysis of the leg, arm, or trunk muscles in up to 75 percent of the cases. In 1954, when Anne contracted it, any news of the contagious disease struck fear in the hearts of people everywhere. Polio had by then reached epidemic proportions, affecting more than fifty thousand people each year in the United States. Dr. Jonas Salk was a year away from government approval of his polio vaccine, which, along with Dr. Albert Sabin's oral vaccine in 1961, drastically reduced the number of polio infections in the world.

Word of Anne's diagnosis spread quickly throughout Stuyvesant Town. The next day, when Marian and her two other children stepped onto the elevator, a woman quickly pulled her children out and ran away from them. "I was devastated," says Marian. "It upset me to feel rejected. But I couldn't blame her. Who would want polio?" Frank asked his patrol car partner if he wanted him to change to a foot post, just in case Frank was contagious. The partner, who had young children of his own, decided against it.

Marian's father, now retired from police work, watched the other children while Frank was at work and Marian was at the hospital with Anne. Other neighbors offered help and support, and the Burkes' church congregation prayed for the little girl's recovery. Marian anguished throughout the ordeal, thinking of a second cousin whose legs had been crippled from polio since the 1930s. She knew some victims died, while others had to be hooked to iron lungs when their breathing muscles were paralyzed.

The spinal injury was already affecting Anne's ability to walk or sit up. She was in the hospital, completely covered up in a closed room, for ten days. No medication could kill the virus or control its spread, so Anne was treated with bed rest and tight wraps of hot, moist bandages. "My sister Eileen and I would take turns going into the room," says Marian. "It bothered Anne that no one could stay in the room with her." Once she was over the worst, Anne sat outside the room, refusing to go inside.

Throughout the ordeal Marian still grieved. "My mother would have been such a staunch rock for me during this time," says Marian. "I felt such a void from her death." That confidence Marian had grown up with, in which she could not even imagine anything going wrong, was broken. "It was such a shock because I had always anticipated everything being perfect. It was very difficult at first when all these tragedies came into our lives."

In the end, Anne came through fine, though her left leg was affected slightly and required six months of intensive physical therapy.

But more bad news soon shattered Marian and Frank. After J.R., Marian and Frank had tried unsuccessfully to have more children. Doctors couldn't find the problem, but advised them that there was little that could be done. In the late 1950s, even to medical specialists, most infertility was accepted as fate. Marian and Frank were dismayed at the diagnosis, but they shook it off and went on with their lives. Soon she recovered and resumed her normal childhood activities. Through the next years, the Burke children stayed busy in their local Catholic church and parochial schools. Before long, Marian had scout troops to lead, baseball and roller hockey games to attend, piano lessons and dancing classes to schedule. She nursed all three children through measles, chicken pox, and other minor childhood ills. Still she was grieving the death of her mother, and she looked for other ways to fill the void in her life.

Marian found a partial answer one day while talking with a neighbor whose daughters had been acting in television commercials, a new venture that was just beginning to grow rapidly in the mid-1950s. Marian came home and took a long look at her children. In her motherly pride, she felt that they were as bright, attractive, and photogenic as any of the kids on TV. That week, she gathered up the best of their photos and met with an agent. Before long, Marian was taking the three to auditions and tryouts all over New York.

The kids enjoyed it. From the start, they were in demand and having fun, and they were thrilled to see themselves in the multitude of print ads and on television. "It was hard work, with long hours," says Marian. "But I took pride in the fact that they were capable of doing so well. I know that I was in the right place at the right time with the right type of children. It was such a boost to our morale, after all we had been through." Anne stayed the busiest, with her red hair, freckles, and huge grin. She starred in a long-running gasoline company TV commercial, and she posed for a bubble gum poster that was displayed in stores during Halloween season for nearly two decades. J.R. was one of two finalists for a role on the hit TV series "Flipper"; had he won it, he and someone in the family would have had to move to Florida for the duration of filming. When he didn't get the part, Marian and Frank were almost relieved that their lives wouldn't be so drastically changed.

Frank and Marian took pains to keep the children's careers from turning them into "stage brats." Marian watched other mothers pull their kids out of school and activities, encouraging them to cultivate friendships just with other child actors. "It was sad, sort of like what happened to Judy Garland and so many others in Hollywood," Marian says. "We made sure it wasn't their whole life. They were always back home to their friends in the afternoon. They still had other interests."

The children's careers lasted until they all reached adolescence and gradually turned their interests to other activities. The pay had been excellent, especially after they moved to a new agency that concentrated on TV commercials. In a decade of modeling, they starred in twenty-five TV commercials and dozens of print ads. Marian pooled the children's earnings into one savings account, which would later pay for three college educations. "Their earnings gave us the wherewithal to do other things, rather than just save for their educations," says Marian.

The family had always had a taste for travel and the new worlds it opened to them. The Burkes vacationed in Bermuda and made annual trips to Florida beaches. Marian's father, Joe Brady, took each of his granddaughters to Europe. Then they found a cottage in Massapequa, a friendly little Long Island beach town forty miles from New York. Marian learned to drive the family car for the first time, now that she needed to make the commute to the beach home and to her college, where she was on the alumni board. "It gave me so much freedom," says Marian. "Growing up in New York, I had always taken public transportation."

Ellen says she felt very fortunate in her upbringing. "We were middle class, but we had a boat, a summer home. We took vacations. We had more than other people around us, but we somehow weren't as spoiled as other children who had less than us. We always had jobs such as babysitting. Somehow my parents were able to combine having a wonderful life and not spoiling us. Our personalities are so diverse, but my mother always made sure we lived in peace and harmony. Those are tough tricks. I don't know how they did it."

Frank had started taking college classes at night in 1947 but dropped them when Marian became pregnant, and when the children were small. Now he returned to finish his degree in criminal justice. Along the way, he had advanced in the police ranks from patrolman all the way to lieutenant, and he was teaching in the police academy by 1965. "Frank made an excellent policeman," says Marian. "People he worked with said he had a great understanding of every situation he found."

Frank's job had little effect on the couple's social life. The Burkes mostly socialized with their group of close friends, made up of bankers, salesmen, small business owners, and their wives. Most of the wives stayed at home with their kids just like Marian.

The long hours were the hardest part of police work. Frank worked rotating shifts around the clock, from midnight to eight, eight to four, or four to midnight. "The four-to-twelve shift was the hardest, because then Marian had to do all the work with the children—feeding them, checking their homework, getting them ready for bed. I tried to help out with the shopping and cooking when I could."

Frank rarely brought his job home with him, keeping it separate from his family life. "I wanted to get away from it. I would talk about the funny or interesting things, but not the criminal acts or the sad occasions."

"Daddy's job wasn't a big part of our lives," recalls Anne. "We were proud of him, the way he went up in the ranks. But he didn't start really talking about his job to us until we were grown-ups. I'm sure he discussed things with my mother, but not in front of us. Later, I was around other policemen, and some of them were the most bigoted people. But Daddy never talked about people that way. We just got a rosy picture; it didn't seem dangerous, just interesting."

Frank says his wife naturally had few anxieties about his job. "Marian was well indoctrinated because her father had been a policeman. In her experience, there was no reason for concern."

In his entire career of police work, Frank only shot his gun two times, both times at fleeing criminals. The only scary time for Marian was one night when Frank was working the midnight to 8 A.M. shift. He had stopped a wild group of teenagers who had tied a Christmas tree on the hood of their car, blocking the driver's view. After Frank signed his name on the summons and left, they called up every Frank Burke in the phone book, finally awaking Marian. When they asked for Frank, Marian told them in her drowsiness that he was working. "Oh good, now we know where he lives," they said, laughing. "He'd better watch out." Marian frantically called Frank, then stayed awake the rest of the night until he came home. "It scared the daylights out of me," says Marian. "And that was the last time you could understand Frank's signature on a summons."

Throughout 1963 and 1964, Marian was caught up in another tragedy. Her brother Bud had just married when his new wife fell ill with cancer. "He was devastated," says Marian. "I remember him stopping in a church and praying, 'God, let me share this with her.'" Soon after, fate played a cruel hand when Bud found out he had intestinal cancer. Marian and her sister Eileen cared for them both, taking them for chemotherapy treatments in the hospital. Bud, just thirty-five, died in July 1964, nine months after he was diagnosed; his wife died a few months later.

Then one day in January 1965, Ellen, fifteen years old, came home from school to an unusually quiet house. Walking through, she found her mother lying on the bed, asleep.

"Mother never took naps," she remembers. "She always had plenty of energy. I thought it was strange. I thought she was sick."

Marian awoke and agreed with Ellen that she probably had a virus. But the fatigue seemed familiar. "If I didn't know better, I would swear I was pregnant," she joked. "Don't be ridiculous!" said Ellen, laughing. After all, eleven years had passed since J.R. was born, and Marian was thirty-nine. She and most of her friends felt they were long past their childbearing years.

That night, Marian let Frank in on the joke. Pregnant—when she was nearly old enough to be a grandmother! Frank laughed but made her a promise. "If you're pregnant, I'll buy you a mink coat." It seemed a safe offer, after all these years.

A week later, when morning sickness added to her fatigue, Marian went to her doctor. By then, she wasn't shocked by the news of the unexpected pregnancy. But it was as if a miracle had happened in her life, a strange and wonderful dream that she had long thought impossible. "I was so thrilled," Marian recalls. "I never thought I would ever again feel a baby in my womb."

The kids greeted the news with enthusiasm. They had all enjoyed playing with the little brothers and sisters of friends, and now they would have their own. Ellen recalls feeling a little embarrassed at first because "nobody else's mother was doing this." Anne was thrilled, and she remembers being very proud of her pregnant mom, glowing and beautiful in the audience of her grammar school graduation ceremony. J.R. had long ago realized the futility of asking for a baby brother, but he never stopped wishing for one. Now he was ecstatic and told everyone the news. "Even another sister would be fine," he thought.

Marian had an uneventful pregnancy, with everything coming along easily and on schedule. She planned to have the baby through natural childbirth, as she had had the other three. It was unusual in 1965, but her doctor encouraged it. "All of my friends were out completely when they had their children, and none of them agreed with me about natural childbirth. But you get something so wonderful for the pain, when all of a sudden it's over, and there's that beautiful child there." On August 25, she visited her doctor, who told her "any day now." She went on to Massapequa with the family and put the finishing touches on some baby clothes she was sewing.

That night, Marian awoke with strong contractions. Frank rushed her forty miles to St. Vincent's Hospital in Manhattan. After six hours of labor, Christopher Joseph Burke was born, on Thursday, August 26, 1965. He weighed seven pounds, six ounces, and had a slight fuzz of blond hair and crystal blue eyes. The doctors inspected him: he had ten fingers and ten toes, and he was alert and wiggly—a perfect little baby boy. Two tiny skin tags, or white moles, were his only flaw.

"He was angelic," says Marian. "Beautiful. He looked like my father-in-law, like a little leprechaun. Of course, I thought he was the cutest baby in existence."

Frank brought Anne and Ellen up to see him and they peered into the nursery, waving at their baby brother. They didn't see the nurses looking closely at Chris' eyes and talking among themselves.

That afternoon, soon after Frank and the girls left, the pediatrician walked into Marian's room and woke her up. The doctor was a trusted friend, having helped the family through Anne's polio and the children's various illnesses. The two women had been on a first-name basis for years, and they had shared the excitement surrounding this unexpected pregnancy.

Yet today the doctor's face was grim.

"Marian, have you seen the baby?"

"Oh yes. He's wonderful."

"Did you notice anything wrong?"

"Oh, those two little growths on the side of his face . . ."

"No, Marian, that's nothing," she said, with a wave of her hand. "We can take those off. Did you notice his eyes?"

"No. What do you mean?" The doctor's tone of voice suddenly scared her.

"They're slanted. The nurses noticed it first. The baby is a mongoloid, Marian."

"A what?" Marian whispered.

"A mongoloid. He will probably never walk or talk. He won't amount to anything . . ." She kept talking, but a wave of deafening shock enveloped Marian, shutting out her words.

"It was," Marian recalled later, "the worst moment of my entire life."

THREE

★ ★ ★ ★ ★ ★ ★ ★ ★ ★ ★ ★ ★

IF YOU WERE TO LOOK in a dictionary or encyclopedia published in 1965, you wouldn't find any listing for "Down syndrome." You must flip back to the M's to see a brief description under "mongoloid."

Today, the inhuman-sounding word offends. But until recent decades, few people even knew the name we use today for this segment of our population. The harshness of the term "mongoloid" reflected the prevailing attitudes and the stigma facing this population and their families.

Marian couldn't even pronounce the word. "I couldn't get my tongue around it," she recalls. "It sounded so horrible."

She also had trouble relating the diagnosis to the beautiful baby she held at her breast. "I just couldn't believe it. I was thinking, 'His eyes are just different. They're crinkly eyes, just like my father-in-law's eyes. They're just saying this and they don't know.' I really believed it would go away at some point."

Still, it was a horrible shock. After the pediatrician broke the news, Marian telephoned Frank; she was crying so hard he could barely understand her. He rushed back to New York from Massapequa to be with her, and they cried together.

"We were in a fog," he recalls. "I don't know how we got through those first few days."

Frank had no inkling what this "mongolism" meant. Marian only remembered a young man from her childhood, a sweet, gentle soul who lived with his mother down the street. And she had noticed a girl and boy in Stuyvesant Town who had the pronounced features of the syndrome.

The doctor was as blunt with her advice as she had been with the diagnosis. "Put him in an institution," she told Marian. "Forget you ever had him. It will be the best thing for you and for your family."

Marian didn't listen, couldn't listen to such talk. One thing was certain: she was taking this baby home with her. "We never gave a thought to the doctor's advice. He was mine and I was going to take him home no matter what."

Had she followed her doctor's advice, Chris would have been placed in Willowbrook State Institution, a crowded, enormous fortress on Staten Island housing thousands of cast-away adults and children. Some of them were mentally disabled or disturbed, but others had no disabilities. Just a few years later, Willowbrook was closed in a great scandal that exposed appalling patterns of abuse and neglect and prompted reform for institutions nationwide. "I don't know how you would give birth to a child who is a product of your love and put it in a place like that," says Marian. "If some of the parents had seen where their children were, I think they would never have placed them there."

Only two people gave Marian comfort for her decision to take Chris home. One was a nun, who advised her just to love Chris as he was. Another was a young intern, who suggested that she bring him back later for more tests.

The nurses didn't like bringing Chris in to Marian's room. "They kept him in the nursery all the time and told me they were taking tests. I had to demand to see him. The doctors were all mixed up about Chris because he was so healthy. They kept looking for things that could be wrong with him."

The delivery room physicians had not realized that Chris had Down syndrome because he had none of the obvious signs. Most infants are diagnosed by the transverse palmar crease, which runs horizontally across the middle of the palm. But Chris, like many people with Down syndrome, did not have a simian line. He had neither the excess skin folds on the back of his neck nor the extreme "floppiness" caused by lack of muscle tone. His eyes were slightly slanted, but even that went unnoticed until nurses pointed it out to the doctor hours later.

When Chris' blood tests came back, the diagnosis was confirmed. He tested positive for trisomy 21, the most prevalent type of Down syndrome, in which there are three instead of the normal two copies of chromosome 21. Normally, each parent contributes 23 chromosomes— one each from 23 pairs—to their offspring. In this case, the 21st pair of one parent failed to separate, either before or during conception. Other variations of chromosome imbalances result in translocation or mosaic forms of Down syndrome, plus other types of birth anomalies.

Chromosomes are located in the nucleus of each cell of the human body. They are long chains of complex chemicals that hold coded information called genes, which command everything from a person's eye color to height. The extra 21st chromosome is a normal human chromosome, and a baby with Down syndrome inherits all the normal genetic code from his family. His appearance then includes not only features similar to other people with Down syndrome, but also characteristics of his family.

Today, we know that Down syndrome affects people of every race, nationality, religion, and socioeconomic status. In the United States, five thousand babies with this genetic anomaly are born each year, one in approximately eight hundred live births. And though the chances increase with the age of the mother and possibly the father, at least 80 percent are born to mothers under the age of thirty-five. The average age of a mother who gives birth to a Down syndrome infant is twenty-eight.

The exact reason for the improper chromosome division that leads to Down syndrome is still a mystery. However, fewer than 1 percent of cases are classified as inherited, that is, an underlying condition that is passed on through generations.

In the body of a person with Down syndrome, where some of the genetic code is duplicated by the genes on the extra 21st chromosome, some signals that tell the body how to develop are mixed. The results are known to affect the entire body in ways as varied as the number of individuals.

Some of these differences are widespread. Nearly every person with Down syndrome has diminished intellectual capacity, probably because of an incomplete development of the brain. There is no "cure" for mental retardation, but people with Down syndrome benefit from early education and stimulation, which can enhance the potential with which they were born. Only a small percentage of people with Down syndrome are severely retarded, requiring intensive, lifelong care with their meals, exercise, and personal hygiene in order to survive. Most fall in the mild to moderate range of intelligence, which means that they can usually be educated, hold jobs, and live fairly independent lives, with some supervision. A handful of people with Down syndrome have even tested above average on standard intelligence quotient tests. But just as these tests don't measure the full aptitude of people in the general population, they also cannot determine the true functioning or mental abilities of a person with Down syndrome.

Down syndrome always affects the nervous system, resulting in slower motor skills and less refined physical coordination. Specialized physical therapy helps diminish these problems.

Nearly half the individuals with Down syndrome have minor or major heart defects; another 10 percent will be born with problems in the gastrointestinal tract. Sometimes there are cataracts, as well as respiratory, hearing, and thyroid dysfunctions. Surgery and medication can correct almost all of these.

Other complications continue to baffle scientists. People with Down syndrome often have a weakened immune system, believed to be the result of a smaller thymus gland. This could be the reason children with Down syndrome are more prone to respiratory infections than other children. They will also develop leukemia, at a rate 15 to 30 times higher than in the general population, and are more susceptible to Alzheimer's disease.

Despite the health complications, when people with Down syndrome are treated with necessary medical care, they now have a life span not much lower than the average population. Advances in heart surgery and treatment will likely increase longevity in the years to come.

It is believed that Down syndrome has existed through the centuries, though there is scant evidence in literature prior to the nineteenth century. The names "mongoloid" and "mongolism" stemmed solely from the writings of John Langdon Down, a London physician who in 1866 was the first to classify various forms of mental retardation. Though a child's mental development can be stymied by a variety of medical and social factors, Down syndrome is the most prevalent cause of retardation.

Down described the characteristics of these children, noting their similarity to the Asian people of Mongolia in their slight stature, slanted eyes, and round, flattened faces. He mistakenly concluded that this disorder was an evolutionary throwback to the Mongolian ethnic group. Other types of retardation, he assumed, were also related to some mysterious ethnic bond.

Down's presumptions were erroneous, possibly influenced too heavily by the discoveries of his cousin, Charles Darwin. But even Down considered these children to have unmet potential. He wrote, "They are cases which very much repay judicious treatment . . . the improvement which training effects in them is greatly in excess of what would be predicted if one did not know the characteristics of the type."

Unfortunately, his hopeful advice was ignored for the following century. By the 1920s, infants diagnosed with Down syndrome were routinely placed in institutions at birth. Some states even enacted laws to force parents to put them away. Despite evidence to the contrary, doctors warned that they would grow into violent and uncontrollable adults.

A few institutions offered loving care and even extended schooling for these children. But most gave neither medical care nor attention to the children's development. Infants were usually strapped to chairs or confined to beds and were not allowed to crawl. The few who survived rarely could walk, talk, or take care of themselves in the most basic manner.

A number of theories were floated about. One scientist thought people with Down syndrome were in a phase of fetal life. Another concluded that they represented a regression to a nonhuman species. Still others saw links between outbreaks of hepatitis and tuberculosis and an increased number of Down syndrome births. All of these have since been disproved.

By the 1920s, scientists raged about eugenics, the study of the quality of society's gene pools. They worried that any "inferior" specimens of humanity would multiply and wreak havoc. So most states required sterilization of people with Down syndrome, even though doctors knew that only a few had ever given birth.

In fact, most people with Down syndrome never even survived childhood. In the 1940s, more than 60 percent of these infants died before their first birthday. Average life expectancy was just twelve years old, with pneumonia being the primary cause of death.

During World War II, thousands of people with mental deficiencies, including Down syndrome, were rounded up and killed in Nazi concentration camps. After the war, when the atrocities of the Holocaust became known, public attitudes slowly began to change. People began realizing that the rights of all humans should be established and protected. Institutions were scrutinized as their drawbacks became apparent. Experts saw that even healthy infants with no disabilities developed slowly and often died when placed in such restrictive facilities.

By the 1950s, many parents refused to put their babies away in institutions. Yet when they took these babies home with them, they were generally on their own. There was little community support for their decision, and few services designed for the special needs of the children existed. In some cities, private special schools had been established and were thriving, but most public schools refused to admit children with Down syndrome. Each set of parents had to learn about their child's development by trial and error, often under criticism by family and friends for turning their focus from "normal" children to the child with Down syndrome.

The public assumed that Down syndrome was caused by something the mother did during pregnancy, so the children were sometimes a source of great shame and secrecy for the family. Many of the children were simply hidden indoors, away from the world, sometimes locked in attics and basements. Their behavior often was unrestricted, and their development—socially, physically, and mentally—was stunted. Eventually, some parents would send their children on to institutions because they lacked resources for their care.

Then in 1958, geneticists found that people with Down syndrome had a total of 47 chromosomes in their body cells, rather than the normal 46. With better medical understanding of the chromosomal origins, some of the stigma was lessened.

A few years later, new studies proved that babies raised by their families fared significantly better than those who grew up in institutions. Children with Down syndrome raised at home tested overwhelmingly higher than children in institutions on every physical, mental, and social test available. The positive news encouraged even more parents to take these children home and provide them with more complete medical care. Death rates fell drastically. By the midsixties, almost 80 percent of these infants were living past their first year.

In cities all over the United States, parents of children with Down syndrome began forming support groups. They set up private day-care and educational programs, and they worked to establish the rights of their children in the communities.

Still, most of the medical establishment saw little value in the life of a person with Down syndrome. Average life span was shortened by heart, respiratory, and digestive problems, often because of doctors' reticence to offer even basic treatment and minor surgeries. Some surveys showed that a majority of physicians would not recommend even minor surgery for a life-threatening condition if a child was mentally retarded.

Part of the problem was, and continues to be, that the average family physician sees relatively few cases of Down syndrome in a lifetime of practice. Old stereotypes die hard, and few doctors accepted positive accounts from parents as proof that people with Down syndrome could enjoy a full quality of life. Scientific and sociological discoveries were viewed with skepticism until they were proven, again and again, by further controlled studies.

Parents and educators found an ally in President John F. Kennedy, whose sister was mentally retarded (not caused by Down syndrome). Kennedy set up university research centers to study mental retardation, and he fostered early education and treatment programs for children with mental disabilities. After his death, his family continued to establish learning and training centers and promote better understanding and acceptance of those with mental disabilities. A few years later, Vice President Hubert H. Humphrey proudly introduced his granddaughter with Down syndrome on a national television show.

Parents, who were seeing progress from the early education, demanded legislation ensuring a full public education. Years would pass before the courts intervened and Congress listened. It was a tough battle, with parents pitted against legions of educators, scientists, and doctors who were convinced that these children were not capable of being educated. The erroneous thinking focused on the perception, fostered by the children in institutions, that all people with Down syndrome were severely retarded.

Others carried their opinions even further. A respected theologian, Joseph Fletcher, even advocated immediate euthanasia for all infants born with Down syndrome in a 1968 article published in *The Atlantic Monthly*. He argued that this population had no meaningful quality of life, so they should be put to death legally upon birth to protect society and individuals from the trauma. Parents, he said, should have no guilt about placing an infant in an institution and hoping for an early death because "a Down's is not a person."

Ironically, Fletcher's definition of human life was "to be self-aware, consciously related to others, capable of rationality in a measure at least sufficient to support some initiative." Though he considered himself an expert, he didn't know that many thousands of people with Down syndrome were meeting these and other requirements on their way to satisfying and fulfilling lives.

Today, when a baby is born with Down syndrome, it is sometimes no surprise to mothers who have had the pregnancy screening tests developed since the 1970s. Most conclusive are chorionic villus sampling and amniocentesis, but doctors also can measure hormone levels in the mother's blood to assess the risk for Down syndrome.

Even if the mother has had no early tests, more parents today have access to thorough information and sensitive counseling once the baby is born. Support and advocacy groups have sprung up in many towns and cities in the United States; their volunteers meet with new parents almost immediately to explain the genetic disorder and its effects on the child's development. They offer hope, encouragement, and practical advice.

For the Burkes, such help was in desperately short supply in the days after Chris was born. All Marian knew was that her son might never walk, or talk. The pediatrician said he wouldn't live a normal life; he might not even live long at all. Seeing the new mother and baby in the hospital bed beside her only magnified Marian's fear, anger, hurt, and frustration. She had taken every care during her pregnancy, just as she had for the previous three. Why had this happened to her?

Marian decided to go home a few days earlier than planned. "I couldn't stand being in that hospital room. It was heartbreaking." Chris had to stay behind for a few more days of testing.

At the register, a nurse handed Marian a sheaf of papers. "What is this?" Marian asked, scanning the print.

"It's a legal guarantee that you'll return for your baby," the nurse replied.

Marian reeled at the new shock. "I couldn't imagine why such a paper existed, or why they doubted I would return for him. I wondered if it was because Chris had Down syndrome. They always acted as if I shouldn't want him."

After signing the papers, Marian felt humiliated and angry. "I went home and scrubbed the entire place from top to bottom. It was therapy. I couldn't wait to go back and get him."

The Burkes told family and friends that tests for a slight heart problem had delayed Chris' homecoming. "We weren't quite ready to tell people that he was a mongoloid. We just couldn't label him." The parish priest passed the sad news along to some of their friends, asking them to pray for the family.

A few days later, doctors allowed the Burkes to come take Chris home. The three older children finally had what they saw as a new toy in the house, and they clamored to play with him.

But Frank and Marian had not yet absorbed the shock. "Those first few weeks were very trying," remembers Frank. "We went through this phase of wondering, 'Why did this happen to us?' And we were bewildered. We thought, 'Where do we go from here?'"

Chris entertained the family by grinning, cooing, grasping hair and noses, and generally being a darling little baby.

Sometimes, Frank would look over at Marian, and they both would begin to cry.

FOUR

★ ★ ★ ★ ★ ★ ★ ★ ★ ★ ★ ★ ★

WHEN CHRIS was a baby, his older sister Ellen, sixteen, and her friends often rushed home from school to play with him. They would huddle around the baby, feeding him, tickling him, and passing him around for hours of hugs. "I felt sorry for the people who didn't have a Chris at home," she recalls. "He was so much fun."

Anne, fourteen, sometimes neglected homework to play with Chris. "He was a living doll, with blond hair and blue eyes and rosy red cheeks. He smiled at us all the time, right from the beginning."

J.R., a rough-and-tumble twelve-year-old, had wanted a little brother for as long as he could remember. Now he shared his room with Chris, putting him to bed at night and waking up with him in the morning. J.R. couldn't wait to teach him basketball and roller hockey, and often carried him down to the playground.

None of the children knew that Chris had Down syndrome.

Marian and Frank were still coming to grips with the shock, and they had decided not to burden the kids with their anxieties.

"I think we wanted to have just a little more time to straighten things out in our own thoughts," recalls Frank. "It was difficult to explain even to our family and friends. My brother was very sympathetic. My mother was along in years, so I don't think she felt the full impact. Marian's father was very positive. He told us not to worry, that Chris would be fine."

To Frank and Marian, such advice was impossible.

Marian was consumed with questions that had no answers. What will he be able to do? What will he look like? How will the children treat him? Had they made the right decision in bringing him home?

"I was afraid he wouldn't be accepted in the world," she says. "I didn't know if I would be capable of raising him. I thought it would be extremely difficult. I envisioned years of stress and training."

She also worried for her family. "The doctor told us that the other children might be hurt by it," says Marian. "I felt bad that I had to present them with this problem. Back then, there was a certain amount of shame attached to having a child who was not perfect. I thought it would affect my children's lives."

Those ill effects on siblings were accepted medical wisdom at the time, in even the most respected quarters. Physicians sometimes agreed with the parents' decision to take a first and only child home, but they usually warned against it when there were other children present.

The reasoning was simple, if uninformed. Some parents were criticized for focusing too much on the child with Down syndrome instead of devoting themselves to their normal children. And the consensus was that it was better to experience the heartache of placing an infant in an institution than to know a greater anguish later on, when the child became sickly or difficult to control. Taking a handicapped child home, they said, would trap the family in an irreversible trauma.

Maybe because Chris' siblings were so much older, none of them felt adversely affected by the attention Chris received. New studies show that their experience is the norm, that children with Down syndrome rarely produce problems in the family structure.

Ellen doesn't remember any difference in the way her parents treated them after Chris was born. "The three of us were secure in our relationship with our parents," she says. "We continued to be cared for in the same way. Any clothes I wanted were bought; any situations that came up were still handled. None of us felt that Chris came in and overwhelmed the family."

Still, Ellen wondered why her mother wouldn't leave Chris, even for a short time, during the first few months. "They were too nervous with this child. They had always had an active social life, and all of a sudden, they weren't going out."

Chris was a month old when Frank enticed Marian from the apartment with tickets to see Peggy Lee on Broadway. But it was a fiasco. "The lights went down, and I started crying," she remembers. "I cried straight through the show and rushed home."

A few weeks later, the family dragged her to the New York World's Fair while Ellen watched Chris. "Mom phoned every half hour," Ellen recalls. "I didn't know why she was so worried."

"I couldn't wait to get back home," Marian recalls. "He meant so much to me, I didn't want to leave him. It was difficult to even go shopping for an hour," she says. She wondered how much time would pass before she would have to tell her children the awful news.

Actually, the children already had a friend with Down syndrome, named Timmy. He was eight years old, a member of a large family who lived in Stuyvesant Town. J.R. remembers that Timmy was different, but nice and friendly. "He was definitely just one of the kids in the neighborhood. I think everyone was taken by how good his brothers and sisters were with him, and how close they all were. He was always in the playground with us."

One day, Anne peered at Chris closely. "I don't know why, but he looks kind of like Timmy," she said.

"Don't be silly," Ellen retorted.

Then that spring, when Chris was about nine months old, one of Ellen's friends mentioned that Chris' eyes were different. "They almost look Oriental, don't they?" she asked Ellen and Marian.

Ellen disagreed, but Marian was silent.

The friend persisted. "See look, this little fold above his eye. It slants up to here." She touched him lightly.

"So what," said Ellen. "Everybody's does that when they're little."

Later that day, Marian and Ellen were alone in the kitchen. "You know," Marian said casually, "Chris has something called mongolism."

Ellen said, "Oh?"

"It's like what Timmy has. It's just a genetic thing that will make him a little different. He may grow up a bit slower than you."

"Oh, that's why you two are so worried over him," said Ellen.

Marian, bolstered by Ellen's mild reaction, soon told J.R. and Anne.

Anne was slightly upset. In the past, she had noticed adult people with Down syndrome. "They had deadpan expressions and shaved heads, and were never dressed nicely. I wondered if Chris would look like that when he grew up."

J.R. listened to the diagnosis but didn't believe it. "I just thought my parents were wrong. I didn't notice anything different in Chris."

Marian breathed a sigh of relief. "The fact that Chris had Down syndrome meant nothing to them. I told them that we all needed to work together with him. From that time on, it was as if he had five parents, not just two."

Looking back, J.R. admires his parents for waiting to tell them. "It gave us time to learn that he was just like anybody else, which is the way we've always treated him. We just loved him as our brother."

Now that Marian and Frank had gotten over most of their early fears, they were enjoying having a baby around. "It was like having a first child all over again," says Marian. "It was, number one, our age difference as parents, but also because he was different from the others. It was a completely new experience for us. We were giving him all the energy and attention that most parents have only for their first child. It wasn't divided as it was when there were two or three small children."

The Burke apartment looked like the home of a first baby as well. Someone would run for the camera every time Chris got a new outfit or learned how to do something new. Soon, framed photos of little Chris decorated nearly every inch of the apartment walls, which led Ellen to remark that her mother was setting up a "shrine to St. Christopher."

But having three teenagers and a baby in one apartment wasn't always easy. Marian and Frank took care to stay close to the children as they entered the tumultuous teenage years. "We wanted them to be independent, but we kept an eye on them," says Marian. "I told them, 'Don't believe what you read about those wonderful teenage years. They're fun, but they're confusing.' I knew from experience that it's important to have a mother who can empathize with you. You have to know what they're going through. You have to let them scream at you sometimes, to get out that anger. They can adjust if you just stick with them. But it's not easy."

Marian found that having Chris around made the family stick together even tighter. "It was marvelous to see the cohesiveness that resulted from us working together with him. The other children always took pride in Chris. They never hid him or were ashamed of him."

Ellen, Anne, and J.R. always included Chris in their activities, just as Timmy's siblings had included their brother. "It probably made it easier, having known Timmy," says J.R. "But there was an interesting thing about Chris. When you get older, it's natural for your friends' little brothers and sisters to be a pain. But Chris was never treated like that. Everyone always treated him a little nicer. He was special."

Some adults had a harder time accepting Chris. A student teacher once told Ellen that her brother was a mongoloid idiot, then described what a limited life he would have when he grew up. "I was disgusted by all these people who thought they were experts because they had read something about Down syndrome," recalls Ellen. "They never said anything encouraging. They always said he was going to plateau. He won't be able to do this or that. He'll be a problem. They thought we shouldn't expect anything from him."

Marian sometimes encountered the same attitudes. "A friend and I were chatting, and I looked at Chris and said, 'Oh, he's so adorable.' She said, 'Marian, he won't be that cute for long. It will go away.' I don't know why she thought she had to say that."

At two months, Chris astonished Marian's friends by flipping himself over while in his carriage. But the pediatrician dismissed this and other signs of his development. "She never gave me any encouragement. She just said, 'Oh, Marian, don't get your hopes up. It doesn't mean anything. It was an accident.'"

As the Burke family continued to celebrate each milestone of Chris' development, Marian began to doubt the horror stories she had heard. Chris talked at eighteen months and started walking at about two years. "He just took a little longer at each phase," says Marian. "He sat up, started crawling, and was toilet trained just a bit past an average age. He wasn't much different from the other children."

Marian hated watching Chris go from stage to stage. He was her last little baby, and he was growing up too fast for her. She may have even postponed a few stages subconsciously. This realization hit her with a force one day when she returned from a short vacation. Ellen, home from college, had been watching Chris and just assumed he could feed himself. So she put his food in front of him and handed him a spoon. When Marian and Frank returned, they were excited to see Chris feeding himself for the first time. "What's the big deal?" asked Ellen. "He was already doing that when you left."

"Well, no, he wasn't," Marian admitted. "I guess he was ready and I wasn't."

Another time, Marian was talking on the phone when Chris, in the other room, began crying with gusto. Before, he had not cried much at all. In fact, he had hardly ever used the full force of his lungs. Marian realized then that the absence of tears was because she ran to him immediately each time she heard the slightest movement or whimper.

"I called Frank at the police academy to tell him about it, and he was in class. But they heard the excitement in my voice, mistook it for an emergency, and rushed to get him. Imagine the surprise Frank felt when he breathlessly called me, only to hear that his baby had been crying!"

Though Marian wasn't ready for Chris to grow up, his siblings couldn't wait, and helped him conquer each new challenge. They brought home flash cards and would spend hours coaxing him to recognize the colors, numbers, and words. He was a quick learner and he loved performing for them. Sometimes it was as if they were competing for Chris' attention to see who could teach him the most.

Marian says she didn't have to encourage them to help with Chris' care. "They played with him constantly," says Marian. "If one put him down, the other would take over. Maybe they wanted to show the world that even if their brother had something wrong with him, he could still learn and be cute and precocious. The children had as much interest in him as Frank and I did. I think each one of them took a bit of him and made him a child of their own. There's an extra dimension there that probably all of us have for Chris."

Learning was incorporated into playtime. Ellen wrote out words in the sand on the beach, and she read to him often. "He picked up on things so quickly," she says.

Anne recalls sitting in front of a mirror with Chris every day, touching and naming his nose, ears, mouth, and eyes, and having him repeat after her. "I think we all made it our goal to make Chris as normal as possible," she says.

J.R., always thinking of sports, taught his brother to throw and catch a ball as soon as Chris could grasp. J.R. loved the mornings Chris would climb out of his crib and jump on his bed to wake him—except when his diapers were soiled.

"I remember Chris being so proud when he learned to do something new," he says. "It was probably because we were all going so wacko over him."

When it was time for Chris to crawl, Marian told the kids, "Let's show him what to do." For weeks, the Burkes crawled on the floor around him until he was following behind them with glee.

Without knowing it, the Burkes were performing a primitive version of what is now called "early intervention." In the early 1980s, educators found that a stimulating program of exercises and games could significantly spur development of muscle tone and the senses of touch, sight, and hearing in children with Down syndrome. Today, infants are enrolled in government-sponsored intervention programs almost immediately after birth, with promising results.

Even as Chris was learning from his family, they were also absorbing some important lessons from him.

Anne says watching Chris overcome his disability made her take her own life and health more seriously. "I was not a perfect teenager, and was growing up in a world where all of a sudden, there were drugs everywhere. Chris made me realize how stupid it was to screw up what I had been born with. I felt I had no right not to give life 100 percent effort. He made me more grounded in reality."

"He taught the kids that everyone is going to have adversity, but you have to rise above it," says Frank. "I know it drew our family closer together."

Marian feels that Chris had a leveling influence on her children. "They knew that when Chris was left with them, they were responsible for him. It taught them a lot."

Frank and Marian also noticed changes in themselves. "Chris brought out a benevolent spirit in us all," says Frank. "We grew to have more sensitivity for others. It brought us out of our narrow, rigid view of the world. And it changed my attitude about a whole range of people, even the ones I came in contact with as a police officer."

"My parents had the maturity to handle Chris," says Ellen. "Their marriage was very solid. They could have crumbled; I have seen other people do that. I think I learned a lot about strength from watching my parents, especially from my mother."

"We tried to get up and get on with life, not let this burden us," says Frank. "The kids saw how we reacted to that. Again, as during the war, I took the attitude that these were the cards we were dealt, this was the hand we would play."

During this period, Frank was embroiled in a different kind of war. In 1967, looking for a shortcut to advancement in the ranks, he volunteered as captain for the New York Police Department's tactical patrol force. From 3 P.M. to 3 A.M., he and his men patrolled the city's high-crime areas, but they were often mobilized to control larger disturbances throughout the city. The men dodged bottles and rocks in the Harlem and New Lots Avenue riots, and tried to control the wave of protests against the Vietnam War. "It was quite a volatile time," says Frank. "But it was exciting work. It gave you the chance to utilize police tactics you normally would never use. Sometimes we would get to the scene before we had enough personnel to take charge and correct the situation. Then you would try to talk with the people demonstrating and ask them to cooperate and move." When hundreds of protesters barricaded themselves in buildings on the Columbia University campus, Frank's patrol was sent in to clear the math building. "There were 300 students in the math building, and we made 190 arrests. After all this was over, I was very proud of the fact that, amid all the complaints of police brutality and use of unnecessary force, there was not one complaint from people arrested in the math building."

Eventually, Frank was promoted to captain. That summer, the family took a three-week vacation to California. They had decided Chris, a toddler, wouldn't enjoy flying cross-country and driving down the coast, so they left him with friends.

In San Diego, the Burkes met with Frank's war buddy Mickey Daly. For the first time, the kids heard how tough life really was for their dad in Stalag 17. "Up to that point, we'd always heard the funny stories," says Ellen. "But that night, I remember Mickey sitting there, this soft-spoken gentleman who looked like a little leprechaun. And he said that he would kill before he would go hungry again. I think those survival instincts Daddy learned were passed on to my whole family."

Throughout the trip, the Burkes missed Chris terribly. On the ride home from the airport, an argument ensued: what would Chris do when they returned?

"He'll run straight to me," said J.R. confidently.

"No, he won't," countered Anne. "He'll come to me."

Marian listened to them, thinking to herself that they were being silly. After all, she was his mother. Of course Chris would come straight to her.

When they returned, they all ran out on the beach, where Chris and the neighbors were playing.

Chris turned his head and caught sight of them. He let out a shout and came running—straight into the arms of J.R.

It was a bittersweet moment for Marian, who was shocked to see that someone else was more important to Chris than she was. "I knew then that he wasn't just my baby. But it was clear that he loved and was loved so much by the other children. I realized how wonderful that was. And I knew that he would go on to make other friends easily for the rest of his life."

FIVE

★ ★ ★ ★ ★ ★ ★ ★ ★ ★ ★ ★ ★

THE BURKES always felt fortunate that they lived in New York City, with all of its lessons and opportunities for their children. Now, as Chris grew older, they began to seek the professionals who could help him reach his potential. Unfortunately, in the late 1960s, even this vast metropolis had little to offer. The few programs that existed had waiting lists and specific requirements for age and ability.

Marian knew Chris would need special therapy, especially with his speech. Children with Down syndrome often have difficulty forming the sounds of language due to smaller mouth structure and poor control of the tongue muscles. And, when young, they sometimes have trouble comprehending the meaning of words, especially abstract expressions.

Chris was no exception. Marian anguished as she watched him struggle to communicate his thoughts.

Today, children with Down syndrome are often in speech therapy as soon as they can form language sounds. But in the 1960s, it was hard to find qualified specialists who would take the extra time and effort required. Marian finally found a speech therapist when Chris was three. It was a long bus ride from her home in lower Manhattan to the office on 115th Street, but she took Chris three times a week.

Later, she enrolled Chris in a weekly program in language development designed for special needs children. "They were thrilled with him," she says. "He recognized their flash cards because we had worked so hard with him on those."

A nearby physician claimed significant results using a megavitamin treatment. Marian took Chris faithfully, though she was never sure if it had any effect. The doctor did offer something of definite value: he gave

Marian hope and encouraged her to do anything she could for Chris' physical and mental development. "He accepted Chris and had respect for him," says Marian. "He encouraged me to take more pride in him than I had. Others felt sorry for me, or couldn't care less. But the vitamin doctor told me that Chris was doing well. He said, 'You'll see wonders from him.' "

At home, Marian tuned the set to the new public television show "Sesame Street." Chris loved to imitate the characters and sing along with them. He set up his blocks in front of the television, making words with the letters they showed.

At night, he would often repeat the lessons for his family. "This message is brought to you by the letter J!" he would yell, forming a J with his arms.

Even then, he was honing his performing talents for the family. "One day we were in the kitchen," recalls Anne. "Chris picked up a banana and started talking into it like it was a phone. It was so cute and funny, and imaginative. Then we found out Oscar the Grouch [a "Sesame Street" character] had done the same thing on the show that afternoon."

Ellen says Chris was a born actor. "He loved to perform for us, from the time he was very little. He was very musical. He had that talent early on. Before he actually verbalized, he was entertaining us."

Marian searched the library for information on Down syndrome, but she found very little beyond complex medical texts. Anne tried again when writing a school paper on the subject. Exasperated, she wrote to former vice president Hubert Humphrey, whose granddaughter had Down syndrome. He replied with an encouraging letter and some information he had found. From that, Anne learned about the newest research and treatments for "mongolism," as it was still called, plus various support groups and services in the New York area.

Marian attended one of the support groups for parents of children with Down syndrome. When she arrived, her hopes were high. But as the meeting progressed, she grew dismayed as the discussion turned negative. "All these women were sitting around talking about all the problems they had had, and how hard it was to bring up their children. I wasn't having any problems. I wasn't finding it difficult. Chris was such a joy. I went a few times, then gave up."

As Marian's older children began leaving for college, she worried that Chris would become lonely. She looked for ways to involve him with other children, enrolling him in preschool groups and Bible classes, where he fit right in with the other children. But when she took him to play at the Stuyvesant Town playground, the mothers would pull their children away from him. "I would just choke up," says Marian. "I didn't know how to handle it. But there was always someone who was intelligent enough to understand. I remember one woman who would always bring her children over to play with Chris." Marian, who was in her forties, felt a little out of place in the midst of all the younger mothers, and she wondered if more friendships would have developed for Chris had she been closer to their age.

Another time, at the beach in Massapequa, Chris toddled over to a little girl his age playing in the sand. When the girl's mother ran over and pulled her away from Chris, Ellen, who was standing nearby, confronted her. "He's not contagious," she said, then turned to Chris. "Come on, let's go somewhere else to play."

The Burkes grew anxious for the day Chris was old enough to enter structured programs designed for children with Down syndrome. Frank had found one such place next door to the 19th Precinct on East 67th Street in Manhattan.

It was the Kennedy Child Study Center, a private diagnostic evaluation clinic for special needs children. One of the first of its kind in the United States, Kennedy combined pediatric, neurological, and psychological expertise, physical and speech therapy, and individualized instruction in nursery school–type classes. The goal was to help slowly developing children reach their maximum potential and find a solid place in their families.

Today, Kennedy accepts infants within weeks of birth. But in the mid 1960s, such programs were virtually nonexistent. Funding was too tight within Catholic Charities to justify what was considered an experiment.

Sister Arthur Marie, then the principal, remembers Frank approaching her to inquire what could be done for his little boy. She told him that Chris was too young but could come in for a brief evaluation. When Marian brought him in, she was told that he was progressing well and would be a good candidate for the school in a few years. They encouraged her to keep up with the speech therapy and language programs, plus any other activities she could find.

"Even then, we were trying to get kids in younger," says Sister Arthur Marie. "We felt that waiting four or five years was wasting precious time." By the time Chris was four, Kennedy had started a play group for younger children, and the school welcomed Chris twice a week.

While Chris played, Marian attended parent consultations with the experts there. Finally, she was hearing positive, practical information about raising her son. "It was great for all of us to chat and exchange ideas, and help one another get over the stumbling blocks," says Marian. Her early fears about Chris' future began to dissolve, and she felt fortunate when she saw him progressing past his peers.

"Some of the children were nonverbal or nonresponsive. But Chris would always call out, 'Mommy! Mommy!' and come running to hug me. He always enjoyed going to Kennedy, and the teachers encouraged me so much."

Chris began attending full-day classes when he turned five, an unusually young age for Kennedy. But he made a big impression on people in the school.

"I'm thinking back twenty years, and I still remember him clearly," says Jill O'Reilly, Chris' first teacher. "He was one of my favorites. He was a regular little boy, and into all little-boy things."

Chris was at about the same ability level as others in his class, she says. "He tended toward the higher scale, just above medium. He didn't make it into the high-functioning class. But he had more practical skills coming in than a lot of other children. He was a self-sufficient little boy."

The most extraordinary thing about Chris, however, was his sociability. "He was sensitive and caring, with a very pleasant personality," recalls Sister Arthur Marie. "He was just a delight."

She remembers bringing visitors into his classroom. "Some children would shy away, but Chris would come over and say, 'Hi, sit down, make yourself comfortable.' He'd show people around his classroom, like a master of ceremonies. He enjoyed interaction with adults."

Every day, Chris rode a school bus to the center. And nearly every day, he would manage to crawl out of his seat belt to walk around. The bus driver complained about it to Marian, adding, "There's only one thing wrong with him. He's too smart!"

One day, a teacher motioned Marian into the classroom. Chris was hovering over a little girl with autism, trying to convince her to join the class in a game. The child was not responsive, but Chris wouldn't give up on her. Finally, weeks later, he persuaded her to join the others. The teachers were amazed. They told Marian, "Even we couldn't get her to do that."

Chris' classes were filled with play activities structured for learning. Finger and sand painting stimulated tactile senses. Games like tag and musical chairs helped develop motor skills and muscle tone. They arranged big, colorful alphabet letters into words, and a few learned to spell their names. Chris continued to amaze his family with the lessons he absorbed so quickly. They were stunned into silence at breakfast one day, when he pointed to a Cheerios box. "Look! there's my name!" he said, touching the letters spelling out "Chris."

But Chris' favorite time in school came when the teachers hauled out big boxes of clothes to play dress-up. "We used to act out stories in the classroom," says Jill O'Reilly. "And we always had a Christmas play. During the year we put on shows for the parents. We had a circus, and the kids dressed up like performers and animals. The more adorable they looked, the more of a hit they were, and the more they enjoyed it."

Though Chris doesn't recall much about Kennedy or his early childhood, he definitely remembers his first magic moment on the stage, in a Kennedy production of *The Emperor's New Clothes.*

"My lines were 'Hark, who goes there?' and then 'Ha ha ha, what a joke!'" says Chris. "It was a lot of fun. That was when I decided I wanted to be an actor, when I was five years old."

It doesn't surprise Sister Arthur Marie. "I'll always remember Chris on stage," she says. "When it was time for people to clap, he'd be bowing. He had a sense of knowing that the audience was very appreciative. That youngster had it in him from a long time ago."

At home, Chris found his siblings' acting and modeling portfolios. He pulled them out and stared at the familiar faces so often that, in time, the photos became dog-eared. It seemed magical to him that Ellen, Anne, and J.R. had once been on television, the wonderful box that brought him his favorite shows. One day Marian walked in while he was looking at the photos. "I want to do that," he announced solemnly, slowly forming the words. "I want to be on television."

Marian sighed. She looked at her son, the same age her other children had been when she whisked them around New York for acting jobs. She knew Chris wanted to do everything his brother and sisters did, but this seemed far beyond his reach. "That would be wonderful," she answered, her heart aching. "But I don't know if there would be any parts, dear."

"Well, you never know!" answered Chris confidently. He had exceeded every expectation of him so far, and in his innocence, he saw nothing standing in his way to reach this goal, too.

Sister Arthur Marie credits Frank and Marian for the confidence and self-assuredness that was evident in Chris even at that age. "Chris has a wonderful, supportive family," she says. "That stimulus and acceptance from the family enhances what they start out with, no matter what degree of retardation they may have.

"Most important was that they came to grips with it themselves. That feeling of rejection, that this is not a perfect child, has to be worked out within the family. It's helpful to see what these kids can do. It helps the family get over the hurt."

Marian threw herself into the promising environment of Kennedy. She was president of the parents' organization, she supervised fund-raising dinners, and she urged others to get involved. She and Frank were regulars at the Sunday afternoon programs for parents, in which they would learn about special activities that would help Chris. On school days, she often volunteered in Chris' class. "For ten kids, we had one teacher and one assistant," recalls Jill O'Reilly. "An extra pair of hands was much appreciated."

The teachers loved to see what Chris would wear each day. Sometimes it was lederhosen (leather shorts and suspenders) brought back from Europe by his sister. Other times, he sported a crisp navy sailor suit or a full-blown cowboy outfit, with hat and boots to match. At all times, he was a clean and well-cared-for child, wearing the latest children's fashions.

Some of the Burkes' relatives criticized them for spending so much money on his appearance, saying they were wasting money that they would need for Chris' care when he was older. But Frank and Marian disagreed. "Marian decked him out in the very best clothes," Frank remembers. "We always thought that was important, to help him be accepted. It wasn't that he wouldn't be rejected by other kids; it was just that they'd have to use another measure. It wouldn't be because of the way he looked."

Dr. Ann Williams, the school psychologist, remembers that such concern was unusual. "At that time, most people didn't do much for these kids in terms of appearance. But Chris really was just a child who happened to have Down syndrome."

"The parents made him," adds Jill O'Reilly. "I was always impressed with what they had done for him and with him. He was a terrific little kid, and they treated him as normal as any normal child. I think that made the difference."

It always surprised Frank and Marian when someone would react to Chris as if his very presence was a tragedy. When Chris was five, Frank took him along to a doctor's appointment in Point Lookout, where they had just bought a summer home. As Chris was flipping through a magazine, the doctor turned to Frank. "What are you going to *do* with him?" he asked.

"Christopher?" Frank asked, stunned.

"Yes," the doctor replied. "Christopher."

"Oh," said Frank. "We're sending him to medical school. He wants to be a doctor."

"He got the point," says Frank. "To me, his ignorance was astounding. I would expect more from a medical doctor. But we learned early on that doctors were not always our allies in this battle. Some of them only want to deal with perfection."

As Chris grew older, Marian and Frank took pains to raise him just as they had their other three children. When he misbehaved, he was always punished. "It was hard to do, but we knew, from when he was a baby, that we absolutely had to discipline him," says Marian. "So many of these children are not restricted in their behavior, and it hurts them later in life."

Fran Slattery, a friend of the Burkes', admired the calmness of their approach. "If Chris did anything that was not acceptable, Marian or Frank would look at him very seriously and say, 'Christopher, you are not to do that ever again.' He would turn back to them with this solemn look, take it all in, and behave. I was never privy to anything harsher than that. They were very patient with him, but firm.

"Down syndrome was something new to all of us," she adds. "They handled everything like such pros, like it was the easiest thing in the world. I'm sure it wasn't. In a way, they're trailblazers. They're the heroes."

Marian and Frank had long since stopped worrying about how Chris would affect the other children. But they were still concerned for the future, when their son and daughters married. Would their spouses and in-laws accept Chris? These fears started to dissolve when Anne became engaged to Tommy Corridan, a neighborhood boy who had taken to Chris immediately. By the time Anne and Tommy were married, Chris had forged a great friendship with Tommy's father, whom he nicknamed "Big Tom." Anne's father-in-law took Chris to the zoo and the beach on weekends and gave him his first two-wheeler bike for Christmas. Chris was also happy when Ellen married another Stuyvesant Town neighbor, Jack Orlando. When the two were dating, Chris liked Jack so much that he sometimes sneaked over to his apartment to say hello. Chris also enjoyed visiting during dinner, when Jack's mother Dorothy would cook lasagna especially for him. "They all showed such love for and interest in Chris," says Marian. "They felt the way we felt, that Chris was just one of the family."

When Chris was six, his sister Anne gave birth to Kara, the first Burke grandchild. Chris was fascinated with her, and he proudly told his teachers at Kennedy that he was an uncle.

Anne and her husband had moved into an apartment in Stuyvesant Town across the playground from the family, so Chris visited often. He would walk over by himself as Anne and Marian watched him from their windows. When Kara began to walk, Chris would take her hand and lead her over to visit her grandmother.

"It gave him a sense of responsibility," says Marian. "I think we always tried what we could to foster his independence."

By then, with the children and friends helping with Chris' care, Marian and Frank had resumed their social life. On weekends, they often took Chris to parties, if other children were present. Their adult friends grew to love Chris and were delighted when he would break into song or dance for them.

"He's always been a big ham," says Fran Slattery. "He would perform at the drop of a hat. He has a good sense of rhythm, and kept up with all the newest music.

"We were astounded by his memory. He could tell you all these things about movies and television. And he always thought to ask me about my children, how they were doing.

"My mother got the biggest kick out of him. She'd say, 'You're telling me this boy's retarded?' She didn't believe it at all.

"But he was surrounded by a wonderful, loving family. He was always a secure, confident, well-rounded person with a great deal of sensitivity to others."

Chris' favorite show stage was the staircase in his cousin Pat Egan's house, where he would rush from the table after dinner to prepare for his performances. When he was ready, he would call everyone in, ushering them to the couch and to chairs he had set up facing the staircase. Sometimes he would sing or lip-synch to his favorite records; other times he told jokes, improvised a short skit, or danced to music.

His family couldn't always understand exactly what he was saying, but they were an appreciative audience, usually clapping and cheering at the right places.

One evening, the night before he was to receive his first holy communion, six-year-old Chris ran in to set up the room. When the adults and other children came in, they saw that he had set up an altar table with candles for mass. Chris played the priest, directing his brother and cousin as altar boys. "He was very solemn," says Pat Egan. "Somehow Chris knew the whole ritual of the mass ceremony, which has quite a bit of detail. He remembered the whole thing. It was quite a performance. We were amazed."

Family friends Pat and Bill O'Neill say Chris always livened up a party by singing or dancing. "He enjoyed the company of adults," says Bill. "He loves a party, and he's not the shy, retiring type.

"When Chris was little, he didn't like to go to the barber, so I would cut his hair. He didn't like to sit still, so we gave him this little toy microphone to play with. That occupied him for the longest time. He would sing into it, pretend he was on stage.

"When he was a little older, and going to a regular barber, he'd tease me about cutting his hair. He'd say, 'There's my barber!' or he'd point to his hair and say, 'How 'bout trimming this behind my ears?' "

Marian didn't confide any anxieties about Chris to her friends. "Maybe [the Burkes] worried, but they weren't the type to wring their hands and lament his condition. It wasn't a subject of conversation," says Pat. "They had their own faith and the great reliance that Chris was watched over by God and their children."

Pat says she could never recall a time when Chris was sad or dejected. "He always made you feel good. People enjoyed being around him."

Around this time, experts and doctors began dropping the term "mongoloid" for the less stigmatic "Down's syndrome." "We were so thrilled to have a new word for it," says Marian. "It sounded so much better. We used 'Down's syndrome' in our regular conversations all while Chris was growing up, so he was comfortable with it. We never had a big talk about it; we just mentioned that that was what he had, and that was why he was a little different sometimes." A few years later, the term was changed from 'Down's syndrome' to 'Down syndrome,' since it was named after the person who discovered it, not a person who actually had the condition. But Chris didn't like the negative connotation that he was somehow "down." One day, he pulled on Frank's arm and pointed to a UPS delivery truck on the street. "Look, Dad!" he said excitedly. "That's what I have. *Up* syndrome!"

The Burkes tended to agree with Chris. His Down syndrome wasn't causing any problems or stress, and the years of hard work Marian had envisioned never materialized. All was peaceful in the family until the spring night of 1972 when J.R. called in the middle of the night. "I've been stabbed, and I'm in the hospital emergency room," he said. He and his date had attended the high school senior prom, then stopped off at New York's Washington Square Park on the way home. A man approached them and demanded their money; when J.R. handed over his billfold, the man stabbed him deep in the leg. That night, when J.R. came home, Frank sat in the room until dawn, watching him closely while he slept.

J.R. recovered and entered the University of Pennsylvania that fall. But the stabbing may have brought on the next tragedy. J.R. was nearing his first college exams when he fell ill with what he thought was the flu. Instead, it was thrombotic thrombocytopenic purpura (TTP), one of the rarest blood diseases in the world. Fortunately, a doctor in the hospital was familiar with the disease and knew that they needed to remove J.R.'s spleen to raise his blood platelet count, which was down to zero. That day, the Burkes got a call from a doctor telling them that their son was in the hospital. "We think your son has a very rare and serious illness," the doctor said. "We need you to come here and sign a permission form for immediate surgery." The Burkes rushed to Philadelphia, and the doctor met them at the door. Marian asked him a dozen questions about the surgery and the length of hospital stay it would require. "You don't understand, Mrs. Burke," the doctor answered. "Your son is gravely ill." He didn't add that TTP was almost always fatal. Only three people had ever survived it.

After the surgery, J.R. was still fighting for his life, drifting in and out of consciousness in his pain. He received last rites twice, but both times he fought back with a tenacity that amazed everyone. J.R. says he knew even then that he got that strength from his parents. "By the time my dad was nineteen, he had been through what had to be the toughest thing in his life. And my mother is as strong, if not stronger, than my dad. I remember battling that disease, thinking that nineteen was a critical age for anyone named Francis Dewey Burke. I felt that if I made it, I would be okay from that point on."

By Christmas, the Burkes were sick with fear. J.R. was not improving. Chris, who was just seven, spent a few nights with Marian's cousin Pat Egan while Ellen, Jack, Anne, and Tommy came down for a grim Christmas Eve. "We were so worried we were losing him," says Marian. "Then on Christmas Day, J.R. looked up at us and smiled. That was our Christmas gift. I knew then that he was going to get better."

Ten days later, J.R. was home recuperating. He suffered a setback when the incisions from his operation became infected, and he was back in the hospital for two weeks. But again he recovered, though he missed six months of college. When he had regained his health, he told his parents that he didn't want to return to college right away. Instead, he wanted to travel the world. "We told him, 'No, we're not going to permit you to do that,'" says Marian. "'You are going to go back and finish your education, then travel.' We felt his schooling was too important. J.R. was angry then, but he has thanked us a hundred times since."

The ordeal had changed J.R. Like his father before him, he was old beyond his years, responsible and serious, and determined to succeed. "I think it made him realize what life was all about, how important it was to live it to the fullest," says Marian.

That year, Chris graduated from Kennedy in a cap and gown ceremony, just before he turned eight. The New York City public school system was ready to accept him, but the Burkes weren't sure it was acceptable to them. At the time, schools did not allow mainstreaming, the practice of integrating special needs children into regular classes, which is common today for high-functioning students with Down syndrome. Many schools did not offer special education classes at all: until the late 1960s, only one fourth of all children with mental retardation had access to special education.

The Burkes hoped they could find a good education for Chris close to home. But when they visited the special education classes in New York public schools, they found them teaching only basic skills, many of which Chris had already mastered. "It was like the students were in a play group all the time," said Marian. "There were children of all different levels and disabilities and emotional problems. It didn't seem to us that the classes were giving the students a structured experience in education. It didn't seem like a place where Chris would learn very much. We could see he could learn, and we thought we needed to do as much as we possibly could for him."

"It was strictly adequate," adds Frank. "We wanted more than 'adequate' for all of our children, and especially for Chris."

Marian and Frank had chosen the place they wanted when Chris was just an infant, after watching a television special called "The Long Childhood of Timmy." It featured their neighbor with Down syndrome, who was leaving home for St. Coletta's School (soon renamed Cardinal Cushing School and Training Center) in Hanover, Massachusetts, near Boston.

"I fell in love with the school the moment I saw the show," says Marian. "I hoped that someday, Chris could go there." Later, she and Frank inquired about private schools closer to New York, but they couldn't find any with the same level of care and training.

"Cardinal Cushing was a lovely, homey sort of place," Marian remembers. "It wasn't sterile. The dining room was charming, and each dorm room was done individually. They had a full range of activities, even a working farm the children could visit. We could see there was love there."

Their plans were criticized by several relatives, who said they didn't understand why they would "waste money" on an education for Chris when they would need the money in the future for his care. But Frank and Marian were adamant. They had taken Chris to visit Cardinal Cushing during school days each year since Chris turned two. "We wanted to get our foot, arm, and head into the door there," says Frank.

When Chris was accepted by the school, the Burkes celebrated. But when the time came for Chris to leave, the idea of sending their eight-year-old son to a boarding school far from home seemed harsh. Marian was apprehensive. "We were so close. Chris and I had spent every day together, doing everything. It was quite a wrench."

Frank gave Marian pep talks, reminding her of their determination to do only what they felt was best for Chris. As the day grew closer, she would look at Chris and fight back tears. Ellen, Anne, and J.R. wondered aloud: could their mother live with the long absence of Chris?

SIX

★ ★ ★ ★ ★ ★ ★ ★ ★ ★ ★ ★ ★ ★

ON FATHER'S DAY of 1973, Chris left home for a two-week visit at Cardinal Cushing School. Frank spent the five-hour drive fortifying Marian, reminding her that the school could teach Chris things they couldn't. And with J.R. in college, they knew Chris needed to make new friends.

Once in Hanover, they stayed a few hours while Chris played with the other children. Then a nun walked over and suggested that it was time they slip away.

Marian wasn't going to leave without a kiss. She walked over and knelt by her son, hugged him, and told him she loved him. Then Frank bent down, his arms outstretched.

Chris jumped to his feet and stood straight as a soldier. "Dad, big boys don't hug," he announced. "They shake hands." He smiled and grasped Frank's hand, then turned his attention back to his new friends.

That was the undoing of Frank. "He just collapsed," says Marian. "He cried for two hours while we drove around. Neither of us could function, so we went back and stayed at a hotel near the school."

It didn't take long for the teachers at Cardinal Cushing to realize they had a live wire on their hands. "I remember the first day Chris was here," says Dolly DiPesa, who was a teacher's aide. "One of the nuns brought him over and said, 'Hold on to him tight, and don't let him get out of your sight.' He'd see something and zoom—he was off exploring. It was hard to keep up with him."

Most often, the objects of his interest were people: the janitor, the cooks, visitors, teachers. Anyone who looked interesting soon knew this little boy who loved to talk. By the end of his first fall semester, he had established himself as both a teacher's pet and a good friend to the boys in his dormitory.

His curiosity and friendliness posed a slight problem, however. Chris was always late because he was always socializing, stopping in classrooms and hallways along the way to class. One day, realizing the teacher would be angry about his tardiness, he stopped to pick flowers for her, presenting them with a flourish just as she started to scold him.

Sometimes he would slip out of class to explore something or talk to someone he saw outside the door. He would drop by the superintendent's office to find out what was going on in the school. Other times, he greeted visitors in the school lobby adjacent to the classroom. With two teachers often giving ten students individual instruction, it was easy to escape detection for a few minutes.

"He was always in the thick of anything happening," remembers teacher Vicky Anderson. "He had a mischievous quality that went hand in hand with his curiosity, and sometimes it was greater than he was. If he saw something he wanted to know more about, he would forget the rules and just go for it. He was a very social, independent kid, with endless energy."

"I liked to hide from the teachers," says Chris. Sometimes he would crouch down under a table in the room to watch the search. Other times, his secret spot was in a storage room along the tunnel that linked the classrooms in inclement weather. "With any other child, you would think they were lost," says Dolly, who was often sent out to locate him. "But with Chris, you just knew he was either hiding on purpose or somewhere socializing with someone."

Chris remembers a time when he realized he had left a paper back in his dorm. He ran out of the room when the teacher wasn't looking and returned out of breath. "My teacher said, 'Chris, have you been somewhere?' And I said, 'Oh, ummmm, right here.' Then my classmates started laughing."

For discipline, the teachers rarely had to do more than talk with him. They realized that Chris had a short attention span and sometimes strayed because he was bored.

"I'm not sure if Chris would meet the typical criteria for being mentally retarded," says Vicky. "He was the youngest in our class, but the majority of the kids were not as bright as him. He was a little out of sync; he needed more challenge academically. I let him slip out for extra math and reading classes, and we engineered extra projects to keep him feeling challenged."

Compared to the whole student body of 150, which ranged in age from six to twenty-two, Chris was about average in academic ability, but far ahead of his peers in maturity and social relationships, say his teachers.

"I always knew I could rely on him for taking charge of a younger kid, helping them find classes, or if I sent him on an errand around the school," says Dolly. "It was easy to forget that he had Down syndrome. I had to stop and remember that he couldn't be expected to understand everything."

He knew how to behave when the time came, Dolly says. "For example, he didn't fool around when he was an altar boy. He had to ring the bells, bring in the wine and water, and assist the priest. He always behaved solemnly in church."

"Chris was always very spiritual," says Father John Keene, who was then the school priest. "He showed great concern for others. He was always asking to pray for his teachers, his family, or just people he would hear about."

He was, Vicky Anderson remembers, extremely cute, with long, thick blond hair and a sprinkling of freckles above his mischievous grin. "He could have easily won best-dressed award at school," she recalls. "Like most boys, he would be disheveled by the end of the day, but he was unusually concerned with his appearance."

Some nicknamed him "The Little Prep" for his favored Izod shirts, khakis, and topsiders. His classmates dressed casually, but Chris often wore a jacket and necktie, and he dressed in suits for special occasions. He carried his papers in an attaché case like a businessman.

"He was quite a kid," says Dolly. "In all my years of teaching, I know they don't make them like Chris. I really attributed it to the strength that comes from their family.

"Lots of kids were there because they didn't have good families and needed the dorm life, because their family was part of their problem," she adds. "Then there were kids like Chris who were just there to get good education. His parents were much more in touch with him."

Though Chris occasionally got homesick, he seemed to adjust well to the school. "At first, a lot of kids cry and won't talk to anyone," says Dolly. "Living in a dorm, they have to learn to do things as a group. Chris didn't have any problem adjusting to that. He got along well with the others."

After weekends home, "he would come back whole, ready for the week," Vicky recalls. "He was a very stable kid that way, so he must have felt pretty secure with his family."

In show and tell, Chris always talked about the other Burkes, and what they had done together on the weekends he went home. He carried around the latest photos of his family, and he gave regular updates in show and tell on what J.R. was doing in college. He was also proud of Anne, who was working at a fashion magazine in New York City, and Ellen, who was an infant-wear buyer for a large merchandise company. And Ellen's husband Jack was preparing for a foreign service career in the State Department.

Once a month, Chris flew to New York, sometimes with his neighbor Timmy, who was an older student at Cardinal Cushing. Some months he traveled back more often for family occasions, holidays, or special events.

When Chris was home, Marian and Frank always welcomed him and let him know how much he had been missed. Marian's cousin, Pat Egan, remembers calling Marian one Friday evening when Chris had just returned from school. She apologized for interrupting them, and Marian said, "Oh no, Pat, we're just sitting here, talking to Chris, and having that wonderful Friday night feeling. I just said to Frank, every family should have a Christopher. It's just such a wonderful thing to have our Chris home."

The first time that Chris went to the New York airport to head back to school, he grumbled a little, recalls Frank. "He started singing, 'I'm leaving on a jet plane . . .'" Then Chris grew to love flying. "He'd come off the airplane with souvenirs, magazines—anything that wasn't bolted down," recalls J.R. "And usually he had two stewardesses in tow."

When the weekends were over, he went cheerfully back to school. "But when he left, Marian and I were forlorn," says Frank. "Often we would confess our anguish and concern, wondering if we were doing the right thing."

When Marian and Frank visited Chris in Hanover, they met other parents of children in Cardinal Cushing and learned that almost all of them received state or local aid for this special education. They even met a minority student from Brooklyn who received a New York City subsidy. "Even though we could afford it, we felt if the city would give us this subsidy, we could put the money aside for Chris' future," says Marian. Frank investigated the situation, then was turned down for a subsidy, but no one could say exactly why Chris was not eligible. Perhaps, if they had applied before he was sent off to the school, a subsidy would have been possible.

Throughout the country, an education revolution was brewing. A year earlier, the Pennsylvania Association for Retarded Children (PARC) had won a lawsuit against its state in which the judge decreed that every child, no matter what disability, had a right to a free public education, and that placement in classes with nonhandicapped children was preferable when appropriate.

Though the decision only affected Pennsylvanians, it opened doors for similar lawsuits across the United States. The Burkes joined in, suing the city to force it into offering either financial aid or an appropriate education for Chris.

The lawsuit came to trial, and the judge agreed with Frank and Marian that the education available in New York was only adequate. She agreed that, as a parent, she would also want to send a child with special needs to a better-equipped school. Yet New York City was in a terrible financial crisis, and she could not find a legal reason for awarding the Burkes financial aid.

The costs were escalating: the frequent travel and long-distance phone calls pushed expenses far beyond the several thousand dollars for Cardinal Cushing annual tuition. Fortunately, the family coffers were beginning to grow. Frank had been promoted to police inspector in 1972, and was responsible for four precincts. Ellen and Anne were out of college; J.R.'s tuition was covered by the remaining earnings from their childhood modeling careers. And, for the first time since 1948, Marian was working outside the home. That first fall, when J.R. had returned to college and Chris left for Cardinal Cushing, their mother didn't wait for the empty home to overwhelm her. She had always wanted to go into teaching, and she decided to try substituting in a Catholic school while she went back to earn the necessary teaching credits. But seventh graders proved a rough adjustment for her. Within a few weeks, she switched to part-time secretarial work at George Little Management, a company that owned and operated trade shows.

Her employers agreed to let her take off Thursdays, Fridays, and some Mondays so that she could be with Chris when he came home from school. When he was out for summer break, she took a monthlong vacation to be with her family at their beach house in Point Lookout, New York.

Eventually, Frank and Marian's life settled into this new routine. Whether or not Chris was home, they had parties, movies, and Broadway shows to attend. When Chris was away, Frank and Marian called him often at school, wrote to him, and sent him packages. Cardinal Cushing offered plenty of weekend activities to keep the students occupied. Chris and his friends frequently spent Saturdays at Cape Cod with Father Keene or one of the teachers. There were field trips, parties, movies, dances, and Special Olympics games. The school had a working farm on the grounds, so Chris made friends with Farmer Al, his wife, and the horses, pigs, cows, and chickens.

The Burkes saw that Chris was content, and they were encouraged by his academic progress. At nine, he was reading at a second-grade level and excelling in math and other studies that were not much different from those taught in regular schools. His language and verbal skills were improving rapidly with the specialized instruction.

Just as Chris was progressing in his academic studies, he was able to satisfy his love for performing at Cardinal Cushing. In the four years he attended the school, he often played leading roles in organized plays. And in the dormitory, he produced impromptu dramas in the evenings.

"Chris was the ringleader," says Sister Eleanor Riordon, the dorm houseparent. "He'd get the other boys organized, then practice in a small room. When they were ready, he would call us all to the main recreation room for the show."

The skits were usually dramas centering on classroom or family situations, or vignettes about, for example, a doctor and patient in the hospital. Music and sometimes a little dancing accompanied the dialogue. Chris often devised makeshift costumes and built props from playroom blocks and furniture. Sometimes he would draw tickets for the shows and hand them around, hawking the night's feature attraction.

"We all enjoyed the skits," Sister Eleanor recalls. "They were very entertaining."

She remembers other students with Down syndrome who showed as much initiative and cleverness as Chris, but none who were as focused on performing. "Others would go through a phase of being interested, but he kept at it. Chris was an actor all along, and very good. Of course, we never thought it would blossom into something in the future."

In class, Chris lapsed into a variety of roles as the mood hit him. The television show "Happy Days" was the rage, and Chris often imitated the street-smart character Fonzie, swaggering into class with thumbs raised and growling, "Aaayyy." Other times, he was a rock star, strumming an imaginary guitar and singing or dancing for the amusement of his classmates. Any time he answered a question or talked before the class, he dropped and amplified his voice like a veteran television announcer.

"It doesn't surprise me that he's doing what he's doing now," says Vicky. "He always had a lot of the qualities: he's a serious learner, very confident yet playful, and loves tackling challenges. He had great ambitions. I didn't doubt them for a minute because he had so much determination and gumption."

Dolly remembers that Chris had a stubborn streak. "He would get a goal in mind, then it was like 'Don't try to stop me till I get there.' "

Chris was always eager to serve as altar boy at mass, which was in some ways similar to being on the stage. And Father Keene often elicited his help in short skits which he used to illustrate Bible stories.

In addition to drama and regular studies, the teachers taught lifestyle skills such as cooking and cleaning, money management, and etiquette. Some of the students, especially those abandoned by their families, had problems with these skills. But Chris already had the basics when he got there, remembers Dolly. "He was socially mature at a young age. He had good table manners, and knew what to do when he met someone."

His outgoing personality made him popular with the girls as he grew into adolescence. Cardinal Cushing was a coed school, with girls living in a separate wing of the same residential hall. There were plenty of parties and opportunities for supervised dating, and Chris enjoyed several nonserious romances.

The girls in his class were older than him, and they looked at him more as a little brother, Vicky recalls. But Sister Eleanor remembers that when Chris was about twelve, he courted a special friend, taking her to the movies and other special events on the weekends. During school days, he walked her to class, carrying her books and holding the door open for her. "He wanted to be grown up, like his brother J.R., and was aware of girls at an early age. He was always very caring, and polite."

The teachers tried to be impartial toward students but found it a challenge with Chris. "It was clear that Chris was a favored boy, the golden child," says Vicky. "He was bright enough to use that to his advantage. He always called me 'Vick,' in a real confident manner, and he knew he could get away with it.

"Maybe he did recognize that what he had was special and unique in comparison with others, and not to be taken lightly. He was aware of things that way. I think Chris knew he was lucky to have so much."

While Chris was in school, Marian and Frank traveled to Europe on vacation. They toured Vienna, where Frank had never been during the war, then drove to Krems, near the site of Stalag 17. There they asked townspeople where the POW camp had been. Everyone rebuffed them, acting as if the place had never existed. Finally, Frank got directions from the police station. Frank could barely recognize the field: a private flying club was on the site where fences, barracks, and guard towers once stood.

From Krems, Marian and Frank retraced his steps on the grueling march to Braunau, stopping along the way at places Frank remembered spending chilly, hungry nights. "In a way it was sort of a triumph to go back," says Frank. "I had the attitude of 'You didn't beat me. I'm back as a free man. I'll follow the march from here to Braunau and I'll do it in style this time.' It was remarkable how many things came back to me." Marian says the trip made Frank pensive at times, but "it was good for him. He explained it to me along the way. He thoroughly enjoyed it."

They even stopped, as Frank had done before, to attend mass at the church in Klam. On the steps sat a little girl, who looked up at them intently.

"She had Down syndrome," said Marian. "Frank and I looked at each other, and thought it must be some kind of sign. It seemed so ironic to us." For Frank, it was a reminder that the worst part of his life was in the past. He had survived the war, and he had come to the full realization that Down syndrome was not the tragedy it had seemed at Chris' birth.

The family still suffered setbacks. At Christmas, a year after J.R. was ill in the hospital, Anne delivered a stillborn baby boy. "It was a low point for all of us," says Marian. Around the same time, Ellen, her husband Jack, and her daughter Sara moved to Washington, D.C., for Jack's foreign service career, wrenching them away from family and friends in New York.

But Chris was progressing rapidly in school, as were the people fighting for better education for children with disabilities. During Chris' second year at Cardinal Cushing, parent organizations scored a landmark victory by pushing Congress to pass Public Law 194-42, mandating a full public education for all students in the least restrictive environment. Throughout the United States, special needs children were slowly being integrated into regular classrooms, and special education classes were upgraded to include more academic training.

In Massachusetts, mainstreaming these children had begun in earnest. Many children who would have received private school subsidies were instead attending local school classes. As a result, Cardinal Cushing was in flux, slowly changing its focus from mentally retarded children to include those with behavioral and other developmental problems.

More of the new children came from impoverished backgrounds, and they were often suffering from early abuse and neglect. They were sometimes unruly, more aggressive toward other students, and frustrated by their own problems in schoolwork and among their peers.

One boy in Chris' classroom had been abandoned at birth and raised in a series of foster homes before he was sent to Cardinal Cushing. He was not retarded, but he had learning disabilities and a range of behavior problems that hampered his education.

The teachers and nuns watched the competition develop between the two boys. "They were both leaders," says Sister Eleanor Riordon. "Chris was outgoing, and this boy was aggressive. He was vying for attention all the time."

One March weekend, the students were walking out of the dining room when the other boy ran his hand down a pine branch, grabbing some needles and cones. He turned to Chris and said, "Open your mouth and close your eyes and I'll give you a big surprise." Chris did it, thinking he was going to get some candy. The boy jammed the contents of his hand in Chris' mouth just as Chris, realizing it was a prank, struggled and gasped, inhaling the needles. As Chris choked up pine needles, the school workers rushed him to the hospital for an examination. Routine X rays did not show the pieces already lodged in his lower lung.

Sister Eleanor remembers the incident as just a prank gone awry, rather than a premeditated attack. But the damage was severe, and Chris was frightened.

He returned to school, remaining in the classroom with the other boy. "He was in a very fragile, vulnerable state," Vicky recalls. "He was honest about his feelings; he didn't try to pretend it didn't happen."

The perpetrator seemed to have a sense of remorse, Vicky says. "I think he felt that the odd consequence of his action was that Chris was still going to get more attention. The school rallied around Chris in a huge way. I felt for both of them. The other boy was struggling with school, trying to get along with the others."

Chris spoke assertively with his classmate, telling him, "I didn't like it; you shouldn't have done that." He wrote about the experience in the school's weekly paper, and the class discussed it from time to time.

"It was a traumatic experience for Chris, and a difficult situation for all of us," says Vicky, who is now a psychologist. "He was trying to sort it through with the boy. I don't think he ever got to the anger. He had sadness and a real fear about what happened, then eventually told the boy, 'Let's be friends.'"

Vicky thinks Chris realized that the other boy was hurt by the incident as well. "It was something very touching to watch. I wouldn't be able to do that. He really forgave him, and it was extremely helpful to the boy."

There were never any further incidents between the two. But for the rest of the school year, Chris was racked with a wheezing cough. The sickness changed him: he was less physically active, and his attentiveness and curiosity withered. When he returned home for the summer, he was lethargic and still coughing. At the beach, he stopped socializing to lie down and sleep. Marian took him to several doctors, but they all blamed his symptoms on his Down syndrome, telling Marian he was just more prone to minor respiratory infections.

That fall, after Chris had returned to school, Frank and Marian met him at the airport in New York one weekend and drove to Washington, D.C., to visit Ellen and her family. Chris seemed well at the start, but by the time they reached Alexandria, he was coughing up blood.

They rushed him to a hospital, and again doctors saw he had Down syndrome and assured Marian that it was only normal for him to have a respiratory infection. Chris took some medicine, went to sleep, then awoke a few hours later coughing up huge amounts of blood. The next day they saw another doctor, who speculated that there might be some foreign matter in his lungs and recommended an operation. But Marian and Frank wanted Chris treated in New York, so they took him back to their regular pediatrician. She scoffed at the other doctor's advice, especially since early X rays showed nothing.

"You know that these kids get pneumonia all the time, Marian," she said.

"But Chris has never had pneumonia . . ."

"He does now," answered the doctor.

Back at Cardinal Cushing, school workers administered special treatments, but his coughing spells worsened. Three times he was rushed to the hospital, where doctors inserted a bronchoscope to examine and probe his lung. Every time, pine needles came up, and every time, they thought the bronchoscope had removed them all. Marian and Frank flew to Boston to be with Chris in the hospital, always returning home days later with the doctors' reassurance that Chris had recovered. Marian wasn't convinced. But the doctors warned that if any pine needles did remain, the operation to remove them would be too dangerous.

"If he had not had Down syndrome, I think they would have operated sooner," says Marian. "But they thought it was not imperative that he go through a major operation, that they could just keep trying to get it up with the bronchoscope. They thought it would be okay if he missed some time in school because he wasn't moving up to different grades like in a regular school."

Chris came home for the summer and seemed to be fine, except for occasional coughing spells. Then in July, in a restaurant, a noodle caught in his throat and he again coughed up blood.

"That does it," said Marian. "This has taken too great a toll on Chris." The next day she called and arranged for the operation in Boston. In August, eighteen months after his schoolmate had shoved pine needles in his throat, Chris underwent surgery to remove part of his lower right lung.

By that time, J.R. had graduated from college and was traveling around the world, from Iceland through Europe and the Orient. He was in Australia when he received a letter that Chris had been hospitalized. The rest of the world didn't seem so important anymore: J.R. cut his trip short by two months, flying home just in time to be by his brother's side after the surgery.

Chris recovered quickly and completely. Within days, he was following the doctors on their rounds, wearing their stethoscopes and pretending to scan their charts.

One doctor had trouble applying his textbook knowledge of Down syndrome to the boy he saw was Chris. He asked Marian, "Are you sure he has Down syndrome?"

"Two tests said he does," she answered.

Chris doesn't like to talk about this time of his life, but he bears a grisly reminder: a surgery scar running from the middle of his back down around his ribs and up through his chest. Deep inside, doctors had found a tiny one-inch pine tree, part of a seed that had sprouted in the warm, moist atmosphere of his lungs.

SEVEN

★ ★ ★ ★ ★ ★ ★ ★ ★ ★ ★ ★ ★ ★

IT WAS ONCE mistakenly assumed that all people with Down syndrome lived in a permanent childhood, never facing the angst of teenage years or the maturity they bring. And Chris, on his thirteenth birthday, still looked and acted more like an eight-year-old child. His freckled cheeks were chubby, usually crinkled into a big mischievous grin. He was excitable and energetic, preferring to run wherever he was going.

But Chris, like most people with Down syndrome, was only a late bloomer. Within the next few years, he matured quickly, both physically and mentally. He calmed down, slowing his pace to a bouncy gait. His voice deepened and his speech improved; he grew slimmer, broader in the shoulders, and almost a foot taller. His white-blond hair darkened, and he let it grow almost to his shoulders, in the style of the late 1970s. When the first few hairs sprouted on his chin, he proudly shaved them each morning, then doused his face and neck with generous amounts of after-shave lotion and cologne.

His family was surprised at how quickly the changes took place. Almost overnight, he switched from "Sesame Street" songs to heavy metal music, which blared a little too loudly for their tastes. His interest turned to writing: he began filling dozens of yellow legal pads with short stories, ideas for television shows, and long letters, which he would send to his favorite celebrities.

Marian says parenting Chris during his early teen years was about the same as when he was a child. "He was still under the control of the schools, and he still listened to us when he was home." One thing she noticed was the way Chris took extra care to treat her like a lady. His manners became impeccable: he opened doors for her, stood up as she entered the room, and pulled her chair out at the dinner table. When they went to a movie, he would cover her eyes with his hand during any violent or sexy scenes, warning her, "Mom, you don't want to see that."

Yet for Chris, the teenage years were bittersweet. "I had a lot of fun, but I had growing pains, too," he says. "Sometimes it was rough."

Changes surrounded Chris in his first year as a teenager. His parents moved to a smaller apartment in Peter Cooper Village, a high-rise community across the street from Stuyvesant Town that was wired for air conditioning. And suddenly he was the new kid at a new boarding school, Don Guanella, where he had transferred from Cardinal Cushing. The move was for two reasons. First, Cardinal Cushing administrators had advised the Burkes to find another school for Chris. The school population was changing: even more students with behavioral problems were being admitted, now that Massachusetts was mainstreaming its educable mentally retarded students into public schools.

The Burkes weren't eager to let Chris try mainstreaming, which had just started in New York public schools, and to this day they do not regret the decision. "Chris was always a leader in his schools," says Marian. "I don't think he would have been a leader in a mainstreaming situation." Marian also felt that the private school classes were more oriented to Chris' needs. "They taught them at the level that they needed to be taught. I realize there are many, many benefits of mainstreaming. But regular schoolteachers don't normally take special ed courses, so how would they know how to teach a person with special needs?"

The second reason for the transfer was that Chris' commute from Boston to New York was taking its toll on the family. Often, the school van to the airport would idle in heavy traffic, and Chris would miss his flight. Other times, weather delays stranded him in the Boston airport for hours, where he would wait with a school worker while his parents anguished in New York. "It was a phenomenal heartache until Chris stepped off the plane," says J.R. "It became obvious that we would save a lot of worry if we found a school closer to someone in our family."

Anne, who lived in Connecticut, had just given birth to twin daughters, Katie and Molly. Ellen, Jack, and their baby daughter Sara were in Bogotá, Colombia, where Jack was working in the foreign service. J.R. had settled in Philadelphia and was building a career in insurance and investment counseling. He scouted the area for a school that would fit Chris' needs. In nearby Springfield, he found Don Guanella, a boarding school established in 1960 by an order of Italian priests who devoted their lives to working with the mentally retarded. Chris visited and liked what he saw. The campus stretched back through two miles of forest, with a pond, an indoor pool, two basketball courts, and a soccer and football field. Every night, students gathered around the recreation hall jukebox to dance and play games supervised by energetic young counselors. Even the food was good, especially when the cooks served up the priests' favorite home-style Italian dishes.

The school's 130 students ranged in age from six to twenty-one, and about a third had Down syndrome. All were classified as retarded, based on a score of seventy or below on intelligence tests, but ranged from mild to severe in disability.

For Chris, the best part of the transfer to Don Guanella was that his brother was just minutes away. Every other Friday, J.R. would drive Chris to the train bound for New York. "My time with Chris was the highlight of my week," says J.R. "It always picked me up and helped me keep perspective on my life. Things I could do naturally took effort for him. That made me realize how foolish it was to complain about things that were, in the big picture, insignificant."

Around this time, J.R. volunteered with an advocacy group made up of parents of children with Down syndrome. At the first meeting, everyone introduced themselves and added a few words about their children. J.R. listened to the sad stories with growing anxiety. One couple had not been away from their son in thirty-five years. Others had children in institutions, where they were adults still in diapers. When it came time for J.R. to speak, he tried to move the discussion past him quickly. "My brother is a student at Don Guanella and he's doing fine," he said, turning to the next person. Then a woman broke in, "My son used to go there. But he had to go home every other weekend. Your family is from New York. What do you do on the weekends he has to go home? Do your parents drive down from New York to pick him up?"

"No," J.R. answered hesitantly. "I go pick him up on Fridays and sometimes he stays with me, or he goes to New York."

"But how does he get to New York?" she asked.

"I take him to the Amtrak station and he takes the train," said J.R. The room fell silent, the people absorbing the news with some shock. J.R. says he spent two wonderful years as treasurer of the group, but he often wondered about some of the people who were so protective of their children. "Some of the sad situations might have been sad because the people were so scared and protective and held their kids back," he says. "What really upset me were the retarded attitudes of the parents."

Still, J.R. acknowledges that the Burkes probably had more to work with in Chris than many other families. "There are so many situations where the potential just isn't there."

For Chris, riding the train from Philadelphia to New York was no big deal, after the years of commuting by plane from Boston. He became friends with the concessions operator in the Philadelphia station, and with the stationmaster in New York. He often played a game with his parents where he would sneak off the train and run to the stationmaster's office. Then, as Marian and Frank searched for him among the disembarking passengers, they would hear over the loudspeaker, "Will Mr. and Mrs. Francis D. Burke please come to the stationmaster's office?"

Frank still laughs about it. "Every single time, we would get to the station before the train came in, and no matter how hard we tried, he always managed to slip away before we saw him. I still don't know how he did it."

Occasionally J.R. drove Chris back home to New York. Chris usually fell asleep within minutes of riding in the car, but J.R. tried to keep him awake by giving him lessons or simple math problems. "One thing I did was to explain what New York City was. We would talk about the five boroughs, so he could get home and tell them to my parents. It was hard work. It took a couple of trips before he got that." Sometimes the lessons were too much for Chris to handle. "I yam what I yam, J.R.," he would sigh, imitating the cartoon character Popeye with a wink of his eye.

"That's what he would always say if he felt we were pushing him beyond his natural capabilities," says J.R. "He could pick up that we were frustrated, and that was his way of making a joke to break the tension."

Chris spent many weekends at J.R.'s home, sometimes bringing his friends along. J.R. would take them to dinner, the movies, and pro basketball games. Chris' friends all knew J.R. from his frequent visits to the school; sometimes J.R. would stop by for a few minutes to shoot a few hoops with them, or take several out for a quick weeknight dinner. J.R. was working long hours building his career, but he monitored his brother's education like a concerned parent, often taking time to talk with teachers and cottage supervisors. He attended Chris' basketball games and other special events.

The first time J.R. attended the Special Olympics games, he was running late and missed the fifty-yard dash Chris had entered. When he arrived, Chris excitedly showed him his ribbon. "I came in third!"

"That's great!" said J.R., and he slapped Chris a high-five. As they sat down to watch the other races, J.R. asked, "By the way, Chris, how many kids were in your race?"

Chris responded with a grin. "Aw, shucks, J.R., I was hoping you wouldn't ask me that. There were only three kids in the race."

One thing Chris didn't like about the new school was its large residence hall, where he lived in a room with twenty other boys. It was a switch from Cardinal Cushing, where he had lived with just one roommate. "That was rough," he says. "There were too many of us. I love my privacy, but I didn't have any at Don Guanella."

Chris' parents got the first hint that he didn't like the arrangement when they took Chris to visit Marian's Aunt Sally in a nursing home, where she had a private room. As they were leaving, Chris turned to Marian. "Mom, can I get a white wig?" he asked.

"Well, Chris, why do you want that?"

Chris looked back at her somberly. "Because then I could put it on and go live with Aunt Sally at the nursing home. I like it there. I could be her roommate." Marian and Frank chuckled at the thought of their son posing as a senior citizen, but they could tell Chris was not just joking. The problem was soon solved when the school began building cottages where the boys could live two to a room.

Chris had other adjustment problems in his first year. The school was far more strict than Cardinal Cushing, where the nuns had a softer style of discipline. Every morning, the priests blared rock music to awaken the students. The boys were supervised almost every minute of the day, at meals, in classes, and in recreational programs after school. At night, the priests monitored their television time closely, often switching the channel to a religious show during a big basketball game or the boys' favorite television shows. Chris, who took his television viewing seriously, sometimes howled and cried when this happened.

Looking back on it, Chris says the most difficult part of Don Guanella was its discipline system. Students were allowed privileges based on merit points they earned for doing chores, being on time, and following directions from their supervisors. "It was very different from Cardinal Cushing," says Chris. "When I got to Don Guanella, I didn't know anything about a point system. I didn't like it because they treated me like I was in the Army. They were always telling me to do this or do that. If I got higher points, I could stay up late. If I got lower points, I had to go to bed early, and I couldn't go on field trips." Chris admits he lost a few points for not keeping his bunk clean. "I was like Jack Klugman in 'The Odd Couple'—real messy."

Except for his chronic tardiness, which, as at Cardinal Cushing, usually stemmed from his gregarious nature, Chris rarely got in trouble. "The worst thing he did was to play his radio too loud," says Father Enzo, who supervised Chris in the residence hall. "He was a good kid. He didn't bother anyone."

The same couldn't always be said for his classmates. Though about half the students were from caring middle- and upper-class families, the other half were troubled kids who had been sent to the school from neglectful or abusive situations. Some had been placed in restrictive public institutions at birth and had not been educated in their early years. Others were borderline retarded, often just slow learners in need of specialized education. People with severe emotional disturbances such as schizophrenia were not admitted into the school, but many of the students had underlying emotional problems that made for volatile social interaction. "They didn't like to be around really retarded kids," says Robert Neely, a supervisor in the residence halls. "Some of them were terrible punks, right off the streets."

To this day, Chris doesn't like to talk about the rough group of students at Don Guanella. "They weren't nice to me at all," Chris says. "They were really emotionally disturbed. If I talk about them now, they'll come beat me up."

Yet Robert says Chris was intimidated but never physically hurt by any of the students. "In the years I was there, I don't recall Chris ever being involved in a fight, which was incredible because everyone else was. The others wouldn't hit him. There was something almost sacred about Chris, because he was so good and so sincere. He would never antagonize anyone or be cruel."

Mostly, the kids would mimic Chris, making fun of the way he stuttered when he got excited or nervous. "He was so emotional," says Robert. "He cried easily, especially in his younger years. He'd get hurt and come crying on my shoulder and say, 'Why are they teasing me?' I'd try to build up his confidence and tell him that everybody has something they have to work on."

Robert says the rougher kids more often preyed on the more gullible students, who would do anything the tougher kids said to do. "Chris was too smart for that. But he sometimes tried too hard to be cool and fit in. It was something he and I had to sit down and talk about, just what it means to be accepted and how you can't do just anything to be accepted in a group."

Chris' eagerness to fit in made him an easy target for the rougher kids' pranks. "They were always getting me in trouble," says Chris. "They'd do something, then blame it on me. This one boy had a rule that I wasn't allowed to pass his part of the hallway. I couldn't even go visit my friends. He got me so wound up. I got in trouble and I didn't even do anything to him."

Another time, Chris came back to his room to find that two large jars of vitamins, which his mother had bought for him under direction of a holistic doctor, were missing. "This other boy took them and went in the fathers' cottage and killed these two little hamsters. He put the hamsters in the garbage and he spilled my vitamins all over them. He killed these innocent little animals. I wanted to beat him up. I said, 'My mother paid sixteen dollars for those vitamins. You had no right to do that.' He never paid me back. It's a very bad memory."

The more delinquent students even terrorized a nun in her nineties, soaping the floors so she would slip when she walked by. The tiny nun crawled into the laundry dumbwaiter to move between floors, since it was hard for her to walk up stairs. Some kids would jam the dumbwaiter, trapping her between the floors, then listen to her cries for help.

Chris tried to be nice to the nun, who spoke broken English, but she insisted on calling him not by his name, but by the number that was tagged to his laundry. "She would say, 'Come here, number 223!' " says Chris. "I really liked her, but she wasn't nice to me at all."

Yet to the Burkes, all seemed peaceful at Don Guanella. The students were polite and orderly under the strict eyes of the priests, and Chris rarely complained. "We had tried to avoid those kinds of students by moving Chris from Cardinal Cushing," says Marian. "We didn't realize that he went from the frying pan into the fire. But I feel it was better for Chris in the long run. He learned so much about getting along with different types of people." And after parenting three other teenagers, Marian knew that rejection and peer problems were inherent to the teen-age years. "No one likes for their child to be picked on. But it's normal. There were things that happened to me in high school that I still remember vividly. And it was the same for my other children."

Chris didn't tell his mother about these incidents until just recently. When he was a teenager, he mentioned the teasing to his dad only once. Frank then came down to the school to talk with the perpetrators. "He's never done anything to anyone," Frank told them. "You just leave him alone, or you'll answer to me." The boys seemed to listen, and most of the teasing stopped.

Before long, Chris began breaking down some of the barriers to make a tentative peace with them. Robert Neely says Chris won them over by using his knowledge of sports and entertainment. When break dancing became the rage, Chris joined the kids on the floor every night, spinning and jumping to the music. A gentle ribbing sprang up between Chris, a big New York Mets and Giants fan, and the kids who cheered the Philadelphia teams.

Through the years, Chris learned to defuse volatile situations by going to the counselors or confronting the other kids without offending them, says Kevin Hay, another counselor. "He would tell them how he was feeling and what they were doing that made him feel the way he was. You can't find that many adults who can do that."

Little problems still came up. Occasionally Chris would provoke the ire of a classmate by blurting out a truthful but tactless comment. In his childlike honesty, he did not always comprehend the nuances or subtleties of a sticky situation in which most people would have stayed silent. "He always had an opinion, and wasn't shy about speaking up," says Robert. "That was one of the things we worked with him on, trying to mature him. His anxiousness and excitement would get him hyper and we'd have to calm him down."

Chris was usually one of the youngest students in his classes. He had started in lower-level classes with more of his peers, but within a few years he had moved up to the highest level with the older students, an unusual feat for someone with Down syndrome. He progressed not only because of his academic skills, which were just slightly above average, but also because of his mastery of social skills.

"Socially, he functioned at a higher level than any kid with Down syndrome I have ever seen," says Ed Kelly, Chris' speech therapist. "That's why he was placed on the higher track. He was in some ways an overachiever."

Placement was based on IQ numbers to an extent, but numbers alone don't convey the success a person will have in a class or in life, says psychologist Bill Ryan, now a school administrator. "There can be a world of difference between two people with the same number. What it comes down to is how skillful you are in interacting in your environment."

A student who is only mildly retarded can memorize lessons and learn to read on a level that includes most books and newspapers. "Where they fall short is judgment," says Bill. "Judgment calls into play abstract reasoning, a memory for the past, and a view of the future. It's an iffy thing for them."

Most of the classes tried to increase that level of judgment by focusing on practical knowledge that would prepare students for life in the world outside. The school issued no report cards or grades; instead, each student was expected to accomplish tasks based on his level of capabilities. They learned to read street signs and employment forms, and they practiced proper manners and behaviors. Many programs centered around nearby malls and shopping centers, where the students learned to shop, paying for items in the right amount and receiving the correct change. They were taught store etiquette: how it isn't polite to handle the merchandise too much or put things back where they don't belong.

General academic courses in math, English, history, and science were tailored with individual instruction and hands-on activities to hold the students' interest. In one class, Chris and his friends produced a news network, covering current news, sports, fashion, travel, and entertainment. They researched a topic in the library, wrote a short segment, then presented the stories as news anchors while the teacher taped it on a video camera.

At fourteen, Chris asked one teacher to help him write a short movie script. For most of the year, they worked on grammar, vocabulary, and dialogue, building the story around a popular Anne Murray song, "Just Falling in Love Again." At the end of the year, Chris persuaded his fellow students to act out the script before a video camera. The story revolved around two soldiers who longed to be with their wives back home.

Don Guanella also offered speech therapy and group discussions with a psychologist who helped the students learn how to interact successfully in their personal relationships. Bill Ryan says that while all the students had some problem with social interaction, the more mildly retarded students were often the most frustrated by their problems. "They carried the largest burden because they become aware of the differences between themselves and the general population. They see how the world treats them differently."

Many of the students were loners, and there were few cliques typical of most teenage crowds. The school workers say that Chris was a little unusual in that he had close friendships. He usually could be found with his two best friends, huddling over some writing or music project or talking about girls. In later years, he and his friends discussed their goals for the future, how they wanted a career and their own apartments.

Teacher Betsy Tompkins says Chris was a normal teenager. "He wasn't a saint. He had days he didn't feel like doing anything. He had his moments of criticism for people. But he was also always right there to give a pat on the back, or to give encouraging comments. He was persistent, and usually was cheering everyone else on. He'd say, 'I know you can do it. Try it again.'"

The main weakness in Chris' personality, say the school workers, was his stubbornness. "If he was doing something he liked, it was like pulling teeth to get him to go on to something else," says Robert Neely. "He would get an idea in his head and stick to it. It was also his good quality. He wouldn't quit on anything."

Sometimes rationalizing didn't work. Once when the cottage group was planning its weekend activities, Chris blurted out, "Let's walk to New York City!" Robert patiently tried to explain that New York was ninety miles away, but Chris wouldn't listen. "No, no, I have a plan. We can go see a show." Robert kept trying, but Chris sincerely believed that his plan was the best.

School days were frequently spent off campus, where the teachers helped students learn to move comfortably in the outside world. Classes visited museums, went bowling, attended cultural events, and learned to maneuver their way through train and bus routes. Betsy Tompkins' class once braved a blizzard to visit Valley Forge on a Revolutionary War anniversary. The students walked through snow that was thigh-deep in places, and they shivered inside the tiny stone hut where George Washington had commanded his troops. When they returned to the bus, Betsy handed out stone cakes she had made from flour and water, and the students melted snow for drinking water, as the soldiers had done for their meals. "She pulled out those cakes and I said, 'This isn't lunch!'" recalls Chris. "And then she said that's the only lunch we're having. I said, 'Get out of here!' It was weird, but fun."

For Chris, it is one of the few field trips he can still recall in detail. Another was his favorite, a week-long trip to Williamsburg. The students prepared for it for six months, making colonial crafts, writing letters requesting tourist information, studying the area's history, and listening to period music. To fund the trip, they set up a mini-business, making and selling hoagie sandwiches around the school. Chris was a top salesman, convincing everyone in the school that they needed yet one more hoagie, until just the sight of the plastic-wrapped packages sent the staff running.

In the spring, the class set out for the journey with more than a little trepidation from the teachers and some students' parents. But the class behaved perfectly and was allowed to stay a few extra days. The pageantry of Williamsburg's historical district fascinated Chris. "I felt like I was back in those times," he says. "The best part was all the music." The people of Williamsburg opened their arms to the students, even hosting a free concert especially for them.

But on other trips to the outside world, the reception wasn't as warm. On one trip to a local mall, one class was asked to leave a department store. "The kids weren't doing anything," says Betsy. "The people who worked there just thought the other customers might view them negatively. I told them we had a right to be there. How else were they going to learn? People don't understand. There's that fear of people who are different. I wanted to say, 'You're not going to catch Down syndrome. It's not contagious.' "

On some outings, people pointed or stared at the students, and sometimes the group was told to sit in a separate area. Such treatment rankled Chris. When he saw a television movie about Dr. Martin Luther King, he was moved by the story of Rosa Parks. "They told her she had to get to the back of the bus and she said no. She wouldn't go back there. I really identified with that scene. I'm glad it's not like that now for the black people and people with handicaps. We have the right to be with all people, too."

Inside the classrooms, the students experienced other lessons in life. When teacher Betsy Tompkins was pregnant, the kids lived through it with her, asking her questions and marveling at the miracle of it all. They fed and cared for the class gerbil, Thriller. When Thriller died, the class discussed the death and decided to give him a fitting funeral in the woods outside the class building. Chris delivered the eulogy at the grave.

In some classes, foster grandparents assisted the students with their lessons. Chris had never known his own grandparents, since they had all died by the time he was a toddler. In school, his favorite was Grandma Rose, who sat in on classes and worked in the mending room. She taught the boys how to sort their laundry, run the machines, and bring it to the cottages. But more importantly, she offered a soft shoulder to cry on when the world seemed unfair.

Chris remembers her fondly. "Whenever I had problems, she'd say,

'Chris, come here.' I'd go hug her and she made me feel better. She loves me a lot."

Grandma Rose says she tried not to have favorites, but Chris was one of two boys she loved the most in more than a decade of working at Don Guanella. "I never thought anyone could be so bright in a place for retarded children. I knew something was different about him when he started writing such long letters to his family. None of them could write long letters like he could. He was really exceptional."

The class pitched in to buy Grandma Rose birthday gifts, and sent her a huge get-well banner when she was in the hospital. Some of the foster grandparents passed away while Chris was at school, and he attended the funerals with his class. "We felt that was an important part of life they needed to experience too," says Betsy.

The school also worked to bring the community in to its students. A nearby high school frequently sent volunteers to Don Guanella, and hosted joint school activities. College sports teams visited, as did celebrities and entertainers from the Philadelphia area. Chris was a favorite with the visitors because he was more extroverted than most students at the school, says Robert Neely. He easily struck up conversations with them, asking them about their interests and taking them on impromptu tours of his school. During the Special Olympics, Chris caught the attention of the "huggers," the high school girls who would assist the athletes and praise them for their efforts. "There were some nice-looking girls, and Chris inevitably got some phone numbers," says Kevin Hay.

"For some of the visitors, it was their first time to be around someone handicapped, and they didn't know what to expect," says Robert. "Chris had a way of easing them. He broke down barriers with his personality."

When Philadelphia Eagles coach Dick Vermeil visited, Chris ran right over and started asking questions about football. "Chris saw a celebrity and there he went," says Ed Kelly. "He wasn't shy at all. He loved meeting new people, which is difficult for a lot of these kids."

If the school needed a master of ceremonies for the basketball banquet, there was Chris. "He was a natural at narrating, or introducing people, or just spontaneously making speeches," says teacher Gloria Luzecki. "He was always comfortable in front of an audience."

Chris' language skills improved dramatically at Don Guanella, where he had daily speech therapy classes. His voice was slightly throaty and gravelly, which is typical of Down syndrome. And like his peers, he was troubled with certain sounds, mostly *k* sounds and blends such as *dr* and *str*. On long words with many consonants, he sometimes dropped the end sounds, or he would leave out filler words such as "at," "the," and "of" in long sentences. Chris often spoke too rapidly, jumbling the words, so Ed had him practice tapping his hands to a sentence to keep a steady rhythm. His stutter, Ed says, was more of a block that happened when he lost his pacing.

Mostly, Chris had difficulty with concentration. "He would start a sentence and wander from the point, but basically his ability to stay on the topic and give you information was incredible. It's not something you see too often in people with Down syndrome. He really and truly was different."

Ed says Chris was a quick learner and a good reader, and he was aided by a strong vocabulary. "He would occasionally use a word that would bowl me over, that you didn't expect from him. He was able to converse about a number of things." Ed credits the difference in Chris to his travels and the experiences he had with his family. "He went places and did things and met people your everyday run-of-the-mill kid doesn't do. His parents made an effort to get him out in the world and get him used to it."

Ed remembers one spring when he was excited about visiting a friend in San Francisco. Then Chris casually mentioned he was going to Poland. That vacation was to visit Chris' sister Ellen, whose husband Jack was advancing in the foreign service. "I was happy to see my sister and brother-in-law and my nieces, but I didn't like Poland," Chris recalls. "I saw all these soldiers with guns [Poland was under martial law at the time] and I didn't know whether they'd shoot or not. I was really scared."

Other times, Chris traveled with his parents to Bogotá, Colombia, again to see Ellen, and Bermuda for a more relaxing vacation. Marian, Frank, and Chris took cruises to the Bahamas, and they traveled to Florida each year. But there was one place Chris wanted to go that the Burkes resisted for several years: Nashville, Tennessee.

At sixteen, Chris had seen a television commercial for a country music station. "I ran upstairs and turned it on my radio, and I fell in love with country music. I didn't even know there was country music until then. I didn't know there was such a thing as bluegrass or hillbilly music!" he says, shaking his head in amazement. It wasn't long before all of Chris' heavy metal and disco tapes lay unused, replaced by an impressive collection of country hits. "I like country music because it tells a story. I like it because they sing their hearts out. And it's honest."

When Chris was home, the Manhattan apartment twanged with the sounds of Alabama and Randy Travis, and the television was often turned to the Grand Ole Opry and The Nashville Network. Chris started sounding like a broken record with his one wish: to go to Nashville. He begged, he pleaded, and he finally wore down his parents.

"They thought they weren't going to like it because they didn't like country music," says Chris. "But they loved it! It was so beautiful and we went everywhere. I learned all about the roots of country music." He returned to school with a cowboy hat, which the priests refused to let him wear.

When he went home to New York, Chris always saw the latest musical hits on Broadway. He raved over the performance of Patti LuPone, who played Reno Sweeney in *Anything Goes.* Sandy Duncan's portrayal of Peter Pan held him spellbound, even during intermission. "He wouldn't get up from his seat," says Marian. "He really lived each moment of it." The Burkes encouraged Chris' love for music by giving him a new musical instrument every Christmas. They even gave Chris a toy set of drums, a gift that they sometimes regretted in the hours that Chris cranked up the stereo with rock music and pounded out the rhythms with gusto.

Chris' musical talent wasn't appreciated much at Don Guanella, where he was kicked out of the band. "I played the maracas. The priest who led us thought I never kept good time. He said, 'You're out of the band!' I thought I was doing okay."

Later that year, J.R. and his parents visited the school for a show that featured an offbeat tune by the band. "They were bad. I mean, they were awful," says J.R. "I poked Chris and said, 'You mean you got kicked out of *that* band?' He was kind of sheepish about it, but we had a good laugh."

Chris fared better in sports, though in his first years he had trouble keeping up with the teams. Chris played soccer and baseball, and he joined the basketball team, but he was shorter, had less stamina, and was not as coordinated as the students who didn't have Down syndrome. Still, Chris faced his limitations with an enthusiasm and determination to improve, says Robert Neely. "He was a spunky little athlete. He was always out there trying. He was kind of a hot dog: he'd strut around the court when he made a good shot."

Counselor Kevin Hay remembers Chris being as concerned with how he looked as how he played. One time before a softball game, Chris was nowhere to be found. The other kids, dressed in their scrungiest dungarees, went on out to the field while Kevin went to look for Chris. He found him in his room, combing his hair. "There he was in this full-fledged uniform, with a hat and softball pants and spikes, new gloves, and a new aluminum baseball bat. I said, 'Chris, you may play lousy but you sure look good.' He didn't mind sticking out. He was always the best dressed in the school."

Chris had his best sports night when his basketball team played the Cabrini College varsity in an exhibition game before a crowd of fifteen hundred local special education students. When Chris got the ball, he pitched it from the center of the court and it fell straight into the hoop. A few minutes later, he tried the same shot and miraculously made a second basket. The Cabrini team looked at him in wonderment while the crowd whooped and cheered. Chris soaked in the praise, running around the court jumping and waving his arms at the crowd.

Another exciting night was when the Don Guanella team played another school at the Spectrum in Philadelphia, just before a pro 76ers game. "That was awesome," says Chris. "When I was going to the dressing room, I saw 'Dr. J,' Julius Erving. I walked over and shook his hand and said, 'I love you very much. You're a great player.'"

J.R. attended many of the games, often bringing his girlfriend Betsy White. On one of their early dates, J.R. had told Betsy that he had a younger brother with Down syndrome, but he didn't go into details. "Chris was just Chris," says Betsy. "To the family, the fact that he had Down syndrome was a minor point. There was no preparation necessary."

Chris was the first person with Down syndrome that Betsy had ever met, but she felt comfortable with him from their first meeting. J.R. and Betsy arrived at the school while Chris was eating dinner with several friends. When Chris spotted J.R., he jumped up from the table and ran straight into his brother's arms. About twenty of Chris' buddies soon surrounded the couple, shaking their hands and welcoming them. They already knew J.R. from his frequent visits to the school. "It was one of the neatest things I've ever seen," recalls Betsy. "The closeness they had hit me hard that day."

Betsy says Chris idolized J.R., who, in return, adored Chris completely. "Chris always wanted to wear the same type of clothes and carry a briefcase like J.R. J.R. was always concerned about Chris' appearance. He would say, 'Chris, that tie looks terrible. Here, let's get you another one.' He would coach him if he said something grammatically incorrect, but not in an offensive way."

Chris says he loved watching J.R. fall in love with Betsy. "He had lots of girlfriends before, but then Betsy came along and it changed him. He had a crush on Betsy. He acted so nice. They always had this sense of humor between them."

When J.R. proposed to Betsy, he made it clear that Chris came as part of the package. He said that in the future his brother might come to live with them. Betsy assured J.R. that she had already expected it and would welcome him in their home.

When J.R. told Chris about his plans for marriage, Chris was excited. "I said, 'Oh great! Now I'll have a sister-in-law!' I was never worried about how it would affect me and J.R. My brother and I have a very special relationship. I thought it was a great idea because I love Betsy very much."

J.R. and Betsy's wedding was a large and formal affair, in which Chris served as an usher. At the reception, Chris cleared the dance floor with an energetic dance routine. "It was around the time of *Saturday Night Fever*, and he was John Travolta," says Betsy. "There was a big crowd around him watching him dance."

J.R.'s business partner, John McKeever, brought a bag of fake-eye-glasses-nose-moustache toys that he and Chris passed around to the wedding party. When the photographer began taking the wedding pictures, Chris pulled his out early. Marian spotted him and started to scold him, then turned around and saw a group of Groucho Marx clones staring back at her.

Betsy is close to her in-laws, and she feels she has learned many lessons in parenting from watching Marian and Frank raise Chris. As the youngest in her own family, Betsy had only a child's-eye view of her own parents' decisions. So as an adult, she observed the Burkes and then applied many of the lessons to the three boys she now has with J.R.

"You know, you read all the books and articles about how to raise children," she says. "Let them know they're loved unconditionally. Support them and show them you love them instead of just telling them. It's a lot of common sense. But all the stuff you read about, that's what the Burkes always did. Chris had that inner security from a warm, secure, loving group around him all the time." When Chris faced challenges or frustrations, the Burkes were always gentle and supportive, telling him, "Keep trying, pal." "They taught him that if you can't do something the first time, to keep at it. I think they handled it beautifully."

J.R. says the only difference he sees in the way his family raised Chris and the way other families raised kids with Down syndrome is that the Burkes treated Chris as just another member of the family. "In a sense, we were willing to let Chris fail, fall on his face and scrape his knees and pick himself up and try again," says J.R. "That's hard to do with any child. But it was so important with Chris."

The family still worked with Chris as they had when he was little, trying to steer him toward activities that would spur his development. Anne had seen a television show about how karate lessons seemed to help develop the side of the brain where people with Down syndrome were weak. But Chris wasn't interested in karate. "I think he thought he'd hurt someone," Anne says. Another time, Anne tried to get Chris to work on a computer, which she had heard was being used to increase the learning power of kids with Down syndrome. But Chris didn't have the necessary hand coordination to hit the keys right. Anne wasn't daunted by that. She gave him a tiny keyboard piano, so he could practice building dexterity in his fingers.

Through the next several years, Betsy watched Marian and Frank struggle as Chris, in his late teens, began to demand more independence from them. "He was sometimes pretty stubborn," says Betsy. "They wanted to give him these freedoms, but there was the same worry any parent of a teenager would have, and a double worry with Chris." Still, they realized that giving their son independence was extremely important for his growth and development, and they addressed each issue as it arose.

Chris rarely disobeyed his parents. "They were kind of strict with me," he says now. "But I listened to them because they're my parents and they know what's right for me." Most of all, Chris argued with them to let him go out with J.R. and his buddies at night. As a teenager, he waited impatiently for the day he was old enough to join J.R. in the neighborhood pubs.

Then prior to Chris' eighteenth birthday, the drinking age was raised from eighteen to nineteen. Then before his nineteenth year, the legal age was pushed to twenty-one. J.R. teased Chris unmercifully, telling him that the drinking age had been raised to twenty-five just to hear his howls of protest. Chris says he wanted to go into the pubs, not to drink, but to socialize. "My favorite drink is a Shirley Temple [a nonalcoholic concoction]. I just love hanging out with my brother. My brother has lots of friends who are my friends, too."

As the saying goes, the Irish take their jokes seriously and treat a serious situation as a joke, a tenet the Burkes seemed to reflect. "It's not that we weren't serious about things," says J.R. "It's just that none of us have ever taken ourselves too seriously. Maybe it's because if we were going to take anyone seriously, it was going to be Chris."

Betsy remembers Chris' sense of humor developing at an early age, encouraged by the rest of the family. "Every once in a while, Frank will come out with this real zinger. Chris is like that, too. He'll make some comment that's so funny everyone will turn around and just be amazed. J.R. was always kidding him, joking around with him, just as he does now with our sons. It's important for them to grow up with that sense of humor."

There was some humor Chris could do without. J.R. once asked Chris if he had ever seen Ray Charles' house. Chris answered no, then J.R. said, "That's okay, neither has he!" Chris howled in protest, "J.R., that's awful! You shouldn't say those things!"

"Chris has a strong sense of humor, but he's always been incredibly sensitive to any kind of joke that made fun of somebody else's situation or misfortune," says J.R. "He would say, 'Stop it, stop it!' but he would be laughing the whole time."

Chris says he knows J.R. only tells him those jokes to tease him into a reaction. "But I don't like to make fun of anybody. That's the way they are, and it's not funny."

Another time, J.R. recalled an old joke about a retarded boy who claps his hands and is given ice cream as a reward, then claps the ice cream cone into his face. Chris was eating ice cream at the table, and J.R. murmured to his father, "Yes, but can he clap his hands?" The comment went over Chris' head, but Frank chuckled. "Mom was furious. She didn't speak to us for days," says J.R.

Chris knew that he had Down syndrome, and he mentioned it sporadically, but he refused to admit that it made him handicapped in any way. He once chastened his father after overhearing a phone conversation in which Frank explained to an insurance agent that his son was retarded. "Dad, you said something bad about me," he said. "You said that I was retarded."

There were times when J.R. and the rest of the family wished that Chris did not have Down syndrome, though they say they didn't dwell on it. J.R., a surfing fanatic who has ridden the waves all over the world, tried fruitlessly to get Chris to go out surfing with him. "He was scared of it," says J.R. "But overall, he was great at trying stuff."

The family had a hard time coaxing Chris to move up to a larger bicycle, even after he went through a growth spurt that made his sixteen-inch bike unwieldy. "It was a stingray bike with a banana seat," says J.R. "It was like a little kid's bike. He was really too big for it. But he liked that his feet could touch the ground. He was scared of the bigger bikes.

So even when we got him a bigger bike, we had to make sure his feet still hit the ground."

J.R. says his relationship with Chris was probably more parental at times than it would have been had Chris not had Down syndrome. "But we've always been really, really close. The fact that he had Down syndrome had nothing to do with how close we were. It was how I would be with any brother I had. But it was neat to always have a little brother, and Chris stayed little a lot longer than other people's brothers stayed little. It has never gotten to the point where he's gotten older and didn't need me anymore, which I guess is a natural thing that happens. On the other hand, it would have been nice for him to mature and experience some of the things he could have experienced."

After he and Betsy were married, J.R. continued to spend nearly as much time with Chris as before. But the marriage brought out new feelings in Chris, Betsy says. "I think he wanted a family and wife for himself. I think it was hard on him. J.R. used to say that sometimes he wasn't retarded enough, in that he wanted things for himself that he couldn't have. He was smart enough to want them and to realize what he didn't have."

The year after J.R. and Betsy married, Don Guanella merged with Elverson, a special girls' school a few miles away. For years, the boys had socialized at dances and picnics with Elverson's students, and had visited the girls' residence hall on weekends. The Don Guanella teachers tried to prepare the boys for daily encounters with the opposite sex, instructing them in basic human sexuality. Visiting experts used puppet shows and short films to discuss AIDS, pregnancy, and the pitfalls of premarital sex in simple language tailored to the students' level of comprehension.

There wasn't much danger of intimate relationships; after the merger, the girls still lived off campus in a new residence hall a mile away, taking buses into school each morning. But because Don Guanella had been all male for so long, the teachers feared that the boys would have problems adjusting. Their worries proved unfounded. Except for a few minor lovers' spats, the merger progressed smoothly, and most of the boys seemed to benefit from the change. "They all had their little problems, just like normal teenagers, and we would counsel them about it the best way we thought," says teacher Betsy Tompkins.

At seventeen, Chris had a definite interest in the ladies, and he was popular with several of them. "I know that he always had someone, little puppy-love-type things," says Betsy. He spent many weekend afternoons at the girls' residence hall, taking walks with his favorites and going on chaperoned dates to movies and dances.

Chris wasn't shy when it came to asking the girls out for dates. "I wasn't nervous," he says. "It was easy. You just need to show your personality and have a sense of humor and some confidence."

Chris says he was in love with several girls during this time, though none of the relationships worked out in the long run. "We would decide to break up, then I would find someone else," he says nonchalantly.

Chris didn't let his romances get in the way of his other interests, especially Boy Scouts. He had joined the troop in his first year at Don Guanella, and by the time he had graduated eight years later, he had progressed to the rank of first-class scout. Today the Boy Scouts offer special programs for physically and mentally handicapped scouts. But in the years Chris was involved, the traditional standards for merit badges were often out of reach for the Don Guanella troop. Part of the problem was that the badges for eagle scout required hours of extensive homework with parental supervision that the school could not offer.

Still, troop leader Harry Hiller ran the weekly meetings and weekend trips as he would with any other troop. "Anytime someone came with us to help out, I'd tell them from the start, 'Just treat them like you would any boys,'" says Hiller. The troop camped out at state parks, scout reservations, and the homestead of Daniel Boone, a nearby historical park. During the day they hiked, fished, and worked on their conservation projects, then they would build a campfire and prepare meals. After dinner, Chris and the other boys would stand up before the fire to tell stories, pantomime, and dance.

Chris has fond memories of his scouting years. "I learned first aid and survival skills and how to cook food over a campfire, and we did lots of hiking. I love nature and hiking through the woods, but I don't like to climb on mountains. That's too hard."

His first-aid training came in handy three times at Don Guanella. Once in a stickball game, Robert Neely gashed his hand deeply on a fence. The rest of the kids kept playing as though nothing had happened, but Chris saw that it was serious and ran to get another counselor. At Chris' insistence, Robert went to the hospital, where the wound was cleaned and sewn with thirteen stitches.

Another day, Robert had taken five boys to a nearby park, where a construction project had left a dangerous open space on a trolley track. Robert cautioned the students to stay close by him, especially Andy, a boy who wore a helmet because he was prone to seizures. Andy resented

Here are my mom and dad in 1948, leaving for their honeymoon.

That's me in the stripes—little Christopher Joseph Burke. I was six months old, enjoying my first Christmas. With me are my sisters Anne and Ellen, my brother J.R., and my cousin Peter Atkins.

My first birthday, with Dad and Anne, at Montauk Point in 1966.

My family loves to travel. We went all over the place when I was growing up. Here we are on our way back from Florida.

Sailor boy Chris is just cruising off for church on Easter Sunday 1971. I liked the clothes my mom dressed me in, but my favorite was the cowboy outfit with a big hat and boots that made me look like a miniature Roy Rogers.

I have six nieces and three nephews, and I love them all, but Nora is "my special one" because she has Rett syndrome and needs my extra loving care. (*People* magazine)

Thanksgiving 1986: My mom and dad posed with my nieces and nephews. From left to right: (back row) Meghan, Nora, Kara; (front row) Sara (holding Michael), Katie, Dewey, and Molly. My nephew Brendan isn't pictured because he wasn't born yet.

J.R. got married and I got a great sister-in-law. From left to right: my brother-in-law Tom Corridan and Anne, my brother-in-law Jack Orlando and Ellen, my niece Kara Corridan, Betsy, J.R., me, Mom and Dad.

I worked for several summers on the beach at Point Lookout, checking people at the entrance gate and maintaining the beach and baseball field. I was twenty years old in this picture, and had just won first prize in the Point Lookout talent show for lip-synching "Rhinestone Cowboy."

Add a white suit and you'd think I was John Travolta in *Saturday Night Fever*. I always loved to dance; I could break dance and do "The Robot" and moonwalk just like Michael Jackson. Here I'm taking over the dance floor on the cruise ship my mom and dad and I took to the Bahamas when I was a teenager.

One of my first moments on stage, and I'm wearing pajamas! I'm the one third from the left; the others are my classmates at the Kennedy Child Study Center. Everybody clapped and cheered for us, and I just loved it. That was when I decided I wanted to be an actor, when I was five years old. (Kennedy Child Study Center)

Here I am, nine years old and trying for a Special Olympics record in the broad jump. I didn't win, but the Special Olympics made me feel like a winner.

Here we're going over the scenes for the pilot of "Life Goes On." Bill Smitrovich is standing. Seated from left to right: Monique Lanier; Patti LuPone; Rick Rosenthal, co-executive producer; Michael Braverman, the creator and executive producer.

This is Kaley Hummel, my very beautiful dialogue coach. She is teaching me all about acting.

I like to go back to my schools and help them raise money. Here I'm visiting Cardinal Cushing, where I lived from when I was eight to twelve years old. Sister Clarinda Zech is one of my favorite people there. (Cardinal Cushing School)

Back with friends at Don Guanella in 1990. I was doing a telethon in Philadelphia that weekend.

the warning and ran away from Robert down the track. Suddenly, he convulsed in a seizure, slipped from the track, and fell two hundred feet to a creek below. "I saw him lying there and I thought, 'This kid is dead,'" says Robert. "The other boys were in hysterics and there was no one else around. But Chris wasn't panicking." Robert and Chris climbed carefully down the rocky cliff by the trolley track to get to the boy. The boy's helmet had saved his life; he opened his eyes as Robert and Chris approached, but he was not moving. "I told Chris, 'This is very, very serious. Stay here and keep him from moving. I'm going for help.'" Chris stayed beside the boy the whole time, talking softly to calm and comfort him. By the time Robert returned, the boy had recovered from the shock of the fall, and though he was bruised, he suffered no serious injury.

Later that year, Robert and some boys were sledding down a hill in the back of the campus during a hard snowfall. By the end of the day, everyone had returned to the cottage except Robert, Chris, and another boy named Danny; the two boys were taking one last ride down the hill. Then Chris came running over to Robert. "Danny isn't moving!" he yelled, pulling Robert down to the bottom of the hill, where the boy was lying, unconscious, in the snow. Robert tried to revive Danny, but he could see the boy had suffered a seizure. By this time, the sky had darkened and the snow was swirling down in a blizzard. Robert yelled for help, then realized no one could hear him. He and Chris rolled the boy onto the sled and began pulling and pushing him up the hill. It was slow going: Danny was six feet tall and weighed more than two hundred pounds, and the hill was covered with a thick layer of ice from the day's sledding. By the time they reached the campus buildings, Danny's body temperature had dropped dangerously, but after a night in the infirmary he was back to normal. "Chris came through again," says Robert. "He kept his composure through the whole ordeal."

Chris has only a vague memory of these incidents. "It's like I'm watching a video of myself and it's not clear. I guess I was just doing what I was supposed to do," he says with a shrug.

As a teenager, Chris was serious about practicing his Boy Scout creed of helping others, a principle his teachers emphasized as well. "We tried to instill in the students that sharing and caring and having love for one another was more important than whether they could write their name or not," says teacher Betsy Tompkins. "Some of the kids didn't feel that way, but Chris did. He had a natural love and empathy for people who didn't have as much as him."

When Chris earned free time in class, he usually chose to spend it helping out in classes with lower-functioning students. At night, he stopped by the younger boys' cottages to tuck them in bed, returning in the mornings to help them shower and get dressed. Robert remembers Chris patiently assisting a physically disabled student who used a walker to move about the campus. Off campus, he stopped on the street to help anyone on crutches or in a wheelchair.

But his Boy Scout lessons didn't always translate to Manhattan. One weekend, when Chris and his parents were walking near their home, Chris saw an elderly woman with a cane trying to cross a busy street. He walked over to assist her, but as soon as he touched her arm, she began waving her cane and screaming at the top of her lungs, thinking he was trying to mug her. "She was hollering at him and he couldn't understand why," says Frank, chuckling at the memory of the scene. "Here was Christopher being a true Boy Scout, and she was afraid of him."

Another time, Frank and Chris were riding in a city bus when someone in the back sneezed. Chris cheerfully called out, "God bless you!" while Frank cringed, waiting for a rude response. "I had to tell him that when you're on a bus, you just sit quiet and don't say anything. Someone might think you're a wise guy and start some trouble. It was hard when the school was training him in one fashion, and we were trying to teach him to live in a cosmopolitan atmosphere. Sometimes it clashes."

By the time Chris was in his late teens, his parents began letting him go out into New York alone for walks to nearby shops and parks. Every Sunday, he awoke early and went out to pick up the newspaper and seeded rolls for his parents. He was punctual and dependable, so Marian and Frank grew worried one day when he had been gone more than twenty minutes. Frank was taking a shower, but he kept peering out the window for his son. Marian was at the other window, which offered a view clear to First Avenue. She looked for the maroon jacket he was wearing. No Chris.

When Frank stepped out of the shower, Marian told him, "I'm going to go find him." As she walked out, an ambulance driver coming into the complex stopped to ask for directions. Marian kept walking, letting someone else help him. "I was on my mission. I was not going to stop for anything."

She walked to the newspaper stand, then to the bakery. At both places, she was told that Chris had been there and left. She walked back and met Frank, who was coming out to look for Chris, too. They separated to search the grounds, then met back, their nerves jangling.

"Maybe he went over to Ellen's," said Frank, knowing in his heart that Chris would have called them if he had decided to visit his sister (who had returned from Poland) or do anything unexpected. When they went back to their apartment to call Ellen, a uniformed police officer was waiting at their door.

"Calm down, don't get excited," said the officer as they approached.

"I'm already excited," said Marian. "Just tell me, where is he? Is he all right?"

"He's fine," said the officer. "However, he was hit by a cab. We have him in an ambulance. He's downstairs and he will not let us take him to the hospital unless you come with him."

The same ambulance Marian had passed was now parked downstairs, with Chris lying in the back. When Marian and Frank ran up, the paramedics were questioning him to see if he was all right. "Who's the President of the United States?" they asked. "Who won the World Series?" Chris answered them correctly, then turned to Frank and Marian. "I'm so sorry," he said, handing them the bag with the rolls he had bought. "I dropped the newspaper somewhere."

"He felt guilty that he had not done his job," says Marian. "He kept saying to us, 'I'm so sorry.' I said, 'Chris, please. You have no idea how happy we are to see you.' I was so relieved to see that he was okay."

They spent the rest of the day in the hospital while Chris had X rays and examinations. They learned that Chris had stepped off into the First Avenue crosswalk just as a cab shot through a red light. The cabdriver kept going, turning the wrong way down a one-way street. A woman at the intersection chased the cab, taking its license, while another bystander called an ambulance. The police caught the driver, who later told them that he thought he had killed Chris.

"I don't know how he survived the hit," says Marian. "It was a cold day, so he was wearing a sweater and bulky jacket. I guess that saved him."

At first, doctors thought Chris had a hip fracture. Then Marian and Frank called in a specialist, who determined that Chris was fine, just bruised. For four days, he stayed in bed for tests while his family and friends visited and sent a roomful of cards, gifts, and flowers. He shared them with his roommate, a young college student.

When Chris was discharged, Marian went over to say goodbye to the college student. "He told me, 'You know, he's one of the luckiest young men I know.' He was a perfectly capable, normal young man. But he said Chris had so much more than he had."

The incident took away some of Chris' confidence. "You'd cross the street with him, and he'd put your arm in a vise grip," says Frank. But the Burkes talked with him about his fears and encouraged him to venture out as he had before. To this day, Chris crosses First Avenue with careful hesitation and always on the opposite corner of the street from where he was hit. And he refuses to get into a taxicab alone.

One place the Burkes didn't worry about Chris was at their summer home in Point Lookout. The tiny community, filled with vacation cottages of mostly New Yorkers of Irish descent, is just three blocks by eleven blocks. "It's safe," explains J.R. "You can only park in the driveways, so you don't have to worry about your kids dashing out in the street from behind a car. The town was immensely important to Chris' development. I think he would be a completely different person if we hadn't lived there, because it allowed him so much freedom."

Chris loved the small-town life. He led the bicentennial parade dressed as a colonial boy, played basketball and softball on the playgrounds, and socialized with everyone on the beach.

The whole town knew Chris. "He was sort of like the mayor," says J.R. "That comfort with other people helped his self-confidence. It's a town of characters, so he didn't stand out that much. There were a dozen other handicapped children who were also a very accepted part of the community, then there were plenty of people supposedly playing with all their genes who were, let's say, strange."

Bernie Kennedy, a friend of J.R.'s, recalls returning to Point Lookout after being away for a few years and seeing Chris zipping around everywhere on his bicycle. "I was surprised to see that he was so independent. He was really on his own. There was no concern he would come to harm, because everyone who knew Chris was keeping an eye out for him. He was part of a larger family, part of the community.

"The key word I think of is 'included,'" says Bernie. "Anything the family was doing, there was Chris. It was natural, but extraordinary. They were steady and unwavering in their treatment of Chris."

Frank Ryan, another friend of J.R.'s, remembers how Chris always greeted people with "How you doing, buddy" or "Hey, pal."

"He never felt out of place. Maybe some people who had not seen a kid with Down syndrome up close would have a tendency to stare, but as soon as they spent thirty seconds with him, he had won them over. He always had such a great personality. He was a very funny kid."

J.R. remembers only a few times in Point Lookout when people pointed at Chris or teased him. "The worst was when they would talk about him as if he wasn't there. Sometimes they'd say, 'Look at that little retarded kid' right in front of him. I would tell them, 'Hey, he can hear what you're saying. You could be more considerate. He's not really different from anyone else.' "

There were few other incidents in Point Lookout. Chris' niece Kara recalls going to the recreation center with Chris, where some boys started making fun of him. "It didn't seem to upset him. I think it bothered him more that I had been there to see it. But that's the only time I remember anything like that happening. I really liked to hang out with him because he knew everyone and he was so much fun to be around."

Sometimes the rejection came from unexpected sources. Once Chris took a strong interest in a teenage girl he knew from a local summer camp, where she was a counselor. He visited her often, until the girl's brother stopped by the Burkes' house and told Frank that he didn't want Chris coming over any more.

"Has he hurt her in any way or done anything to make you feel this way?" Frank asked.

"Well, no," answered the boy, "I just don't like him being with her. He's different."

"As we all are," replied Frank. With some reluctance, he and Marian told Chris that he was not welcome to visit that home anymore. "My heart broke in about twenty pieces," says Marian. "We were so disappointed that someone we knew had been so insensitive. Chris was very affectionate, and I think people were somehow scared that he was sexually inclined. But we never saw that in Chris. If anything, he was less interested in sex than other teenagers."

Still, the Burkes didn't worry too much about Chris because he seemed to be making friends easily, though not always in his peer group. He preferred the company of adults, especially the family friends who were J.R.'s age. Even as a youngster, Chris accompanied Frank to a "men's club" of neighbors, where he joined the men in songs and piano playing. Chris also played with many smaller children, including his niece Kara, who is seven years younger than him. Kara says Chris was one of her best friends growing up, and that they never "outgrew" each other. "Sometimes when I was younger, I didn't understand why he got special treatment. He wasn't really spoiled, he just got so many things. We got along great together, but at times he was more like a younger sibling than an uncle."

Kara and Chris saw each other frequently in those years: at Point

Lookout, in New York, or when Kara's family would visit Chris at school. Chris always stayed with them the week after Christmas and over New Year's Eve. And each June, when Chris got out of school, he would stay with Anne for several weeks while Marian and Frank were working. Chris liked his time there so much that he asked his parents if they could build him a little house next to Anne's.

Chris stayed busy at Anne's, babysitting her four daughters and even helping Anne change the girls' diapers when they were babies. Anne's husband Tommy would also pay Chris to do small jobs around the house, such as chopping wood for the fireplace or cleaning out the garage.

Kara, who shared Chris' interest in entertainment, let Chris borrow one of her prized possessions, a book with the names and addresses of teenage celebrities. Then she lent him her special videotape, on which she had painstakingly recorded dozens of televised interviews, news clips, and music videos of singer Michael Jackson. But when Chris took the tape to the video store to be duplicated, the store worker mistakenly erased it. Chris was devastated; no one could console him. He cried and kept apologizing to Kara, who, though not happy, understood that it wasn't her uncle's fault. The accident left an indelible mark on Chris. Ever since that day, he has pulled the tab on the back of his videotapes right after recording, so that they cannot be erased or recorded over. He also went through his sister's videos and did the same thing. When she tried to record a show, none of her used tapes would work.

By the time Chris was eighteen, he had an enormous library of videos and cassette tapes that rivaled any small store collection. But he always wanted more, and he was not shy about asking people for them. Many of the tapes in his collection were gifts from his family, his friends, and even people who didn't know him well but eagerly obliged his requests.

Chris had a funny knack for getting total strangers to do favors for him. Jimmy Fiesel, a family friend, recalls seeing Chris standing by the ocean, looking out at a fifteen-foot band of seaweed that lined the shore. An older man walked by, and Chris turned to him and talked him into carrying him through the seaweed to the clear part of the water. "We were cracking up watching it," says Jimmy. "Chris always had this persuasive way about him."

Jimmy, whose family's summer home was next door, was a few years older than Chris and often watched him when the adults went out at night. "We were always getting into water fights, things like that. He loved that kind of mischievous fun."

Chris was more serious when he served as an altar boy in the local Catholic church, where he impressed the neighbors with his uncommon sensitivity. At the end of mass one evening, he asked the priest if he could make an announcement. "I'd like for all of us to pray for Thurman Munson," he said, referring to the New York Yankees baseball player who had died in a plane crash that week. Then he led the congregation in a brief prayer. "It was overwhelming," said Fran Slattery, a family friend who was in the church. "People were crying."

Another time, Chris broke the news to Fran that Emma, a mutual friend's mother, had passed away. "Fran, let's you and I say a little prayer for her right now," he said, and he bowed his head.

"I was amazed," says Fran. "But Chris is very spiritual. The church has always meant a great deal to him."

Chris wrote letters to his Great-aunt Sally, who lived in the nursing home. Then one night Chris overheard her daughter Pat Egan saying that her mother was giving her a hard time over something. Later, Chris pulled her aside. "I want to talk to you, Aunt Pat," he said solemnly. Then he explained to Pat that maybe she should be more patient with her lovely mother. "She's not quite herself. She didn't mean to upset you," he said. Pat never forgot it. "He was just a teenager, but he had more sensitivity than our own children would have had at that age. That insight he had was something."

At school, Chris was always concerned about counselor Robert Neely because his father was ill and his mother had died a few years before. He always asked Robert about his father and reminded him to leave water and food nearby so his father could reach it when Robert was at school. One day around Easter, Chris suggested that he and Robert go visit his mother's grave at a nearby cemetery. "Chris went over and said a prayer, then he put some flowers on her grave," says Robert. "He was always sensitive and caring and picked up on things like that."

Chris' concern for others sometimes took unexpected turns. One summer he walked around Point Lookout knocking on doors with a cup in his hand.

"I'm raising money to go to Hollywood and help the handicapped," he told Mary Fleming, a family friend.

"That's nice, Chris," said Mary, and she handed him a dollar. Marian caught wind of that venture and made him return the money he had collected.

"I explained to him that fund-raising was serious business," says Marian. "You had to have someone backing you with a legitimate cause. It was tough because he was always so concerned. He was always interested in people raising money to help various charities, like Sally Struthers and her organization for underprivileged children. From an early age, he felt very strongly about helping the handicapped, and just wanted to do something about it."

The Burkes had always encouraged their children to take part-time and summer jobs, and Chris didn't feel he should be an exception. As a teenager, he made the rounds of local businesses, asking if they needed help, but he had no luck. He saw a boy delivering newspapers, so he tried to sell his family's used papers down the street. He and his niece Kara sketched pencil drawings and painted seashells to sell on the beach. Later Chris sold first-aid kits for a school fund-raising project. "He talked nearly everyone in town into buying one," recalls Marian. "He even sold one to the parish priest."

When Chris was seventeen, he earned his first paycheck at the company where Marian worked, George Little Management. Chris and Marian commuted by train from Point Lookout each morning, then Chris worked as a temp, collating papers and stuffing envelopes with brochures for an upcoming trade show. He was responsible and efficient, but also fun to work with, says Doris Reap, who supervised him. She remembers Chris liked to talk about how he was going to be a movie or television star when he was an adult. He told her how he wrote letters to his favorite singers and actors, including Marie and Donny Osmond, and planned to meet them in person someday.

Doris says when she told Marian about Chris' plans, Marian just laughed and shook her head. "He keeps raving about all this and I don't know what to tell him," she told Doris. "We have to tone him down because he really thinks he will be a movie star. I don't think it's good for him to have such goals because he'll never make it."

Chris saved his earnings to buy a videocassette recorder so that he could record and study the movies he loved. He was a whiz at understanding the VCR manual. He set up the VCR expertly, learning how to use all the buttons to program it to record the late-night movies. His favorites were the classics—*The Wizard of Oz, Singin' in the Rain, It's a Wonderful Life*—and he watched them over and over till he could recite the dialogue by heart.

Chris got his first steady job at eighteen, when he was hired by the nearby Town of Hempstead to maintain the baseball field and beach area in the community of Point Lookout. Every morning, he woke up by himself, fixed breakfast, then got to the park by seven to sweep the walks. For the rest of the day, he worked out of a little booth where the bases and maintenance equipment were stored. "It was like a second home to him," says J.R. "He had an umbrella there, and he'd sit in his beach chair, listening to music and making sure the field was taken care of and the garbage was picked up."

The storage area had a phone, and before long Chris was receiving harassing calls. Then one night, someone tipped over the booth, destroying it. "We figured out it was the other kids who worked there," says J.R. "I went down to them and said, 'I thought you might want to know that I'm Chris' older brother. I'm bigger than all of you, and I have a short temper. You do something like this again, you'll have to answer to me.' We're nice people till you cross us, and then we're not."

Frank spoke to Chris' supervisor, who called a meeting of all the beach workers and told the boys, "It takes little minds to pick on a kid like Chris." After that, they left Chris alone.

On days and nights when Chris wasn't working, he stayed busy in the Anchor Program, a camp in nearby Lido Beach designed for teenagers and children with a range of handicaps. He attended Anchor all through his teenage years, taking classes in everything from art to sign language to yoga. His favorite was the music activities group taught by twin brothers John and Joe DeMasi. The twins worked at night as professional folk-pop musicians, and they had both studied classical violin before joining the Anchor Program on a whim. When they met Chris, he was a young teenager and they were in their mid-twenties. A fast friendship developed, one that continues steadily today.

Joe says they gravitated toward Chris at first because he was so outgoing and had the same passion for music and acting as they did. "He viewed himself as an equal, which is how we viewed him. Other kids, it was more of a teacher-student relationship. But Chris was always a helper. We were more like advisors."

Chris has a positive attitude that is infectious, says John. "He's always smiling. When you're around him, you feel like you can go to the moon. He always sees the good; he always sees the fun. I laugh when he's called handicapped because he's more advanced than a lot of people I know, people who are always complaining about their lives. Chris handles life great."

The camp was the twins' first exposure to people with handicaps, but now, after working nearly two decades with thousands of them, they say that the creativity so abundant in Chris is not a rare exception. "You wouldn't believe the talents they have," says John. "But the difficult thing is, there's usually no outlet for it. There's often no way for them to express their creative sides. One reason they respond so well to music is that it is honest. It gives them a language."

Chris often helped the twins come up with ideas for the group, which often numbered in the hundreds. One summer, he suggested that they make their own video to the song "We Are the World," imitating their favorite stars. Chris posed as Stevie Wonder; a black boy impersonated Bruce Springsteen. "The kids had no prejudices. They didn't impose limitations on themselves," says Joe.

Other times, the group ran a pretend radio station. Chris called himself "Double B, Billy Burke," and spun his favorite country and rock tunes between bits of comedy and deejay patter. The group also video-taped skits, mock television commercials, and other music videos, including one to the Michael Jackson song "Beat It." The most involved projects were the send-ups of popular television shows, including "Star Trek." The group wrote a short script, devised sets, made costumes, and picked out theme music. After several rehearsals, they acted out the story before the video camera. "It was fun," says Joe. "We'd tilt the camera from side to side, and they'd run back and forth, to make it look like the Starship *Enterprise* was being attacked."

Chris especially liked the nights the DeMasis played in concert and at dances for Anchor. He often joined the twins on stage, break dancing and moonwalking to the songs. Then he got the idea to start a fan club for what he called the DeMasi Trio, himself being the third member. "He asked us for pictures, then went and typed up this thing about us and mimeographed it," says Joe. "At one dance, he showed up with a stack of these flyers and handed them out to everyone."

Normally, Chris' attention at dances was centered on his current girl-friend. He would sit with her in the audience holding her hand, or they would dance together, requesting love songs and slow dances. Chris would sometimes ask John and Joe to announce their anniversary, even if it was just one month. But then in his late teenage years, Chris met a girl at Anchor whom he dated for nearly two years. They wrote each other love letters and posed together for a portrait, which they sent to their friends and family. J.R. and Betsy double-dated with them at one Anchor concert. "He was very proud of her," says J.R. "He put his arm around her when they watched the show. It was not too different from any twelve- or thirteen-year-old crush."

Joe DeMasi says Chris has an unusual freedom in his life because he was never inhibited. "He just does what makes him happy and doesn't worry about what people think of him." Chris didn't hesitate to break into song or pick on a guitar or banjo. He liked to surprise people by showing up at Anchor in makeshift costumes, impersonating his hero of the day. Once he was Kenny Rogers: he wore a cowboy hat and boots and played on his guitar. Other times, Chris posed as a reporter by wearing a visor with a piece of paper sticking out of the top like a press card. He made the rounds of the camp, interviewing people about their current activities. He would go home and write up stories, then come back the next day to hand out the handwritten or typed copies of *The Handicapped Citizens News,* as he called his newspaper. Each story was framed with headlines, sometimes drawings, and always the byline "Chris Burke, reporter."

The Burkes encouraged and supported each new activity, and they loved watching his creativity bloom. But his inventiveness also brought out conflicting feelings, because it showed a glimmer of what might have been. "When we'd see what he did with limited capabilities, there was always the thought 'What would he be like if he didn't have Down syndrome?'" says J.R. "That's always been a frustration. I think he would have been a very talented person. On the other hand, one of the beauties of Chris is that he is so uninhibited. The world is very black and white to him. It's the gray stuff that screws all of us up. Maybe he would not be what he is today if he had the capacity to give deeper thought to all things."

One night, as Chris entertained the family with accounts of his experiences, Marian looked over at her cousin and sighed. "I look at what he does, and I just wonder. If Chris had not been born with Down syndrome, I think he would have been someone really important. I think he could have made an impact on the world."

Yet Chris never felt his Down syndrome was keeping him from doing anything. He talked often about helping the handicapped, a group he saw as somehow separate from himself. He was extremely comfortable with the fact that he had Down syndrome, as the family soon learned. When Chris was nineteen, the daughter of a close family friend gave birth to a little girl, who was then diagnosed as having Down syndrome. Even though that family had known Chris since he was born, it was devastating news to them all to find that this first grandchild in the family had Down syndrome. Chris had overheard the news, but he had not commented on it. Then the grandfather of the weeks-old baby came by their summer house to talk with Frank. Chris bounded down the steps greeting the man heartily. "Congratulations! I just heard that the baby had Down syndrome! Isn't that great?"

The man looked at Chris with shock on his face, while the room went silent. "Yeah, I guess it is," he answered.

Marian says the incident showed them all how much self-esteem Chris had, and how comfortable he was with his life. "I think it helped break down something with the other family, though it took them some time to get over it. Maybe you would think that knowing Chris would make it easier, but it didn't. It's a big thing to swallow."

By the time Chris was nineteen, the Burkes had begun to worry about him. His fascination with the entertainment world had grown to an obsession. He was not as physically active as he had been in the years before, partly because he preferred to spend his time in front of the television, watching his favorite movies and television shows. Every Sunday when the newspaper arrived, he would pull out the television listings, marking the shows he wanted to see. "If Michael Jackson was going to be on 'Entertainment Tonight' on Tuesday night, Chris knew it," says J.R. Chris set his VCR to record dozens of movies, which he would watch repeatedly, studying every key scene and repeating the dialogue.

Ellen, Anne, and J.R. argued with him about it and tried to get him to turn off the TV and go outside. Chris would go to the beach with them for a few minutes, then rush back inside to catch reruns of his favorite, "Little House on the Prairie." MTV also fascinated him, as did any musically related movie. He danced along with the music, singing into a "microphone" he had fashioned from the end of a baseball bat wrapped with aluminum foil. "Betsy and I used to get frustrated in Point Lookout," says J.R. "We'd say, 'This is such a useless thing for him to do.'"

Chris also loved family sitcoms such as "Growing Pains" and reruns of "The Brady Bunch," which rankled Anne. "I would look at him and say, 'Oh God, he's too old to be watching this.' Maybe it was just me not being fair to him as an individual. I always wanted him to be more like people his own age."

Chris' siblings saw his growing TV habit as an ominous sign that he would become more inactive in his later years. "My fear with it was that it was becoming a big part of his life," says J.R. "He was living vicariously through some of the shows. He believed that some of the things he saw were really happening. I always pressed him to make sure he didn't think it was real."

Frank didn't like his son's preoccupation, but he saved his criticism for the times Chris stayed up till midnight watching reruns of "The Honeymooners" or his favorite old movies. Marian didn't mind it at all, since she felt it was an outlet for him, and he seemed to be learning so much from it. One thing was certain: Chris was expanding his memory far beyond what any of the Burkes ever expected. Over dinner, he would regale them with monologues on his favorite actors, mentioning obscure movies and television shows in which they had played only small roles. "He knew every little thing about the actors and the parts they played," says Betsy Burke. "We could ask him who wrote this episode, and he would know it. It was amazing."

His young nieces even noticed his passion. "You never want to watch a movie with Chris," says Anne's daughter Meghan, fourteen. "He'll tell you the best part. He'll tell you the endings of movies. He is just obsessed with TV."

Chris felt justified in watching so much television. After all, he was going to be an actor when he left school; he was just preparing for his career. He would casually mention to his family and friends, "I'd like to be on 'Growing Pains'" or "I'm going to be on television someday."

"Never, ever did we take him seriously with that," says Anne. And as his family grew more critical of his ambition, Chris slowly stopped mentioning it to them. "I didn't really listen to them about it," says Chris. "But I didn't know if it would happen. I thought I could be on TV. But I didn't know."

It was around this time that Chris noticed something unusual about the people he watched on the screen. "There wasn't anyone like me!" he says. "There wasn't anyone with Down syndrome. There weren't many people with handicaps at all." He began writing short television stories that included a part for a young man with Down syndrome, to be played, of course, by himself. He even sent a few to the television show offices, though he never received any responses.

Then one day in 1985, Chris saw something that changed his life forever. There, in the TV listings, was a show featuring a boy with Down syndrome. He was ten-year-old Jason Kingsley, a guest star on an episode of "The Fall Guy." Chris called J.R., telling him, "You've got to watch this show! It's going to be so great! It's going to tell all about this boy with Down syndrome."

Chris set his VCR and waited anxiously for the big night. In the show, Jason played a boy who witnessed a murder and ended up with Colt, the main character played by Lee Majors. The show was a landmark: it was the first time a person with Down syndrome had a major role on a regular prime-time series. It also dealt frankly with questions about the capabilities of people with Down syndrome: it showed Jason speaking several languages and talking about attending regular classes in a public school. In the end, Jason competes in the Special Olympics, with the help of guest stars Larry Holmes, Bruce Jenner, and Lou Ferrigno.

It wasn't Jason's first step into the limelight, however. Emily Perl Kingsley, Jason's mother, is an Emmy-Award-winning writer for "Sesame Street" who first introduced Jason as a participant on that show when he was three. The same year, Jason played a role in the hour-long NBC drama "This Is My Son," which chronicled his own young life from the perspective of his mother.

When Jason was born in 1974, doctors advised Emily to tell family and friends that he had died at birth, and to place her son in an institution. "They told us he would never walk or talk or sit or stand. They said he would be a vegetable." Instead, Emily took Jason home and enrolled him in an infant stimulation program. He was only the second child to enter this experimental treatment in Westchester County, New York, but the results were evident early on when Jason began talking, and later when her son began to read at three years of age.

"We got so gung ho about what the kid could do, we would go anywhere that anyone would invite us to talk about it," says Emily. Jason and Emily were interviewed on "Donahue," "Good Morning America," "CBS Sunday Morning," and a dozen other shows. They traveled around the United States speaking to numerous professional organizations and in classes at elementary schools, high schools, colleges, and medical schools.

Jason continued to appear on "Sesame Street," playing spelling games with Big Bird and romping naturally with the other guest children. "I'm proud to say 'Sesame Street' was one of the earliest shows to routinely feature kids with Down syndrome and other disabilities regardless of the content of the show," says Emily. "We want young impressionable kids to see that kids with disabilities can be playmates, that there's nothing to be afraid of or tentative about. They belong there and have a right to be there. It was always our hope and dream that other shows would follow suit, but it's been very sporadic."

When Jason was seven, Emily heard that the soap opera "All My Children" was planning an episode in which a character undergoes amniocentesis. Emily called the producers and told them, "You've got to do this right. You can't perpetuate the old myths and stereotypes." She later met with them, bringing photos of her son and more advice. "Let's show that Down syndrome is perhaps not the disaster people think it is," she said. "In your audience are thousands of people who have kids like this. Similarly, there are many who are watching who are pregnant, and are going to have kids like this. You don't want to send the message that Down syndrome is a tragedy when people are living with this in their daily lives. You have a responsibility."

The producers listened to Kingsley, then surprised her by asking if she would appear on the show with Jason. She agreed, provided she could write the scene. In the story line, the pregnant character runs into a neighbor and her child with Down syndrome, played by Emily and Jason. The pregnant woman sees that the child is cute, capable, and personable. Also, the dialogue touched on the growing resources and programs available to help these children develop into productive, independent members of society.

After the show aired, ABC received a flood of letters praising the way the subject was covered and asking for more information. Though it aired in 1981, it is still discussed today as a model of responsible entertainment.

Three years later, producers contacted Emily to see if Jason could play the young boy in "The Fall Guy" episode. His role was originally small, written with brief and simple speaking parts. But Jason played his scenes so well, comprehending the direction and performing complicated sequences, that his role and dialogue were expanded. Eventually he was in forty-nine of the sixty-five script pages. He memorized the entire script, including his costars' lines.

At the time, Jason was one of only a handful of people with Down syndrome who had ever been featured in mass media. Seeing Jason on the show gave Chris hope that his dream was within reach. When his family tried to dissuade him from his dreams of being an actor, he now could point to Jason's success to show that it was, indeed, possible. He wrote to the local station for the Kingsleys' address, then for several weeks he worked on a letter to send to Emily and Jason.

Emily still has the letter Chris sent her. "My name is Christopher Joseph Burke and I have Down's [*sic*] syndrome too just like your son Jason," he wrote. "He looks very cute with Lee Majors and Lou Ferrigno and Bruce Janner [*sic*]. And I also agree with what they are doing with Jason. Sounds like he is a winner." Chris went on to mention his interest in Special Olympics and the newspaper he had started in Point Anchor, *The Handicapped Citizens News*. "That is my favorite hobby to do and I have to know what Jason is intrest [*sic*] in school and getting avolved [*sic*] in sports and what he is learning, something like staying away from fights and not get avolved *[sic]* in it."

Chris laughs about the letter now because, he says, "I made so many spelling mistakes." But he was thrilled when Emily wrote him back. Before long, the two were pen pals.

"I was impressed with him," says Emily. "I considered him my friend. It's neat to have someone to correspond with who is so different from yourself, yet have that relationship and ability to communicate."

That summer, Emily invited the Burkes to a picnic she held at her home each year for hundreds of parents and educators in Westchester County, New York. When she finally met her pen pal, she marveled at his poise and self-confidence.

"What stood out was how beautiful he was. He was so sparkly, so bright. He was thin, he was tall, he was handsome. He was all the things we wanted our kids to be."

Through the years, Chris and Emily continued to correspond and meet occasionally. "Chris' letters were delightful. He wrote about his family, his life in school, all the things he was doing. I would write to him about his hopes and dreams and plans. For me, it was a rare opportunity to get to know someone a little older than Jason, to get insights into his future."

Jason was still a boy, and Emily had often wondered what he would be like as a teenager. "We didn't have many people to look to for a really clear view of what the future was going to be for our kids. When we looked at adults with Down syndrome, we were, generally speaking, looking at people who didn't have the advantages of early programs, or heavy-duty academic educations."

She knew Jason would be more advanced than the adults with Down syndrome who had been placed in institutions, or those who were raised without early education, who were not reading well or speaking clearly. "When I saw Chris, I saw that a young adult with Down syndrome could be this attractive, this capable, this smart, with such a great sense of humor. He was the fulfillment of all our dreams. He was a real inspiration."

Emily encouraged Chris to do more writing, and she asked if he would write an article for the *Down Syndrome News,* which is distributed in the United States and internationally to parents and educators. "I was straight with him. I said, 'We don't often have people as articulate as you to tell us what it is like to have Down syndrome.'" Chris wrote that article, which appeared as a letter to the editor in 1986. In it, he explains that he has Down syndrome and asks if he can be a reporter and photographer for the *News*.

In one letter, Emily asked Chris, "What do you want to do when you get out of school?" Chris answered, "In time, I thought it would be nice to be an actor." Emily was cowriting the CBS television movie "Kids Like These," based on her experiences raising Jason through his childhood; the movie won several awards after it aired in 1987. Chris wrote and asked her about it, saying, "Please keep me posted on it so I can be on TV." Emily responded that the roles in it were too young for him to play, but she told him to keep trying. "I knew there weren't many parts, but I thought he would be a natural for any that came up," she says.

Those same ambitions which Emily encouraged were causing fits with the Burkes, and especially J.R. As a child, J.R. had seen firsthand how demanding and rigorous show business could be, and he knew firsthand about its pitfalls and disappointments. But now Chris had a role model and a hero in Jason Kingsley, whom he would mention when J.R. told him he was being unrealistic.

Dick Benson, a friend of J.R.'s in Philadelphia, remembers J.R. telling him point-blank not to talk to Chris about acting. J.R. said the Burkes didn't want to encourage him, and that Chris would be looking for ways to put a wedge in the family's decision against it.

Dick sometimes would pick up Chris at the train station when J.R. was busy, and inevitably Chris would mention his favorite subject. "He'd casually say, 'Oh, I just read a great book about acting.' When I didn't respond, he'd say, 'Aren't you allowed to talk to me about that?' He was conscious of the fact that I had been warned about it, and he had great fun teasing me. He'd say, 'Dick, we can talk about it. I won't tell J.R.' "

Chris had even less encouragement at Don Guanella. The school places great emphasis on training students for employment so that they can be self-sufficient after graduation. Classes repeatedly focused on basic work skills and attitudes, including lessons on how to search for employment, conduct yourself in a job interview, and get along with people on the job. Career counseling was ongoing, in classes and in individual sessions. Higher-functioning students were required to take jobs in the community, often while being supervised by school instructors in their first few weeks.

At nineteen, Chris was assigned to a maintenance job at Cabrini College in the suburbs of Philadelphia. Chris and the other students took a bus, two trains, and a van to reach the campus on time. He enjoyed his job, but he made it clear to his teachers that he was destined for Hollywood.

The teachers had heard it before. Many of the teenagers at Don Guanella wanted to be rock stars, pro basketball players, or, like Chris, movie and television stars. "That's why we got into career counseling so much," says Peggy Carney, one of Chris' teachers. "We thought most of them would be working in McDonald's, or in workshops, or at camps for children, if they were lucky. Acting is not a steady job for most people."

Gloria Luzecki remembers teaching Chris how steeply the odds of acting were stacked against him. "We pointed out the numbers of people who study acting and how many people are able to make a living from it. It's not something most people can do. We said, 'You can dream your dream, but in the meantime, you need to make money.' "

"I think what we tried to do was say this is a dream, and not everyone reaches their dreams," recalls Betsy Tompkins, another of Chris' teachers. "We felt it was beyond reach, but didn't want to squelch any hopes.

"His dreams far exceeded our own," she adds. "That was the extra spark in Chris. Other kids were go-getters; their goals were just not as astronomical. Some of them would have been content just to find a good foster family, or to find a job in a shelter workshop."

Ed Kelly, Chris' speech therapist, also tried to downplay Chris' fascination with acting and movies. "We said, 'It's fun, you can have a good time with it, but you've got to concentrate on your studies, you have to learn math skills.' " Ed could picture the ever social Chris working as a maître d'. "I'd say, 'Chris, a job in a restaurant would be nice.' He'd say, 'Yeah, yeah.' "

He even confided his ambitions to the school's mother superior, Sister Mary Gibin. "He always said, 'When I'm big, I want to be a movie star.' I would tell him, 'That's nice,' and encourage him. To myself, I was laughing. I never thought he could go that far."

Chris was adamant. He was going to be an actor, like his friend Jason Kingsley. "He argued with me all the time about it," says Peggy Carney. "His argument was that he should pursue it because he wanted to be an actor. We came back and said, 'All right, if you want that, let's work harder on your reading, on your speech.' "

Some of the other students would roll their eyes and tease Chris the moment he began talking about his ambitions. "They would say, 'Sure, sure, Chris,' or someone would tell him he was being immature," says Robert Neely. "At the time when he was saying it, even I would get onto him about it. I would say, 'It's nice to dream about, but right now we're here, and we have to do what we do here.'"

But Robert saw some talent in Chris. Many of the older boys liked to perform for the younger students, using wooden benches for a stage or gathering everyone in the auditorium for bigger productions, such as talent shows. "Chris was always a hit," says Robert. "He was constantly the entertainer. Wherever there was a group of people and he had the chance to do something, he would get up and do a skit, or tell jokes, anything to get a reaction."

Many times the group would pantomime singing groups, dressing in black pants and white shirts and performing complicated dance routines while they sang. Other times Robert would give them an actual play and try to get them to stick to the lines. "But usually I just let them go," he says. "They often did a lot better doing the impromptu things." Chris preferred to perform the stories he had written, some of which he would work on for months. He also liked to direct others in productions of his stories. "I remember him standing there and pointing to where people should stand and saying how they should act it out," says Robert.

When Robert read about a local acting workshop for students with disabilities, he thought of Chris. He signed up the handful of boys who were interested, then drove them to classes at Cabrini College every Monday night for two years. It was here that Chris first learned the finer techniques of improvisation and acting. The class worked before a camera, learning where to stand for the best angles. They built sets and devised costumes for characters, then learned how to position themselves on a stage while they acted out scenes from plays. "Chris was always one of the first to volunteer," says Robert.

In school, Chris' teachers knew that they could motivate him to work harder if they could find a way to apply lessons to the world of entertainment. Ed Kelly coached Chris on diction by having him read from scripts and plays. "He'd jump through hoops for you if you were able to make it interesting," says Ed. "Almost everything he did, he put it in that context. He was a very creative student, and fun to work with."

Sometimes the teachers used skits to demonstrate and practice lifestyle skills, such as walking into a store and asking for help. Ed Kelly remembers Chris embellishing the exercises into interesting minidramas.

"Everyone else would just pretend to walk in the store and ask where the sunglasses were. Chris would have this whole scenario of 'My friend and I are lost, and we're trying to get to the basketball game . . .' He had a flair for making ordinary exercises fun and dramatic. In some way or another he was always acting and performing, at all types of things, in little ways."

Throughout the year, the school staged shows for visiting parents. Chris never had a starring role, but nearly everyone still recalls his performance as a monster in a musical based on Michael Jackson's "Thriller" song and video. On stage, Chris rose from a grave in gory makeup, slicked-back hair, and Army jacket, then danced up a storm. He can still re-create the routine, a mixture of moonwalking and the mechanical "Robot" dance step that was the rage that year.

Chris kept working on his stories for television, sometimes enlisting the help of his best friends, who shared his love for show business. He kept sending letters to his favorite celebrities—rock and country music singers, movie and television stars, and people he read about in the newspaper.

"Where you saw Chris, you saw paper and pencil," says teacher Gloria Luzecki. "I remember Chris taking the initiative to write letters to anybody. He had an abundance of confidence."

The whole school learned about Chris' letter-writing skills after Robert Neely asked each of the boys in his cottage to write to a politician. Most of the boys wrote to a local mayor or councilman, but Chris picked the biggest: then-President Ronald Reagan. Chris studied newspaper articles about discrimination of people with handicaps, then wrote that he felt everyone needed the chance to work and learn to be independent. After the letters were sent, the group waited impatiently for answers from the politicians. But there were no answers until weeks later, when a letter arrived bearing the presidential seal. Inside was a one-page letter from President Reagan, who applauded Chris' views and said he agreed with them. "I was so excited about the letter," says Chris. "I wanted to put it in the newspaper."

"It wasn't a form letter," says Robert. "It really seemed to be a personalized letter. Chris was so proud of that. He made a hundred copies of it." The letter caused a stir in the school, where it was read over the intercom during class time and passed around to teachers and students.

Chris also wrote for the *Don Guanella News and Views,* the school paper that was sent throughout the school and to parents, staff, and benefactors. He wrote the story about Jason acting on "The Fall Guy"; other times he would report on favorite movies, the Special Olympics, or basketball games they had played.

At twenty Chris, using a nom de plume, authored a monthly advice column patterned after "Dear Abby" and called "The Mystery Writer."

Students and teachers would send him letters about their problems or concerns, and Chris would find a solution. Peggy Carney remembers one in which a student wrote that he was always angry; he felt as though he was going to punch somebody. Chris had a snappy answer: "Go hit a punching bag instead."

That spring, Chris looked forward to his last school prom. He quickly asked the girl of his choice, a student with Down syndrome who shared some classes with him. Chris urged his best friend Andy to ask out an attractive girl he knew so that they could double-date. Then on the night of the prom, the boys dressed in suits and met the girls, handing them corsages they had bought. A disc jockey spun records while the students danced and socialized. Chris started teasing Andy about his date, who obviously had a crush on the boy. "She'd laugh and slap his leg. He really loved it. I loved teasing Andy. I started saying their names back and forth. He said, 'Knock it off, Chris.' His face was solid red like a tomato. It was fun."

Back in New York, the mood was more somber. Though Marian and Frank were excited that Chris was about to graduate and come home, they wondered how he would adjust to a new life in New York with two career-oriented parents. Frank had retired from the police force and was working as a security consultant for the New York Bank for Savings. Marian had just been promoted to manager of George Little Management's National Stationery Show. "We both enjoyed our new lives," says Marian. "We were both involved in careers that were so different from what we had done before."

Around this time, J.R. sent Chris to a local organization that tested students with disabilities and gave them direction for employment opportunities. Both J.R. and Chris were interviewed by the workers. They asked J.R. how Chris got home to New York, just as the volunteer advocacy group had asked him years before. J.R. told them that he took Chris to the Amtrak station, then Chris would take the train. The people nodded, unimpressed. "Who buys his ticket?" they asked. J.R. said that he did. "That's not doing Chris any good, now is it?" they responded.

J.R. was surprised. He had never thought of it, but now he realized that he had been leading Chris by the hand, buying him a ticket and a snack and even sometimes helping him find a seat on the train. "They were rightly critical. Where other people thought that what we were doing was fantastic, these people said, 'There's a hell of a lot more that you could do. You're holding him back.'" After that meeting, J.R.

started working with Chris more and more on money and tried to give him responsibility.

But graduation was looming just a few weeks away. Don Guanella takes students up to twenty-one years of age, and Chris would turn twenty-one that summer, just months after graduation. Marian and Frank drove down for the big day, as did Ellen, Anne, and their families. The other children had pitched in to buy Chris a fancy new typewriter, which Anne had hoped would get him to stop filling up the dozens of yellow legal pads that he carried with him everywhere.

The day was difficult for the Burkes, but mostly for J.R. During the ceremonies, J.R. stood in the back with the camera, but at times he grew too upset to watch and had to step outside. "It really hit home to me that now we were talking about the rest of his life. He was sheltered and isolated a bit when he was in school. Now we were talking about real-world stuff. He was going to have to go out and get a job. We had the same fears you would have for someone coming out of high school or college, but it was so much more dramatic in his situation. It was very tough for me."

Chris got emotional too, while saying goodbye to his friends at the reception afterward. The students were all talking about their future plans. Several were going to work with their parents, who owned small businesses. Another had found a job on a farm. Many came from small towns and had jobs waiting there. "It made us nervous that Chris had no job possibilities at that point," says Ellen. But Chris had big plans, and he had no hesitation announcing them to everyone. "I'm going to Hollywood to be an actor, and help the handicapped," he said confidently.

The Burkes cringed when they heard his words, repeated over and over through the day. Chris was returning to New York with them, and they worried that he would not be able to find even the most basic, manual-labor job. His hopes for an acting career seemed ludicrous.

It was an anxious time for them all. "We didn't know what was ahead of us with Chris," says Marian. "We knew that acceptance was at a very low level. I remember feeling that up until then, we had had control. With school and vacations, our lives were in place. Now everything had changed. It was very, very scary."

On the drive back to New York, while Chris dozed in the back seat, Marian turned to Frank. "Dear, this really is the first day of the rest of our lives," she said with a weak smile.

EIGHT

★ ★ ★ ★ ★ ★ ★ ★ ★ ★ ★ ★ ★

"FORGET IT, CHRIS. Just forget all this Hollywood crap." J.R. was angry, spitting the words out at his brother sitting beside him. "You don't know the acting business. It's hard, it's crazy. Damn it, Chris, it's just not going to happen. I hate to tell you, but it's not."

Chris turned his head away from his brother and stared out the window. "Don't curse at me," he said quietly.

The two glowered, silent in the Point Lookout beach house. Chris was in the last days of his summer maintenance job for the town of Heampstead. There were no job prospects waiting for him in New York, and he was holding firm, determined to pursue an acting career.

Frank and Marian were also worried about their son and his lofty goals. "I think any parent of any young person would feel the same way in this situation," says Frank. "We didn't know any show business people. It just seemed impossible."

The family was having a hard enough time finding even a job-training program for Chris. J.R. looked into a school for adults with handicaps in Philadelphia, but the tuition was far beyond the family's resources. Ellen checked out a job-training program for people with learning disabilities in New York, but it also cost thousands of dollars. Even more discouraging, she learned that its graduates often encountered problems finding jobs when they had finished. Marian and Frank considered unskilled job options such as those in the cleaning industry, but they weren't comfortable with the thought of Chris working in an unsupervised atmosphere where someone could take advantage of him.

The Burkes also checked within their offices and called several friends to inquire about possible job openings for a stock boy or messenger.

Many times, Chris dressed carefully in his nicest jacket and tie, and showed up for interviews at companies around the city. Sometimes, the person suddenly wasn't available to meet him. Other times, he was sent from department to department within a company, but everyone he needed to talk with was on vacation, or out sick, or in meetings when he arrived.

After a few weeks, the search seemed futile. There were no more job prospects on the horizon, and Chris grew restless trying to fill his long hours at home while Marian and Frank were at work. He was familiar with the neighborhood surrounding Peter Cooper Village and Stuyvesant Town, and he felt free to move around it as he pleased. In the mornings, he visited neighbors and shot hoops on the basketball court in the village playground. He took long walks in the park, and he hung out at local music stores and the video store where he checked out dozens of movies each week. But in the afternoons, his favorite place was across the complex at his sister Ellen's apartment, where he would baby-sit his nieces Sara, eight, and Nora, five, when they returned from school.

Nora loved to see him arrive, and she would grin and giggle for him when he ran to hug her. But she couldn't stand up to greet him or even say hello. Nora had Rett syndrome, a degenerative disease that confined her to a stroller and held her development to that of a small infant.

It had all started a few years earlier in Warsaw, Poland, where Ellen's husband Jack Orlando was stationed as a foreign service diplomatic officer. Nora was a healthy nine-month-old baby learning to stand and talk when Ellen began noticing that she was dragging her legs behind as she crawled. As the months passed, Ellen's worries grew as Nora slowly regressed in her development. She stopped crawling, was unable to stand up anymore, and could barely sit in a chair. She no longer spoke the simple words she had mastered in the previous months. Ellen took her to several doctors in Poland, but they were as puzzled as she was.

"I could see something was wrong," says Ellen. "I was thinking it was a virus or lead poisoning, or even that some Communist had come into my house and done something to my child."

Ellen and Nora left Warsaw and stayed with Marian and Frank for a few weeks to seek help from New York doctors. When Ellen first returned to New York, Marian was as worried for her daughter as for the baby. The stress had taken its toll on Ellen; she had lost twenty pounds off her thin, tall frame. Marian nursed her back to health while encouraging her to seek the best medical and therapeutic help for Nora.

"She was there to bolster me up," says Ellen. "She never let me falter. She told me to cope with it, to find what I needed and continue on. If I had not had them to come home to, I don't know where I would have gone. Without the support of my family, I don't know how I could have done it."

Physical therapists advised a rigorous treatment that Ellen realized she could find in Warsaw. She returned to Poland and placed Nora in a therapy program there. It didn't seem to help: Nora's decline continued.

Though Ellen and Marian had not discussed Nora's condition with Chris, he could see the difference in her from his other nieces and nephews. One day, a few weeks after Ellen had returned to Poland, he pulled Anne aside. "I am so worried about Nora," he told her. "I think there's something terribly wrong."

Anne had the same fears, and she was relieved that she finally had someone to confide in. "Chris was the only one I could talk to about Nora. Everyone else kept saying that it would all work out, that she would be fine. But Chris would admit that he was scared, just as I was. We had very adult conversations about it."

A few months later, Jack was reassigned to the United Nations in New York. Ellen was overjoyed to move back, where she could continue her search for help. It wasn't easy. Ellen found the medical profession extremely difficult, just as Marian had twenty years before with Chris. Many of the doctors refused to believe that Nora had ever been healthy.

"I know my whole personality has changed because of what we went through with Nora," says Ellen. "Nobody even wanted to diagnose her. One doctor told me to just put her in an institution and have more children. My husband had to pull me off her."

Then Anne suggested she gather up her photographs and put them in two albums. In the album of photos from her first year of life, Nora was chubby, active, and alert, standing and sitting up and feeding herself. In the album from her second year, her limbs were limp and useless; she lay in her stroller like a tiny infant.

Ellen took these albums to yet another neurologist, who finally believed her story about Nora's regression. Within a year, the doctor confirmed that she had Rett syndrome, a neurodegenerative disease that starts to show its effects in healthy baby girls when they are from six to eighteen months old. It is irreversible: there is no cure, and little treatment.

Rett syndrome is still a mystery, though it is the leading cause of severe mental retardation in females. It occurs about once in every fourteen thousand female live births. The cause could be genetic, perhaps a faulty X chromosome. Its victims rarely walk or talk, even with intense therapy. In previous years, it was misdiagnosed as autism, though the children who have it are social and love to be cuddled. A strong parents' organization named the Rett Syndrome Foundation works to promote research, treatment, and better understanding of the condition.

Ellen was devastated by the diagnosis, as was her family. The Burkes had known so much sadness through the years; Marian had never quite gotten over the early death of her mother and her only brother. J.R. had battled two recurring episodes of the rare blood disease that had nearly taken his life years before. Upon news of Nora's diagnosis, Marian looked up at the sky angrily. "No more, God," she said firmly. "This family has had enough now. We cannot take any more."

Ellen looked to her mother's example for strength, but sometimes the frustration and sadness overwhelmed her. "When this came up, it was the last thing in the world I wanted to have to cope with," says Ellen. "I never wanted to be in that world with a child who had a handicap. It wasn't a problem I wanted to struggle with personally. Even though our family, with Chris, went along beautifully, with no great traumas, I still didn't want that for myself. I always understood that it's lonely, knowing that your situation is different."

Ellen had been nervous about birth defects during her pregnancy with Nora, and she requested amniocentesis even though her doctor told her it wasn't necessary. She was only thirty, and he felt that since her parents had been older when they had Chris, there was no genetic link to Down syndrome that should worry her. The tests came back fine, and Nora was born without complications; she had no health problems until the Rett syndrome showed.

Ellen doesn't compare Nora to Chris or wish that Nora had Down syndrome instead of the more severe Rett syndrome. "They're so completely different. If I wished at all, I would wish only for a perfect child."

For the next few years, Nora attended a preschool program at Columbia University, in upper Manhattan. But when she outgrew that, Ellen found there were no private schools in New York City for children with severe handicaps. She had to rely on the public school system, which concerned her greatly. Then she heard about P.S. 138, a citywide program serving the handicapped student population. One of the program's five locations was at 400 First Avenue, only a few blocks from their apartment in Peter Cooper Village. Ellen visited the school and met with teacher Tom Roeder, who assured her that Nora would be given an excellent education.

Nora went to school each day, and the teachers worked with her to stimulate her mind and activate her weakened muscles. She entered the school just as Chris returned home from Point Lookout and began his search for a job.

Chris regarded Nora as his special little angel, frozen in an infantile life, but as sweet and loving and responsive as any baby. He joked with her, hugging and tickling her to make her smile and giggle. He took her on walks or to the playground, and he helped bathe and feed her. They watched "Sesame Street" together or played music while Chris danced for her. Chris soon learned Nora's favorite books and he would read to her, holding her close against his chest.

Ellen says Chris was one of the best babysitters she has ever had, conscientious and gentle with both of her daughters. "I can trust Chris implicitly," she says. "I have no qualms about leaving him with my children." Chris also had the patience to stay with Nora for hours on end. "Nora is quiet," says Ellen. "Other people could get a little bit bored with a child like Nora. But Chris didn't."

Chris says working with Nora is one of his favorite things to do. "She needs my attention and love and care and I try to help her. She has to communicate with us with her body language. I want her to learn how to walk and talk. I want her to learn to have freedom."

Nora, now ten, recognizes Chris when she sees him, no matter how long it has been between visits. "She really reacts to Chris," says Ellen. "She smiles and laughs with him."

As much as Chris enjoyed being with Nora, he and his family knew he needed to find a job. "I didn't want to be some bum, sitting around and watching TV all day," says Chris. "I wanted to make money and take care of myself." He also wanted to make new friends: though he had an active social life, it still revolved mostly around his family and his parents' adult friends.

One day, Ellen heard of a place a few blocks away that offered classes and job training for people with various handicaps. Chris enrolled in the classes, but it was obvious he did not fit in. Most of the students had physical impairments, or behavioral or mental problems. The teachers had so rarely worked with high-functioning people with Down syndrome that they mistakenly thought Chris' short attention span, and his varying degrees of comprehension and judgment, meant he could not learn. "They were not patient with Chris," says Marian. "Within a few days, the teachers decided that Chris wasn't benefiting from the classes. They placed him in a sheltered workshop on the premises, where he would be paid a few dollars for a day's work.

The next week, Ellen dropped in to visit Chris at his new job. She walked into a cavernous room where twenty people worked on an assembly line stuffing small items into boxes and bags. The room was silent except for the barking voice of the woman supervising them, who would not allow the workers to talk or leave their seats. "Many of the people were psychotic or had mental problems. It was like something out of *One Flew over the Cuckoo's Nest,*" says Ellen. "And there was Chris, sitting there stuffing these things into bags. I almost had a heart attack. It broke my heart."

She cringed when the woman screeched at Chris, treating him as if he was stupid. "I never, ever saw Chris behave the way he behaved around her. He was acting retarded. We got him out of there really fast."

It was a week that Chris would never forget, though he wishes he could. "I hated it," he says, rare anger creeping into his voice years later. "They wouldn't let me talk or do anything. I said I'll never go back to a workshop again."

Marian found some occasional part-time work for Chris in her office. Chris would walk with her to work and then stay busy filing, stuffing envelopes, and running copies. Marian's assistant, Priscilla Rosado, says that Chris was "super-duper ultra responsible" and would always ask questions to make sure he was doing something right. "He was so methodical, and always willing to do what we needed, and he worked very hard for us."

When Priscilla sent Chris to run copies, she knew she probably wouldn't see him for a while. "He would stop by to say hello to everyone. Even if he hadn't been in the office for a couple of months, he would remember everybody's names and all about their families. He had no reservations about going in to talk with the vice president or president of the company. Everybody enjoyed it when he came in, and everybody made a little time for him."

Still, there were no real job openings in the company that Chris could take. It was frustrating for the Burkes, considering how well Chris handled work responsibilities. Each new day, the vast metropolis of New York City stretched out before them with the promise of all the opportunities they had wanted for their children. Yet for Chris, the doors seemed closed.

"People don't make allowances on both sides of the coin," says Frank.

"They don't make allowances for their lack of ability in certain things, and they don't make allowances for their abilities. There are a lot of jobs handicapped people can do, but they have to be given the opportunity to prove it."

"At that point, we would have paid someone to have Chris work in a nice safe atmosphere," says Marian. "It was a foolish thought. It was more important to Chris and his development for him to earn money. But we were just desperate."

Marian drew Ellen aside one night to discuss the situation. "It would be great if he could even find a volunteer job somewhere," she said. "It might lead to something else once they see what he can do."

Ellen mulled it over, thinking about how well Chris cared for Nora. The next week, she approached Tom Roeder, Nora's teacher. She told him about Chris and how involved he was with Nora's care at home. "Could Chris volunteer in your class and help out with Nora?" she asked. Tom didn't answer right away. There were no volunteer programs at P.S. 138, but he could use an extra pair of hands in his class. He met with Chris, who told him how he had always wanted to help. He talked about Nora and the way he took care of her. Tom instantly liked Chris and wanted him as a volunteer, but first he wanted Chris to meet with Pat Mulholland, the unit teacher.

The next day, Tom made a visit to Ellen's home. Chris was there, playing with Nora on the rug. He sang with her, hugged her and kissed her, and had her giggling. "The love between them was so alive. And I could see that he could physically manage her and was gentle in positioning her. He got so much response from Nora that it helped me in knowing what she was capable of doing. He let me know what toys and stories she liked best. Here was Chris, who was going to be a volunteer, showing me things about this child who was in my class."

A few days later, Chris put on his blue blazer, a dress shirt and tie, and his best gray flannel pants. Pat Mulholland still remembers her shock when she saw him, so poised and mannered, and learned he had not been able to find a job. "I was appalled that he had been through these programs and no one had placed him. One problem with our kids is that they sometimes don't have social skills. He had them. It should have been easy as pie to find him a job."

Pat eagerly approved him as a volunteer teacher's aide in Tom's class, and Chris started helping out the next day.

The Burkes were ecstatic. "It was such a wonderful opportunity for him," says Ellen. "It gave him his own lifestyle and let him make friends and contacts on his own. He was learning job skills, he was learning how to deal with people, and he was in a safe and controlled atmosphere."

Chris says he was very happy when the volunteer job came through. "I loved working with the students. And the best part was that I had my own friends to hang out with. They were like my family. There were parties and we went out on Friday nights. I was like a social butterfly."

Within a few weeks, Tom and Chris were the best of friends. They lunched together often at a nearby diner, ordering the same bacon, eggs, and french fries. Chris quickly nicknamed Tom "Red" for his hair color, and a running joke sprang up between the two in which they pretended they were brothers. "We both had fair skin and reddish hair, and he joked that we were both so good-looking, and got better-looking every day," says Tom.

Tom says that one of the greatest bonds he and Chris had was a love for and understanding of each other's family. "Some of the background was different, but that closeness, that loving family was the same experience for us. He talked about his family all the time, and told me all about them. There was a whole lot of sharing and love, and a deep sensitivity. Mr. and Mrs. Burke gave him the support he needed, but they also allowed him to take risks, to get out there and participate in the things he enjoyed. They encouraged his interests. I think a lot of what Chris was able to offer the children came from home. If you see your parents as giving, loving people, it rubs off on you and you embrace that yourself."

Chris worked with Tom and the classroom paraprofessionals, who assist the teacher. Chris helped them teach the students how to use pictures and objects to communicate their needs and feelings. He helped lift students from their wheelchairs and into adapted equipment where they could make the most of their physical abilities. He also taught the children how to shop in community stores and prepare simple meals and desserts.

At the first, Chris stuck close to his niece Nora, but before long he began spreading his attention to all the children in the class, telling them jokes and trying to get them to laugh. They responded well to him, says Tom. "Chris displayed a deep respect for the dignity of each child in the class. He spent a lot of time getting to know them, discovering their personalities and learning what made them happy."

Ellen remembers how Chris would get close to the students, hugging them and rubbing their arms. "All of the kids were severely handicapped," she says. "Many of them had been institutionalized for years. As a result, they were very spastic. It was difficult to look at some of them. Their legs didn't have bracing when they should have, so they were twisted backward. Some of them had big crooked teeth and drooled. But Chris knew them all by name. He would go up to them and their faces would light up. He had a great rapport with them."

Sara Albert, a para in Tom's class, recalls that she was worried about working with Chris at the beginning, but Tom told her to just let Chris move around and get a feel for what they were doing in the classroom.

"Chris was a little shy at first," she says. "But after a few weeks, he started asking me all these good questions. He was very interested in what we were doing. And he was so proud of Nora. He would talk about her and introduce her to everyone who came into the school."

Chris was fascinated with Sara's background as a native of Puerto Rico, and he asked her to talk to him in Spanish so that he could learn the language. During quiet times, he talked with her about the history of the island and its current events, sometimes bringing in articles he had found.

Sara developed an almost motherly relationship with Chris. Once Sara praised Chris for his work, calling him "a good boy." "He said, 'Sara! I am not a boy. I am twenty-one years old. I am a man!' I said, 'Okay, but my son is older than you and I call him a boy, too.'"

Chris was not yet making many friends outside the classroom, though. In fact, many of the school workers weren't sure how to react to his childlike honesty and friendly teasing. "A few people didn't realize that Chris had Down syndrome," says Ellen. "Sometimes they were insulted by something he said or did."

Tom says the incidents mostly stemmed from Chris' friendliness. "Sometimes maybe Chris' sense of humor was not in sync with what other people saw as humorous. And then a few people just don't have a sense of humor; some of them were the same people who had difficulties with me at times. But there are limits to which you can joke around with people depending on how well you know them. It was just an area he needed to work on, making those judgments."

Pat Mulholland was aghast at some of the things she witnessed between Chris and the other workers, and she moved in to quash it. "When the others would tease him, it was more traumatic for me than it was for Chris," she says. "I told them, 'What are you doing, working with these kids and picking on Chris?'"

Some coworkers didn't like the way Chris would pat them on the back or hug them when he didn't know them well. And though his friends usually hugged him back comfortably, they warned him against his favor-

ite trick of coming from behind someone and embracing them unexpect-
edly. "The staff would rat on him because he wasn't supposed to do
that," says Pat. "I told him, 'It's okay for us, but it's not okay out in the
community.' Sometimes he would cry a little and I would say, 'Oh,
Chris, I know it's tough.' It was hard for him to learn not to do these
things he had done all of his life."

Chris gave serious thought to his work and how he managed his job,
says Tom. Chris was good with the children, but he had to learn to keep
his attention on the task at hand and follow it to completion. For example, Chris could get distracted by something more exciting happening
outside the classroom, and Tom would have to remind him to finish
what he was doing.

Chris worked well as a team member in the classroom, and he always
volunteered for extra projects or offered ideas for activities, says Tom.
And though many people with Down syndrome find employment difficult because of the intangible gaps in their judgment, that did not pose a
problem at P.S. 138, Tom says. "Chris' role in our school certainly ac-
commodated any limited sense of judgment. There was always a para or a
teacher around to guide him. Chris was able to use the abilities he had."

Initially, Chris had some problems accepting positive criticism about
his performance. "He would get upset with me if I was challenging him
to change his behavior," says Tom. "But he was always able to talk about
things; he never shut me out. Chris had to learn that the criticism wasn't
something personally against him; it didn't mean that I didn't like him. I
was just pointing out behavior he needed to learn to be a better worker."
Chris responded better when Tom explained why it was important for
him to be either behaving in a different manner or doing the task in a
different way. "We want to give any worker the understanding instead of
just giving an order. In anyone, it's hard to face something in yourself
that is not perfect, something that takes an effort to overcome. But
Chris showed a spirit of learning and improving. Over time, his anger
and frustration decreased. He'd say, 'Okay, Tom, thanks for telling me
that.'"

From the start, Chris was punctual and consistent in his attendance.
Every morning, he would wake himself up, get ready, fix a quick breakfast, and head over to the school before 8 A.M. One day Frank noticed
that Chris was going in even earlier, at 7 A.M. "Chris, I don't want you
going over to the school before everyone is there," he warned. "It's just
not safe." For the next week, Chris slipped out just as early. At night,
Frank argued with him about it, but Chris was obstinate.

Finally Marian stepped in to ease the friction. "Frank, I didn't want to tell you this," she said. "Chris is going in early because he is making you a Christmas gift." Frank says he felt like a heel, and even more so a few weeks later, when Chris presented him with a wooden sign he had carefully carved to read "Frank's Place." Frank hung it on the wall behind the bar in the Point Lookout beach house, a solemn reminder that Father didn't always know the full story.

Just as Chris loved going to work early, he hated to leave. In the afternoons, he would say goodbye, go out the door, and return minutes later with another question or comment for Tom. "Some days he said goodbye six or seven times before he left," says Tom. "It makes you feel good to have someone care about you that much. He missed seeing us till the next day, and we missed him, too."

Tom remembers that Chris was a snazzy dresser. "He had a real flair for matching clothes. It's pretty casual here; he didn't stand out. But sometimes he just looked so cool that people would mention how great he looked."

"We were aware that Chris still needed vocational training," says Marian. "We were delighted that Pat, Tom, and Terry took the time to help Chris and train him."

As the year went on, and the other workers got to know Chris better through school parties and events, they began to understand and appreciate him more. For the first time, he was making age-appropriate friendships, says Pat. "We would go have a few beers after work, and I was a nervous wreck because I knew Marian and Frank probably didn't want him to do that. But he was fine."

Tom sought Chris' help when he needed any information about music. "If I needed songs for a program about, say, friendship, Chris could always tell me the names of several songs, who wrote them, and when they came out. Then he would go home and make copies for me from his tapes."

Chris took center stage at social events, dancing and requesting the latest hits. One time he brought his drum set to play at a school party. He pounded on them late into the night, happily sharing the stage with the band. Marian grew worried when he didn't return home, and she went up to the school to check on him. She had a hard time getting Chris to leave his newfound friends on stage to come home.

Para Beverly Logan remembers another party where a group of emotionally disturbed girls were hogging the dance floor. "They thought they were hot stuff. Then along came Chris, dancing up a storm. He stunned them; he was really good."

Usually Chris spent his free time at the school as he had at Don Guanella, writing letters, stories, and short television screenplays. Tom and Sara helped him with his spelling and grammar, but with Beverly it became a running joke. "He would come ask me how to spell some word, and they were always tough ones. I would say, 'Gee, Chris, I don't know. I can't spell.' Then when I needed help spelling, I'd always go to him."

His coworkers learned more intangible lessons from him as well. "As adults, we didn't just go up to someone and say we loved them," says Tom. "It doesn't come easy. Chris would say, 'You know, Tom, I love you.' It's corny, but it's something that comes from within him. After a while, I found myself being able to say it back to him."

Beverly remembers that when people asked Chris about his Down syndrome, he would correct them, saying, "Oh no, I have Up syndrome, not Down syndrome."

"It was not just a clever twist of language. He really lived by that. I think he knew what his limitations were, or what they were expected to be. But he was always positive and confident."

That fall, Chris found out about some acting classes being conducted by the Young Adult Institute, a private nonprofit agency serving adults with disabilities. In 1957, YAI was founded by a small group of parents concerned with the lack of programs for their adult children who were mentally retarded. Now it offers classes, job training and placement, residential and clinical services, family and educator training, and a variety of support programs. The only problem was that the classes Chris wanted to take were held at night, in the Lower West Side of Manhattan. The route from the Burke home was circuitous, involving two bus changes. Frank and Marian were reluctant, but Chris persisted and finally won out.

On the first night of classes, as Chris boarded the bus, Marian was lurking nearby in the shadows. Chris didn't stop to talk to strangers, and he moved assuredly through the crowds. When he reached the bus stop near the Young Adult Institute, Frank was hiding in an alley. He watched his son cross the street with the light, then tailed him, ducking in doorways along the way. After Chris walked into the YAI building, Frank called to report to Marian, then returned home. The Burkes had asked a YAI worker to watch Chris when he left classes, to make sure he got on the right bus. Still, Marian waited anxiously at the window, turning out the apartment lights so she could see the corner where he would get off the bus. When Chris returned, he spotted his mother through the window and waved up to her with both arms, yelling, "Piece of cake, Mom!"

In time, the Burkes learned not to worry about Chris, even when his classes ran past 9 P.M. He took two or three courses a semester, studying filmmaking and improvisational theatre as well as vocabulary and practical academics. He attended the dances held at the school, making several good friends. "He came in with such seriousness," says Eileen Himick, YAI supervisor. "He was a hard worker, very intent. We had to get him to relax a little. We wanted him to have some fun with it."

"The thing I remember about Chris was how he'd get involved in everything and make it bigger than it was," says Helena Blum, one of Chris' classmates at YAI. "He knew how to do improv right away, and he was very talented. He's a very smart, intelligent person."

Paul Gussow remembers that when he first joined the improv group, Chris helped him out and made him feel comfortable. "If you forgot your lines, he would remind you. He was very studious and he had a really good memory."

In filmmaking class, Chris got a small part in *Sticky Fingers,* a videotaped parody of Mafia movies. "I was the cop," he says. "I was playing Frank Burke. My father showed me some steps, things like how to arrest people." In the film, Chris looks slightly nervous in his big scene, in which he argues with the Al Capone–type character, then takes him in to jail.

But Cesar Telli, who played the Mafia boss, says Chris was experienced before the camera. "He knew how to get his words across and everything. He was a real pro."

Chris, buoyed by what he was learning in his classes, talked more and more about his dreams of being a professional actor. "He always said that someday he wanted to go to Hollywood and make it big," says Cesar. "I told him, 'You've got me with you. I hope you'll do it.' "

Chris wasn't getting much support for his dreams from anyone else. His family still worried about his preoccupation with acting and the long hours he spent watching movies and television. "We were really strongly against this," says Ellen. "No one wanted him to be so set up for disappointment. It probably strengthened him. He had to fight and swim upstream. It made him more determined."

Tom Roeder understands the Burkes' reticence and admits he would have the same qualms if his own children set their sights on acting. "You don't want someone always trying to reach something you don't think is attainable. I don't think anyone in their wildest dreams could have anticipated how much he would be able to accomplish."

Paraprofessional Maureen Walsh recalls Chris showing her a list of goals he had for his life; they were mostly centered on acting. "He was going to be an actor by the age of twenty-three. One said something about having his own TV show, and the next was to be in the movies. First I thought, 'Oh, what is this?' Later, I thought, 'Hey, maybe I should write some goals down myself.' "

Chris made no secret about his ambitions around the school. He carried books and magazines about acting, reading them in quiet moments during classes. He frequently talked about acting and showed people his letters to Jason Kingsley and other actors. "He expressed his dreams really well," says Tom. "People thought he was nuts."

Sara Albert says Chris even brought in Spanish movie magazines, asking her to translate them. "He was ambitious, but in a good way. He never mentioned money, just how he wanted to be an actor. He had faith in himself."

"I have to admit I was skeptical," says Beverly Logan. "If any of our coworkers had had the same ambitions, I'd have had the same reaction. But you could see that determination. For Chris, there was never any doubt. It didn't matter what anyone else thought."

Chris' favorite student (other than his niece Nora) was seven-year-old Erin Gillis, whose mental development is stunted to that of a toddler as a result of an unknown genetic disorder. Still, Erin is a beautiful little girl, with blond hair and clear blue eyes who loves to laugh and sing and play her battery-operated piano. Chris immediately "adopted" her as his little sister. "He knew what she wanted or needed before anyone else," says Beverly Logan.

Chris sent notes home with Erin, telling her parents what she had done in school that day. Sometimes he gave her presents, including some Disney albums from his childhood. One day he supervised her in a community integration activity with children from a local elementary school. "He was helping her plant seeds with them," says Tom. "He told the other children all about her abilities and her personality. I remember how happy he was seeing Erin around the other children, and being the person responsible for her."

At Christmas, Erin played an angel in the school's concert. She was wheeled on stage with wings pinned to her back, a halo above her golden hair, and a sweet smile on her face. Chris sat between Erin's parents and kept saying, "Aren't you proud? Look at her. She is so beautiful."

Chris was just as enthralled with Erin's father, Jim Gillis, a veteran movie and television actor. When Jim came in to pick up his daughter from school, Chris talked with him about his dreams to be an actor. "He wanted to know everything about show business," says Jim. "He asked lots of questions; he wanted to know how to act. I said, 'Chris, there really isn't any how. You're just doing who you are, just playing yourself and showing what you have in your heart. If it's there, if people can see that, if I can look at you and you can give me that energy and express your feelings, then you are an actor.' "

Chris asked to see videotapes of Jim's work on television shows and in the movie *Tiger Warsaw*. Jim says Chris, like an adoring fan, kept him excited about acting, and he tried to do the same for Chris. "I told him, 'Sure you can be an actor. You can be anything you want to be, whether it's an acting job or working at the school.' I tried to keep his energy up about it. I said, 'Everything's against you.' But I saw that he was so charming and enthusiastic and positive. What was important was that he be able to first get into the door, with a casting director or a director. Then they couldn't help but love him and know that he's so expressive and energetic that they've got to hire him."

At home, Chris stayed busy writing short television scripts. He would watch his favorite shows, then draw out a story line involving a character with Down syndrome—to be played, of course, by himself.

Meanwhile, three thousand miles away in California, producer-director-writer Michael Braverman was busy writing a script for a television series pilot titled "Desperate." Even though the script was in its early stages, Warner Brothers Studios wanted to produce it, and ABC was interested in the series idea for its fall 1987 schedule, though its executives had to first approve the script.

Much of the story centered on the captain of a small fishing boat who was haunted by people and situations from his past. Because so much of the plot was internal, Michael saw that he needed someone to whom the main character could express his thoughts, someone innocent and nonthreatening to serve as a sort of conscience.

Michael, who had written, produced, and directed for the series "Quincy, M.E." had once written an episode for that show about doctors who were withholding heart surgery from infants with Down syndrome. The show had a small part played by a Canadian actor, David McFarlane, who has Down syndrome. Another time, Michael had met with a group of children with Down syndrome and their parents while researching a "Magnum, P.I." episode—which was never produced—

about Special Olympics. Now he turned his thoughts to creating a pure, innocent character for "Desperate." The inspiration hit him: a teenager or young adult with Down syndrome would fit that bill.

When Michael described his idea for a character with Down syndrome to executives at Warner Brothers, they were nonjudgmental. ABC executives were dubious but cooperative. So Michael approached the casting director to see if she could find the actor they needed. That December of 1986, auditions were held in New York and Los Angeles, and more than fifty young men with Down syndrome responded, including Jason Kingsley. Jason was good and experienced, but he was too young for the part. So his mother Emily made a suggestion to the casting agent: call Chris Burke.

Marian was in the kitchen when the phone rang that night. When she answered, the casting agent explained to her about the pilot movie, and how Michael was writing a part for a person with Down syndrome. Marian first found it hard to believe, until she was told that Emily Perl Kingsley had recommended Chris. "Can Chris come in this week for an audition?" the casting agent asked.

Marian let the words sink in. "Hold on, let me ask him," she replied calmly. She called to Chris, who was watching television in his room. "Christopher, this lady wants to know if you would like to try out for a part in a movie for television."

Chris came running into the room. "Yes, yes, yes!" he yelled. "I'm going to be in a movie! Ha! A movie!"

Marian made the appointment for the next day, then hung up and turned to Frank, who was standing nearby with a quizzical expression. "Warner Brothers would like to interview our Christopher for a part in a television movie," she said, smiling and shaking her head at the thought. Frank took in the news with more than a little shock, then turned to look at his son, who was dancing around the room with glee. Marian quickly warned Chris not to get his hopes up too high. "There are many others trying for this same part. You'll just have to go in and give it your best, but if it doesn't work out, maybe there will be other chances in the future."

Chris nodded but didn't let her caution dampen his spirits. "I waited for this chance all my life," he says. "I didn't know if I would get it. But I wanted it so bad."

The next day, Marian casually told her assistant Priscilla Rosado that she was taking off work a little early to go with Chris to an acting audition. "She refused to get excited," says Priscilla. "She was so unbelievably calm. She didn't really want to talk about it. She was the one who had both feet planted on the ground."

Marian says she was excited inside, but she knew that the appointment didn't mean a job. "This was something we had been through with all our other children during their modeling and acting careers," she says. Chris walked up from P.S. 138 to Marian's office, then they walked to the Warner Brothers office in Rockefeller Center, where Frank joined them. Chris went into the room with casting director Phyllis Hoffman while Frank and Marian waited outside. He stayed behind the closed door for what seemed an eternity to Marian, reading parts of the "Desperate" script in front of a video camera. "They asked me all sorts of questions," says Chris. "I just told them all about me." He also mentioned his niece Nora, and his lifelong ambition to be an actor.

The next day in Burbank, Michael received the tape of Chris' audition. He popped it into his VCR and immediately knew he had found his actor. "Chris stood out right away," he says. "He was extremely articulate. People with Down syndrome have something called hypotonia, which affects the muscles in the tongue and makes it difficult for them to speak clearly. But Chris was very high-functioning and very articulate. He had a perfect look, which was a nice bonus. And he sounded very natural."

For the next two months, Michael wrote and polished the script, then waited for ABC to approve it. It was a big decision: ABC would be committing millions of dollars to produce "Desperate." The odds of getting an idea for a series to air as a pilot on a network are about two thousand to one. First, the studio takes the best ideas presented by dozens of writers, directors, and producers, then submits them to the networks. Of the roughly 250 pitches ABC receives from various studios such as Warner Brothers, it commissions only about 30 pilot scripts to be written. From those 30, fewer than 15 scripts are actually produced as pilots. The networks only choose the ones that they think can translate into a profitable series. After these pilots are produced, executives screen them and choose fewer than 10 to run as series in the new fall schedule. The drama pilots that don't make the cut are usually broadcast as television movies. "Desperate" beat the odds: by February, ABC had approved the script and given Michael the go-ahead to produce the pilot movie of "Desperate."

After the audition in New York, the Burkes had been waiting on pins and needles for a call from Warner Brothers. As the weeks grew into months, the subject came up less and less. If Chris brought it up, his parents carefully warned him that it might not work out. One of the other boys could have won the part. ABC may have decided not to produce the script. They crossed their fingers, though in their hearts they felt the chances were slim. Chris listened to them, but his faith remained set on this part. He prayed about it at night and talked it over with Jim Gillis, Erin's father, at school. In time, his interest turned back to his volunteer job and his classes at YAI.

Then, on a Monday evening in late February, the phone rang. Marian answered, and a woman identified herself as an employee of Warner Brothers. "Do you think you could have Chris out here in L.A. this Wednesday?" she asked. "We would like him to audition for the TV pilot he tried out for in New York."

This time Marian lost her calm demeanor. She held the phone to her shoulder and called out to Frank. "You should have seen my mom's expression," says Chris, dropping his jaw and widening his eyes in pantomime. "She said, 'Frank! Frank! Chris is going to Hollywood!'"

It all happened so fast that the Burkes barely had time to tell their family and friends. Frank was taking a short vacation from his banking job, from which he was about to retire, so he and Chris flew straight out to California and rushed to the studio as soon as they arrived. When Chris met with Michael Braverman and Warner Brothers executives, they were even more impressed with him than they had been from his performance on the audition tape. "I wasn't nervous," says Chris. "They were very nice. I liked Michael right away." Chris read them scenes from the pilot script and talked to them about his desire to be an actor. Warner Brothers agreed that Michael had found the man for the job, so Frank, Chris, and Michael rushed to ABC's corporate offices, where Chris gave a repeat performance for the network brass.

Frank sat outside the doors during both meetings. "I wisely turned down an offer to be an observer," he says. "I didn't want to have Chris' attention diverted by my presence." Chris rejoined his dad a little later, while the executives talked behind closed doors. A few minutes later, they called Chris back in the room. "Chris, you have the part!" Michael told him, shaking his hand and patting him on the back. Chris gave a big whoop, then literally danced through the hallways with joy, stopping to give Frank a bear hug.

"We were so elated over the fact that Chris had done this on his own," says Frank. "Whatever he did, whatever he said, it was enough to handle it."

They flew back to New York in first class, their coach seats upgraded by ABC. They had only a few days to repack their bags for the trip to Key West, where the pilot was being filmed. Chris went to P.S. 138 the next morning, heading straight to the classroom to work with the children. He told a few people about the audition and his shot at TV stardom, showing them the scripts and the dialogue he had to memorize. He spent his free time that day casually working on his lines. The news spread like wildfire through the corridors and classrooms of P.S. 138. Maureen Walsh remembered Chris' list of goals, on which he had said he wanted to be an actor by age twenty-three. "He beat it by two years," she says. "It was amazing."

Frank was retiring from his banking job that very week, so he told his coworkers that he would have to leave just a few days early. "You can fire me if you want," he joked. Instead, they threw him a hurried going-away party on Tuesday night before he left.

On Wednesday, a limousine picked up Chris and Frank to take them to the airport. They flew to Key West, where another limo delivered them to a luxury gulf-view suite, their home for the next eighteen days.

It was the first time Frank and Chris had traveled together without Marian. "We were like 'The Odd Couple,'" says Chris. "Dad was Oscar."

Chris studied for his scenes, which were to be shot a few days later. Then he and Frank ventured down to the set to watch some of the filming already in progress. "It was all so new to us," says Frank. "We were even excited about seeing the director's chairs with the stars' names on the back."

The crew was busy performing its Hollywood magic on the surroundings. Frank and Chris got a surprise when they walked into an abandoned building where a scene was being shot. Trash covered the floor; cobwebs hung from the rafters. Frank mentioned the filth to a crew member, guessing that they had a big cleanup job to do. He told Frank, "Oh no, this was clean when we got here. We had to trash it up to make it look this way."

Chris was thrilled at every sight. "It was the first time I had ever been on a movie set," he says. "Everything surprised me. The sets, the cameras. The way they make everything look. The way they do the lighting."

Frank and Chris began to learn the intricacies of being on a set. "We were so inexperienced we didn't know up from down," says Frank. "But nobody gives you a crash course on being on a movie set. We had to get used to being aware of moving out of the way of the crew and the lights. We had to learn how not to walk into a scene they were shooting. It was all behavior that was completely strange to us."

The role Chris had won was that of Louis, a teenager with Down syndrome, who is the son of Dory Mae (played by actress Meg Foster), a feisty woman who owns a rowdy little bar. She and Louis are good friends of Noah, the captain of a small charter fishing boat. Noah wrestles with some haunting memories of his past as a naval officer, and his feelings for Deirdre, his former fiancée, who has just shown up in Key West on business. Eventually Deirdre, a radical leftist, entangles him in a conspiracy to arm Irish terrorists.

Just three days before shooting began, Michael had chosen John Savage to play Noah, the lead character. Chris got excited that first day when he saw John, a star from the movies *Inside Moves* and *The Deer Hunter.* "John was very nice to Chris, and understanding of Chris," says Frank. "Christopher immediately becomes very affectionate with some people, and he was that way with John. I had to explain to him that John had a very big part in the movie, so he couldn't be banging on John's trailer door and going in and visiting all the time."

A fast friendship also developed between Chris and Meg Foster, who has starred in the films *Ticket to Heaven, Carny,* and *The Wind,* and on television in "The Trials of Rosie O'Neill," "Miami Vice," and "Cagney & Lacey."

Meg describes Chris as a "remarkable human being, extraordinarily passionate and talented.

"There's a joy and love of life and being in the moment which is an actor's goal. Chris doesn't have to work for that. He is the moment. He is the actor." She says he knew all the words to Michael Jackson hits and would sing and dance spontaneously when the mood hit him.

Chris had a limited role, with simple dialogue, but he was in several of the key scenes. He worked roughly six of the eighteen days they were in Key West. During the day, they ate catered meals on the set. At first Frank admonished Chris not to eat too much of the food, thinking heavy portions would add to the production expense. "I didn't know how their catering worked," says Frank. "We finally realized that they had plenty of food and it didn't matter how much we ate of it. It would all cost the same for them." At night they were on their own, with expenses covered by a per diem allowance. "It was all such a new life for us," says Frank. "We felt a little like royalty at first."

At night, Frank worked with Chris on his dialogue. Often, Chris would write his lines on paper, then repeat them over and over while Frank read the other parts. During their free time, they went sightseeing and swam in the hotel pool, but Frank usually kept Chris shaded from the sun so his fair skin wouldn't burn. "I loved Key West, but it was really hot when we were there," Chris says. "The most fun I had was hanging around John Savage and Meg Foster." Chris didn't ask for autographs, but he and Frank took lots of photos of everyone on the set.

The cast and crew had been told they would be working with an novice actor who had Down syndrome, but beyond that, they were told just to treat Chris the same as any other actor. There were no special provisions, and the show had no backup actor to step in if Chris had trouble with the part, because Michael felt Chris could handle it. They were going to sink or swim with Chris. "They didn't explain much," says Chris. "I just learned to listen to my director. Michael helped a lot on the set of 'Desperate.' Daddy did too."

Michael advised Chris to listen to him, and only him, for direction. "I had to keep him focused. That was the hardest thing to do. He knew his lines extraordinarily well." Sometimes Chris' timing was off, or he would forget a line he had just repeated several times. Both are problems inherent to all actors, but even more pronounced in newcomers, and even more obvious with Chris.

Chris was mostly distracted by the overwhelming experience of being in the middle of such a frenetic production. "He was amazed with the enormity of the situation, the newness of it all, and the rapidity with which we shoot," says Michael. "On a pilot, we go through five or six script pages a day."

The laid-back residents of Key West shared some of that same amazement, from the day the eighteen trucks rolled into town with their loads of equipment and props. Then the cast and crew invaded some of the main areas of the sleepy little resort town, staging fistfights, a funeral procession, and romantic interludes while crowds watched from the fringes.

Chris was in a half-dozen scenes with John Savage. In one long scene, he amazed everyone by memorizing not only his lines, but those for John as well. The two had a strong on-camera relationship in which they joked and teased each other like brothers. The character Noah would say to the character Louis, "What Indian tribe do you belong to today?" Chris would answer, "Iroquois," or "Navaho"—words that sometimes would trip him up.

After a few days, Frank learned that on breaks, while the crew was setting up the lights and camera for a new scene, he needed to take Chris back to the trailer to relax or work on his lines. It was tough, since Chris preferred to socialize at any free moment. But Frank saw that Chris' attention span suffered if he got tired or too wound up from talking all during his breaks.

Meg Foster was amazed at how Chris kept his energy and enthusiasm even when the working hours dragged long. "His father could tell when he was getting tired but I couldn't," says Meg. "His father knew more about his concentration and how far he could push himself." Still, Meg says Frank was a far cry from some of the overbearing stage parents she has seen in twenty years of show business work. "Frank's such a wonderful, down-to-earth, gentle man. He stayed around when Chris was filming scenes, but he allowed Chris to establish his working relationships and have his adventure. He had confidence in Chris. Their relationship is fabulous. You would want to have a parent like Frank, and wish you were Chris. They are a gracious family, a humble family. Working with Chris, and meeting his father, was a very enriching experience for me."

Meg recalls how Chris was so aware of what other people were feeling. "He has an amazing barometer to know what people are going through at any given moment, in a way that's so selfless and loving, I was almost taken aback. It's charming, beguiling, and very powerful. I saw it all along, but I remember in particular one instance. We were shooting a scene in a cemetery. I'm usually quite gregarious on the set, but I was having a quiet moment, just sitting and thinking. Chris came over and said, 'What's wrong, Meg?' I said, 'Oh, nothing.' Then he put his arms around me and gave me this big hug. I didn't even know that was just what I needed."

Though Meg had never worked with anyone with Down syndrome before, she didn't worry about the challenges she might face. "I don't consider Chris handicapped, and I didn't when I met him. He has less of a handicap than many people who don't have Down syndrome."

Meg says Chris was a little nervous at first, but everyone kept encouraging him just to be himself. "To anybody walking on a set, it can be very confusing. There are a million questions." She remembers that Chris took pains to learn everything correctly, from set jargon to camera movements. "It's so interesting when you're doing a scene sometimes, and your impulse is to move, but due to technical things and time, you're not allowed to move. In television, there's not a lot of time to choreograph those movements like you would for a stage play. But Chris learned very, very fast."

She noticed that Chris trusted his instincts, like a seasoned professional actor. "All actors have to take direction for the camera to make a shot work, because there's only a small space within that environment.

You could see him thinking about where the camera would move in a very professional way."

His excitement about being in the movie shone through in the scenes, she says. "Chris just has an extraordinary truth about him as a human being that the camera catches. It's undeniable. When the camera rolls, he can't lie. At certain moments, even when he's directed a certain way, a totally different thing comes through his eyes. He has this acceptance of himself, and he is so accepting of others. When you accept your limitations and you know what they are, you all of a sudden are boundless. You don't use them as crutches. The audience responds to that. There's something profound about it. I don't think he's aware that it happens on screen, but that's what I see. It would be the same if he were playing Hamlet, because your eyes can't lie. He doesn't know how to manipulate himself that way as an actor."

Meg said goodbye to Chris after eighteen days, when he flew back to Los Angeles to be in some of the interior scenes that were filmed on a soundstage in Warner Brothers Studios. Chris was amazed when he saw what awaited them at the stage: exact replicas of the cockpit, pilot house, and engine room of the ship they had used in outdoor scenes in Key West. Chris and Frank stayed for another week, then flew back to New York.

The next day, Chris resumed his volunteer work at P.S. 138. Everyone wanted to hear about his adventures in moviemaking. He excitedly showed them pictures of John Savage and Meg Foster and Michael Braverman, and he talked about all that he had learned about camera angles and lighting and movie magic. He told them that he thought the pilot would be picked up for a series by ABC, and that he would be moving to Hollywood to continue his role.

His coworkers took that prediction with a grain of salt. Chris had had his fifteen minutes of stardom, and now it was back to the routine of daily life. "There was good reaction around here to the 'Desperate' part," says Maureen Walsh. "But we just thought it would be a fleeting thing."

"We were saying, 'It's a once-in-a-lifetime thing. He'll never get this,'" says Terry Egan, a coordinator at P.S. 138. "It's not that we didn't have faith in him. It just seemed implausible. At the time, you never saw handicapped actors on television, certainly not on the three major networks."

Chris and Meg Foster, who then lived in Manhattan, stayed in touch by phone. "This was his dream, to be an actor," says Meg. "He couldn't believe it was happening, that it was manifesting itself for him. He was excited, but he was pragmatic about it. He said if it didn't happen, he was still grateful for the moment. But he was very much looking forward to having an acting career."

By April, ABC had screened "Desperate" and decided not to produce it as a series. When Michael Braverman called with the news, Frank and Marian were disappointed, though also a little relieved. "We had talked about what might happen if it was picked up, and we really didn't know what we would do if it was," says Marian. "It would have brought great changes in our lives, and I'm not sure we were ready for that."

Tom Roeder recalls that Chris was disappointed, but not dejected. "He seemed to accept everything so well. He saw it as something wonderful, that he had been given that chance."

A few weeks later, Michael called Chris again with the airdate for the pilot, then sent the Burkes a final tape of the movie. Marian's coworkers badgered her to bring in the tape; when she did, they all crowded around to watch it. "We were all so disappointed that it hadn't been picked up," says Priscilla Rosado, Marian's assistant. "But Chris took it like a trooper. Marian was keeping private about it the whole time. She said, 'Well, okay, it's over with now. Maybe this will get it out of his system.'"

But the experience had the opposite effect on Chris. "When it didn't get picked up for a series, I was kind of . . . desperate!" he says. "I was worried that would be it, that I wouldn't have another part. I pushed myself; I worked hard. I tried to maybe get on other shows."

Chris talked with Meg Foster about it. "It happened once. Why can't it happen again?" he asked. Meg answered, "If you want it bad enough, it will."

"A lot of people wouldn't express their excitement about things like this, but Chris does," says Meg. "He has that enthusiasm and self-esteem. In that way, I thought he would work again." She encouraged him to keep looking for other work, but she cautioned him that acting careers didn't happen for everyone. "Screen Actors Guild is the least-employed union in the nation. There are very few people who actually get to work just in acting without holding down different jobs to support themselves."

Chris gave a copy of the tape to his friend Jim Gillis, who suggested that Chris find an agent who could bring him more work. Jim sent a letter of referral to the young adult division of his agency, Abrams Artists. Chris followed through with it, sending the pilot tape to the agency, then meeting with Claudia Black. Claudia remembers that when

Chris came in, she and the other agents were flabbergasted. "He was all dressed up, and he sat down and crossed his legs and started to tell us about himself. We just sat there with our mouths open. He wasn't like a child or a teenager; he was a very determined young man. We saw every aspect of his personality in that first meeting. You could tell when things were tender to him, especially when he talked about the kids he worked with. We could see how interested and excited he was to meet someone who could possibly get him into this field. He wanted so much to be a part of it."

Claudia says that after meeting Chris, she realized that the part in "Desperate" was minimal compared to what he could do. "He was capable of so much more. Unfortunately, it's not every day that something comes along for someone like Chris. When we called around, people would say, 'How bad is he?' But we had a few good responses. We looked at a few scripts, but there were not many we felt were right for him."

Claudia advised Chris to have professional photos made, which they could send out to casting directors. Frank and Marian had put Chris' earnings from "Desperate" into savings, but they let him use three hundred dollars of it for the photos. "We said, 'Oh, nothing's going to come of this,' " says Frank. "He had his fling with show business, and that was that. But he's the one who worked, he wants to have the photos made, so let's let him do it." Chris made an appointment with the photographer, sat for the photos, then sent them back to the agency, along with extra copies of the pilot tape.

Chris had already taken the tape of "Desperate" to P.S. 138, where his friends gathered to watch it. And nearly every Friday afternoon, when the children were allowed to watch television and movies, Chris would casually produce it again. For many of the children, it was a favorite selection, not so much for its story but because they loved watching Chris in his scenes. Several of the classes and staff members watched it repeatedly, while Chris filled them in on behind-the-scenes happenings during the filming.

Chris also took the tape to the Young Adult Institute, where he had resumed his classes immediately after filming the pilot. "When Chris came back, he was still the same old Chris," says Eileen Himick, the YAI coordinator. "He wasn't coming in and bragging about it. Then when the pilot wasn't picked up, Chris didn't mope around. He wasn't angry. He was confident something else would come along. There was no change in that determination. It was as if he saw the path that none of us could see."

Ellen's family moved to Washington, D.C., for a few months, then on to Vancouver for Jack's next State Department assignment. Chris was devastated when the family moved, and to this day he still wells up with tears at the memory. "It was very hard for me to say goodbye to them," he says. "I burst into tears. It was very, very tough for me."

By this time, Chris had joined an improvisational class and a theatre company named Intentional Acts. Of the dozen members, Chris was the only one with Down syndrome. The rest were mildly retarded or had emotional or learning disabilities, but those disabilities didn't stop them from taking their work seriously. In earlier years, the company had toured professionally around the New York area and selected its members through interviews. Now it had open membership, but it still drew some of the brightest and most ambitious of the YAI students.

Teacher and acting coach Mark Buchan, who was then in a professional improv comedy company, led the group through a range of theatre skills. They would develop their own characters, write a short script with monologues around them, then put the characters together in scenes and perform. Mark says one difference with Chris was that the characters he developed were always involved somehow in helping people with Down syndrome or other disabilities. "He was always conscious of the fact that he had Down syndrome. It was a recurring theme; his characters would either help someone with Down syndrome or they would set an example that people with Down syndrome can have dignity."

At the time, though, Chris was not setting the best example with his behavior in class. He had a short attention span and liked to talk and make comments about what was going on, sometimes to the detriment of the class situation. Eventually, Mark developed a code system so that he wouldn't have to stop the class to berate Chris. He would simply tap his nose to signal that Chris was getting out of line, and Chris would behave. Then once, while Mark was performing an animated acting sequence before the class, Chris tapped his nose in the same way. "It was like he was telling me that I was getting out of line," says Mark. "I was furious. I took him out in the hall and talked with him about it. He was very shaken that I was angry, and was sincerely sorry."

Mark says Chris was in some ways a real challenge for him. "He had respect for me and loved me, but he sometimes acted as if he didn't have much to learn from me. My goals in the class were as much to help students develop life skills as acting techniques. We worked on his ability to settle in, to be a part of what we were doing. I wanted him to let go of that need to have his ego fed."

But with his stint in "Desperate" under his belt, Chris viewed himself as more of a teacher than a student. He often asked to lead the class or work as Mark's assistant. At any chance he would break into an impromptu speech or apply a lesson to his experiences in show business. Other times, he would sit back, eyeing the other actors on stage, and give them advice in a directorial tone. Mark tried to dissuade him from that; he worked at getting Chris to be more of a team player. "He would perform his scenes, then want to leave. He was never interested in being an audience member, which is an essential part of the work."

Yet Mark could see that Chris was a talented actor. "He had his emotions at his fingertips. He creates an obviously appealing character, with real emotional range. He can be very intense, and he loves to perform." Mark says Chris merged with his characters completely. "There are certain degrees to which actors commit themselves to a character, where they're not monitoring themselves or editing what they're doing. Chris has that essential skill or gift, more so than most actors. It was quite exciting to watch."

Mark says he thought of Chris more as an actor than a person with Down syndrome. "He had a good deal in common with actors I know who have had commercial success. He was single-minded in his ambition. He had a terrific capacity to get attention from people, and a limitless desire for attention. He worked on his career the same way those successful actors work on their careers. He was one of the most ambitious actors I have ever met. It was a good kind of ambition: he would never have stepped on someone else or hurt another actor to get what he wanted. Chris just viewed himself as a star before he was a star. He talked all the time about wanting to get on another pilot and have a television series. I thought he had delusions. I know thousands of actors who want to be in a television series. It never occurred to me that someone with Down syndrome could have their own show."

Out in California, that very discussion was making the rounds in the ABC corporate offices. Even months after they had screened the pilot, ABC executives were still raving about Chris' performance. "He really lit up the screen," says Chad Hoffman, who was then ABC's vice president of dramatic series development. "He captivated you. I remember his eyes, how they would invite you in. There was something very welcoming and heartwarming about him, that made you both enjoy watching him and feel really good about being with him. Sometimes in scenes with other actors, you would find yourself being drawn to him. He had a magical quality; that's what made us realize that even though 'Desperate' didn't work, we should try something else with him."

In August of 1987, Chad called Michael Braverman for a meeting. They had breakfast with Susan Harbert, another ABC executive, at Dupar's, a coffee shop in Studio City. Very quickly, Michael learned Chad's mission: to talk him into creating a series built around Chris.

Michael was surprised, though he says it is not unusual for a network or studio to see something valuable in an actor and try to find a vehicle for his or her talent. Tom Selleck reportedly starred in a half-dozen pilots before "Magnum, P.I." hit gold. And dozens of actors have used small roles in series as a springboard for spin-offs, just as "The Mary Tyler Moore Show" launched Valerie Harper into "Rhoda" and "The Jeffersons" sprung from Sherman Hemsley's occasional appearances on "All in the Family."

Michael recalls that Chad asked him what approach he would take in developing a series around Chris, and if he would be interested in such a project. Michael told them he'd have to think about it. He was busy writing a feature film for Tri-Star and was deep in research for another ABC series idea, tentatively titled "Judge and Jury." "I didn't have time to do it all. I wanted to work with Chris again, but at the time, I thought the other projects had more promise. I really didn't have much hope for the project involving Chris."

Chris and his family knew nothing of the meeting between Chad Hoffman and Michael Braverman. They all anticipated September 16, 1987, the big night that "Desperate" would air. On the Sunday before the show, Chris pulled out the television listings as he had done for many years, but this time, there was his name listed right there in print with all the other actors that would appear on TV that week. J.R. sent postcards announcing the show to all his friends and family. He also called the local television talk show "A.M. Philadelphia" to tell them about his brother. The show invited Chris, Frank, and Marian to stay at the Adam's Mark Hotel in Philadelphia, then interviewed J.R. and Chris just before "Desperate" was to air. After Frank checked in and surveyed their room, he remarked to Marian, "I don't believe this son of ours. He has been responsible for so many trips and hotel stays. He is really something."

Beyond the talk show, there was very little media coverage of Chris' role in "Desperate." So with little fanfare, the Burkes gathered in Point Lookout with a few close friends on the night of the broadcast to watch what they thought was Chris' once-in-a-lifetime spot in the limelight. When the opening credits rolled, everyone clapped and cheered while Chris sat back smiling. Though the Burkes had watched the tape repeatedly, nothing quite matched the thrill of seeing Chris on television and knowing that millions of people were also watching. The myriad of flashbacks and plot twists confused a few of the friends, but they were thrilled to see Chris' easygoing charm and humor translated to the small screen.

Fran Slattery, a friend of the family, remembers how the excitement had built in the months after Marian first told her about the pilot. "We were all ecstatic, thrilled. Everybody watched it and we all decided Chris was the best thing on the show."

"He came across so well," says Bill O'Neill, a family friend. "He looked very natural. He was himself. It didn't look as if he was playing a part. We expected him to be nervous trying to act. We were biased, but we could see that he had done a great job."

In Connecticut, Anne watched with some of her friends. "Nobody liked the show, but everyone thought Chris was wonderful," says Anne. "I was quite surprised at how natural he came across." During the scene where Chris walked with others in a funeral procession, she started laughing. "He looked so forlorn, and I was thinking, 'What in the world did they say to him to make him look so sad?'" Another scene bothered her: in it, Chris stares into an aquarium with wonderment, his eyes wide and his mouth hanging open. "That was the only scene that didn't look like Chris. It made him look stupid. But everything else was very natural for him, especially the relationship with John Savage's character. I was so proud of him. I thought he was great."

The Burkes soon settled back into the normal routine of their lives, and the memory of the show faded into the background, upstaged by some news that Marian and Frank felt was infinitely more important than anything show business had offered. After a year of volunteer work, Chris was going to be hired by P.S. 138 for a salaried position.

It started when the P.S. 138 district office, located upstairs in the 400 First Avenue building, ordered the school to convert a service elevator to one operating exclusively for the students and teachers. The elevator needed to be manned by an operator who would help the children navigate their way around the building. Pat Mulholland had just become assistant principal, and she approached the district superintendent about hiring Chris. "I said, 'This is deplorable. Our entire district is serving children with handicapping conditions and we don't have anyone like that employed. I'd like very much to put Chris on the payroll.'"

Pat soon found that it wasn't a simple request. The New York City Board of Education worried about the liability of hiring someone with a disability to operate heavy machinery. And they were not sure he was capable of supervising children with severe handicaps. But Pat and coordinator Terry Egan persisted, drawing up a serious proposal and convincing the district supervisors that Chris could handle the job. The papers were put through in December. Chris was already operating the elevator as a volunteer when his status became official on February 3, 1988. His hiring broke a barrier in that school district: Chris was the first person with a mental disability to be hired as a paraprofessional, which is usually a teacher's assistant position but can include other functions. His salary was about ten thousand dollars; he had full medical and dental coverage, belonged to the municipal employees union, and had civil service status.

"Our prayers were answered," says Frank. "It was so much more important to us than his fling with show business. It represented the kind of long-term employment that we knew Chris would need for the rest of his life." Frank told Chris that he was following in the footsteps of his grandfather, Henry Burke, who had been an elevator operator during the Depression. And the family celebrated as much as they had when Chris had been on television.

"Everybody looked upon it as an incredible opportunity," says Ellen. "We weren't betting on the chance that someone in show business would call again. This permanent job was more important than anything else."

The significance wasn't lost on the staff at P.S. 138. "It put him on an equal par with everyone else," says Pat. "At times, it caused a little duress with his coworkers. Some of the staff were hanging on financially by their bootstraps. The hardest people to sway on any issues, whether it's racism or sexism, are the ones not doing so well themselves, the ones who are in competition for the same jobs. I'm sure there was some jealousy."

His performance was held up to the same standards as that of anyone else, which required a few adjustments in the habits Chris had picked up as a volunteer. At his first few staff meetings, Chris sometimes tuned out of the talk, or went to watch a movie on the adjoining room's VCR, as he had done before he had been hired. Pat pulled him aside to remind him that he was now a bona fide staff member, with all the duties and responsibilities that entailed.

Another problem came up when the children were involved in activities that interested Chris. "He wanted so much to still be a part of things

going on with the students," says Tom Roeder. "Sometimes it was difficult to include him since he had to run the elevator."

At first, Chris also had some difficulties learning his new job. Navigating the cranky, slow-moving old elevator through the building's floors is
not an easy task, says Pat. "It's quite stressful. The elevator does what it
wants to do. People are yelling at you and you have no control over it."

The elevator went to all eight floors of the building, but Chris was
told to only carry the children and teachers through the bottom three
floors of classrooms. Above them were five floors for the school district's
administrators, who were supposed to use the main elevator in the lobby
of the building. Problems intensified when the main lobby elevator
broke down, as it does roughly once each week. With the lobby elevator
broken, anyone going to the upper floors had to either walk the stairs or
board Chris' elevator. Squabbles would break out if someone grew impatient while Chris allowed extra time for a disabled student, or if Chris
advised the extra riders to take the stairs. "I liked my job, but I didn't like
it when people got impatient," says Chris. "They would say, 'I need to
get to my office,' and I would tell them, 'The children come first. These
children are severely handicapped and they can't walk like you do. They
need to get to their buses. They have to get home to their families.
Think of others, then yourself.'"

These little conflicts were sometimes stressful for Chris, but when it
got too bad, he would go talk it through with Tom or Pat or Terry, who
helped him find an approach to deal with the complaints. At first, Terry
would step in to help out if things got too busy or stressful. Then Chris'
confidence began to soar as he learned to deal effectively with the situations that came up on the elevator. He took his job very seriously,
following his instructions to the letter, no matter who tried to talk him
into an exception. One day he even refused to take the school district
supervisor up to the top floor. The man got off to walk the stairs,
chagrined but understanding that Chris was just doing his job.

Chris' coworkers say Chris got so good at his elevator job that he
probably would have advanced to another job eventually, possibly as a
teacher's assistant. He sometimes got bored during classes, when there
wasn't much activity, and he would sit and read, or write letters. When
no one was around, he would turn up the volume on his cassette player
and dance around the elevator. "Sometimes I'd walk out of my office and
see him in there with his headphones on, bopping away to the music,"
says Terry. "I'd stand there for a while until he noticed me, then he'd get
embarrassed and say, 'Oh, gotta go,' and close the doors."

Everyone in the school became acquainted with Chris, now that he was shuttling them from floor to floor every day. "He got to know people on a personal level," says Tom. "He wasn't satisfied with everyday small talk. He had a genuine interest in people and a real concern for them." Chris always called people by name and asked about their families. In time, his coworkers started calling on him to babysit for their children on weekends, and they invited him to parties and outings.

With Marian's help, Chris held a formal Christmas dinner for the staff at his home. His coworkers recall that Chris was the perfect host, greeting them at the door in a natty coat and tie, and introducing his parents. He said the blessing before dinner, then engaged in a lively conversation. Even now, some of his coworkers remember his impeccable manners and social graces of that night.

The camaraderie grew as Chris' coworkers realized he could take a good-natured joke. His friend Maureen Walsh remembers stealing Chris' elevator when he was on break. "I'd take it to the other floors, and he would have to come searching for me."

When Tom Roeder entered the elevator, he and Chris would tease each other lightheartedly. Chris would entice Tom to start singing, either by humming a song or by holding out a pen like a microphone. Then as soon as Tom would start singing, Chris would hold his hands over his ears and say, "Tom, please! Knock it off! My ears are hurting."

Just as often, Chris would talk seriously about the work Tom was doing with the children. Of special interest to Chris was the community involvement program in which students were integrated into activities at regular schools. Chris wrote Tom encouraging notes, praising him for his hard work. "I think it's great what you're doing," one note said. "Our students need to be out there with other children."

Tom had created a work experience program for the older students, in which they operated an ice cream stand in the park and worked part-time in neighborhood stores. Frank, now retired except for occasional consulting work, helped Tom set up a program for jobs at the local police-academy museum and volunteered to take the children around to various programs in the city. At the start of the school year, before the work experience program was expanded, Tom and Pat discussed ways to get the employees excited about it. "In order to get this program to work, we needed to have the staff look toward a common philosophy," says Tom. "We wanted them to understand why our students belong in the community." They decided that the best person for the job was right outside in the elevator.

So Chris was invited to address the entire school district staff in a special meeting about the program. Maureen Walsh was amazed at his nonchalance. "I told him the only thing I would ever say in front of a big crowd would be 'Fire!' But giving a speech didn't bother him in the least."

The day came, and Chris strode to the podium like a veteran lecturer. He talked about the dignity of work and told what his own job had meant to him. He used many educational buzzwords he had picked up from Pat Mulholland and Tom Roeder, lines about how people with disabilities needed to belong in the community and be exposed to other people so that they can develop independence and solid friendships. But instead of just parroting lines, he wove them into his own experiences, talking about his appreciation of the opportunity he had been given, how much he valued his friends at P.S. 138, and how great it felt to belong to the group. Many of the people in the audience who didn't know Chris were astonished at his poise and the extensive vocabulary he used. Although his words jumbled a little when he talked too fast, and his sentences sometimes rambled, his message came through loud and clear. "I think it had a profound impact on the staff," says Tom. "It helped bring them together, and it got them to participate wholeheartedly in the work program."

Little did they know that out in California, show business executives were deep in plans for their own work program for Chris. After meeting with ABC, Michael Braverman had mulled over the idea of a series for Chris. When he approached Warner Brothers executives about producing such a series, they thought it had promise, but really wanted him to spend his creative energy developing other projects.

Michael still had a few concerns about Chris' ability to carry a television show. Shooting a dramatic television series is one of the most demanding jobs in show business, both physically and mentally. An average workday can last twelve to fifteen hours, and though work is scheduled mostly during weekdays, it sometimes spills into nights, holidays, and weekends. Production runs from July to April, with only an eight-week break in May and June. Michael felt that Chris was strong enough for the job, but only if he was surrounded by an experienced cast who could shoulder separate story lines.

"I didn't think it was possible for him to be the lead character in a show," says Michael. "Somehow he had to be surrounded and insulated so he could function at his best. I was thinking in terms of an ensemble cast, with five or six people, so that he would only have to work 20 to 25 percent of the time."

During the development, the Writers Guild strike broke out in Hollywood. Many projects, including this one, ground to a halt from March to August 1988, while screenwriters negotiated for better working conditions. When the strike was over, Michael met with ABC again, presenting them with ten different ideas on how to use Chris in a series. "The family idea is the one I proposed the strongest. No family shows had ever really dealt with having a special child. I could couch it in a lot of humor, balance Chris against that humor, and keep it buoyed up. I wanted it to be honest and emotional, without being saccharine or maudlin. If it was moving in that direction, we could go to something fun. I wanted to keep it on a tone that made Chris accessible to the audience, rather than having them view him from a distance as we often view handicapped people in our personal lives. I wanted the audience to get close to him, and the way you do that is to use humor."

Chad Hoffman at ABC had made it clear that he wanted the family to represent the working-class people who have to earn two paychecks to get by. "We wanted it to be a typical American family, with a unique child. I wanted it to deal very honestly in its portrayal, yet be optimistic, showing that this family could survive and thrive. If we could show that these people could triumph in a small way with their lives, it was possible that other people could find a way to do so as well."

Family dramas were not common at ABC; the last significant one had been "Family" with Kristy McNichol, which had gone off the air in 1980. ABC did have a new yuppie-style hit in "thirtysomething," but now Chad wanted a drama from the other end of the spectrum. "I didn't see that audience being represented on television," says Chad. "I felt extremely passionate about it. I wanted to show them they weren't alone in their experience, that you can have your dreams and they can come true. But I wanted it to be realistic, not sugarcoated."

More than a year had passed since Chad first spoke to Michael about building a series around Chris. Michael had not spoken to the Burkes during that time, because the plans were still nebulous. But by November of 1988, with a pilot script nearly finished, Michael felt confident enough about its chances to call the Burkes. He also wanted to check on Chris' health and make sure that Chris would be available if the script was approved by ABC. When Michael called, Marian answered the phone. She greeted his news calmly and agreed with him that she probably shouldn't tell Chris about the plans until they were more concrete.

Marian told Michael that Chris had been hired at P.S. 138 as an elevator operator, and that his health was excellent. What she didn't tell him was that she was skeptical about his plans: though it sounded exciting, she didn't want Chris to jeopardize his real job for just another quick stab at stardom.

A few weeks later, ABC approved the script, deeming it strong enough to warrant the huge expenditure of a pilot production. Michael called Chris to tell him the news. "Can you come out to California to meet with me about it?" Michael asked.

"When can I be there?" countered Chris excitedly.

Michael didn't tell Chris that the whole pilot had been built around him, or that they were set on using him in it. Instead, he warned Chris that this was just another audition, and that other actors would be trying out for the part. "Even though we had always discussed Chris, and we were more or less set on Chris for the part, to protect ourselves we auditioned other people with Down syndrome," says Michael. Again a casting call was sent out, and more than fifty young men with Down syndrome responded. Jason Kingsley was not one of them, because he was busy in school and also too young for the part. "Even in the far corners of my heart, if I had wished it was Jason, we couldn't have stopped our lives to go out to California and make the commitment that the Burkes have," says Emily Perl Kingsley.

Chris asked for vacation time at P.S. 138, then flew out within days of Michael's call. Again he made the rounds of ABC and Warner Brothers executive offices. None of the other cast members had yet been hired, so Chris read part of the script with Deedee Bradley, the "Life Goes On" casting director. Deedee remembers that Chris was much more articulate than the other young men she had interviewed for the role. "Every now and then a word was hard to understand. But he was wonderful. He had a warm, appealing quality that came across right away." Deedee read the lines for father Drew Thacher in which he talks with his son Corky about his struggles to make it in regular classes at a public high school. "I got to the line that said, 'When is the last time I told you how proud I am of you?' I looked up and tears were welling up in Chris' eyes. I started crying, too. I was so shaken by it." They left the studio for the ABC offices, where Chris and Deedee again choked up on the same lines, then embraced in a hug. Just like before, Chris waited with his father in the hallway while the executives discussed the audition. Minutes later, Michael called Chris back in, and shook his hand vigorously saying, "Chris, you've got the job!" Chris threw his arms around him in a bear hug, then ran out into the hallway. "I got it! I got it!" he yelled, dancing around his father.

Chad Hoffman remembers that after Chris left, the executives sat in the office, basking in a warm glow. "We all felt so good, not only because we felt it was a good decision businesswise, but also because we felt we were doing something of value. We wanted to make this a show that spoke to the audience, dealing with an interesting and different situation. But we were also giving someone like Chris the chance to prove that they can be total human beings. They can have lives of meaning and purpose, and live lives like a lot of other people. Despite their qualities that make them different, they can function, and belong to the world at large. If we could send this message, here's Chris Burke who can do this show, it's possible for other people to do that. We all felt we were doing something we could be proud of."

Chris flew back to New York and greeted the staff with the big news about his role as Charles "Corky" Thacher in the yet-unnamed pilot movie. He would play a teenager, the middle child in a working-class family. The plot for the pilot revolved around his struggle to succeed in regular classes at a public high school he attended with his precocious younger sister.

During quiet times in the elevator, Chris repeated his lines slowly, enunciating each syllable. On his breaks he studied them some more, and he even tried to persuade Maureen Walsh to type out his dialogue separately. She balked when she saw the sixty-five pages, most with at least a line or two for Chris.

Chris also wrote his lines down, as his father had taught him to do during "Desperate." Tiring of that, he would practice writing "Corky Thacher," and "Charles Thacher." He also tried out different names for the show, including "Corky's Life" and "The Corky Thacher Show." A few weeks later, Michael, determined to keep it an ensemble show, settled on "Life Goes On."

One day, Terry Egan hopped on the elevator and was startled to see Chris poring over Edgar Allan Poe's poem "The Raven." "He usually had movie and acting books, so I said, 'What is this, Chris? You're becoming a Poe fan?' "

"No, Terry, I have to learn this for my movie," Chris responded casually.

Terry was taken aback. What kind of show was this? It all seemed so strange, seeing Chris day to day studying these lines while running the elevator between floors. "He had a job here, and that was great," says

Terry. "But as things got more and more serious, and he was asked to go to different things, people began saying, 'Wouldn't that be weird if he got it?'"

When Chris left that March to film the pilot, a staff member stepped onto the elevator and noticed his absence.

"Where's Chris?" he asked.

About ten people answered in unison, "He's in Hollywood making a movie!"

The man started laughing. "No, really. Where is he?"

The crowd assured the man it was true, then started talking excitedly about the details. Slowly it was dawning on them that Chris had not been so crazy all along in the two years he had regaled them with his show business dreams. "Maybe his ambitions were right on target after all," said one coworker. The rest of them smiled and shook their heads in amazement at the thought.

This time, Marian took off work for a few days to accompany Chris and Frank to California. Just before shooting began, Chris came down with a horrible fever that left blisters on his tongue and face. At dinner the night before the first rehearsal, he could not even eat the steak he had ordered. That night, Marian gently rubbed petroleum jelly on the areas and coaxed him to go to bed early. She worried that he would not be well enough to work. But the next morning, when Chris jumped out of bed at daybreak, his mouth was healed. He paced around the hotel room excitedly, imploring his parents to hurry so that they could get to the rehearsal early.

On that first day, he met his costars and the pilot crew, some of whom had also worked on "Desperate." He actually had more experience in front of a camera than one other member of the cast, Monique Lanier, who played Corky's leggy blond half-sister. Monique had just moved from Utah, where she had starred in several theatre productions.

The rest of his costars were veteran actors with pages of show business credits. Bill Smitrovich, who plays Corky's father, Drew Thacher, has had featured roles in theatrical performances and movies including *Her Alibi, Silver Bullet, Renegades,* and *Crazy People.* On television, he played a bad cop on "Miami Vice" and a good one on "Crime Story," among other parts. In addition, he has an education degree with a minor in special education, and he had helped with a workshop for retarded citizens in Connecticut.

Patti LuPone, the much celebrated Broadway star, was picked for the mother, Libby Thacher. She trained at the prestigious Juilliard School in Manhattan, then toured the United States for four years, appearing in classical plays with the John Houseman acting company. New York City fell in love with her in *Evita*, for which she won a Tony and a Drama Desk Award. Her portrayal of Reno Sweeney in *Anything Goes* earned her a Tony nomination, as did her work in *The Robber Bridegroom*. Performances in London productions of *Les Miserables* and *The Cradle Will Rock* brought the Laurence Olivier Award for best actress in a musical, the first ever bestowed upon an American. She was also the first American actress to play a principal role with the Royal Shakespeare Company. Her film credits include *Witness, 1941, Driving Miss Daisy,* and her portrayal of Lady Bird Johnson in the television movie "L.B.J."

Kellie Martin, who was chosen to play the younger sister Becca, was just thirteen, but she had been an actor for almost half her life. She got her first acting job at the tender age of seven on the series "Father Murphy," and she has not had much free time since. She's been on television shows including "thirtysomething," "The Tracey Ullman Show," "Valerie's Family," and "Highway to Heaven," and in movies such as *Troop Beverly Hills, Body Slam,* and *Jumpin' Jack Flash.*

From the start, Bill was comfortable working with Chris. The others were apprehensive. Patti LuPone had never been around anyone with a handicap, but the sensitivity of the script had moved her, making her eager for the challenge. She recalls seeing Chris on the set before she met him. "I said to my husband, 'That's Chris.' I could tell from his back, the way he was walking. I had a sort of leeriness about it. But from the moment I met him, it was okay. He has such an outpouring of love. He has no pretense." Chris immediately told her how much he had loved her performance in *Anything Goes,* and he sang her one of the songs from *Les Miserables.*

Kellie Martin remembers that when she auditioned for the part of Becca, she asked Michael Braverman if he was indeed planning on using an actor with Down syndrome. When he told her yes, that Chris had been chosen and he did have Down syndrome, she was shocked. "I couldn't imagine how they could have someone with Down syndrome carrying a TV show," she says. Kellie knew very little about Down syndrome; she had only seen a television documentary about it, which focused on some severely handicapped children in institutions.

Just before the shooting for the pilot began, Kellie did a reading with Chris, covering the entire script. "I was a little afraid of him. He came up to me and gave me this big hug. I didn't know what to think." Then Chris sat down to read, and he knew all of his lines from the script. "I didn't even know all of mine," she says. "The thing that really blew me away was that he already knew 'The Raven.'"

Each day Kellie worked with Chris, she became more comfortable around him. "In the beginning, I never thought I'd warm up to him. But it naturally happens to everyone who knows Chris. He is so gentle, and loving, and he always wants you to feel comfortable."

Now they were all family, at least for three weeks, as they brought Michael's words to life before the camera. This time, Chris was more comfortable with his acting than he had been with "Desperate." There had been more time to study the script, and a dialogue coach helped explain his scenes and drill him on his lines.

Chris also liked the fact that he was part of a film family that was in some ways similar to his own, with a story that mirrored some of his own life experiences. But the differences were apparent from the start. Chris, now twenty-three, was playing an eighteen-year-old who was being mainstreamed in regular high school classes, much to the concern of his parents, who couldn't afford to send him to private schools. He struggles in math while his little sister Becca agonizes over how his presence will hurt her budding social life, especially a particular unrequited love for a football star. Then Corky is accused of cheating in his English class, and in a serious parent-principal meeting, he proves his innocence by reciting the opening lines of Poe's "The Raven."

It was a simple, Hollywood-style resolution to a conflict, sweet but wrenching. The cast and crew grew nervous as it came time for Chris to deliver the longest lines he had ever spoken on film. The set was quiet as everyone hovered behind the lights and camera to watch the scene. The director called out, "Action!" The cameras rolled, and the actor playing the teacher delivered his accusing lines. Then Chris took a deep breath and recited:

> Once upon a midnight dreary,
> while I pondered, weak and weary,
>   Over many a quaint and curious volume of
> forgotten lore—
>   While I nodded, nearly napping,
> suddenly there came a tapping,
>   As of some one gently rapping,
> rapping at my chamber door—

Director Rick Rosenthal yelled, "Cut!" and the silence broke with cheers and applause from the crowd. A few people were crying openly. "Patti LuPone had tears in her eyes—real tears!" recalls Chris.

After the filming was completed, Chris and Frank flew back to New York. The next day was as normal as all the ones before show business had called: Chris went in to work, shuttling the children on the elevator. He resumed his classes at YAI, though he would often rush home early to see if Michael had called. At night, he prayed for the pilot to be picked up.

The Burkes were anxious too, but for a different reason. They worried that the show would be picked up and completely upset the order of their lives. Marian was committed to her job, and knew she didn't want to leave it. And they hated to think what Chris would have to sacrifice for his chance at acting. "He had a nice job with benefits and pensions just a few blocks away from where they lived," says Anne. "They were wondering if it was the right decision to make for him, to let him go do something that might be over in a month or two. They knew it would mean a drastic change in their lives. But it was something he had always wanted. How could they not let him?"

Kellie Martin also had apprehensions. "I didn't know if I wanted it to go to a series because it was a really hard show to film. I worked nine and a half hours on the set every day [the maximum allowed for an actor under sixteen years of age]. But after I saw the finished product, I wanted it to go so much."

The reaction was similar over at ABC. "Everybody loved it," says Chad Hoffman. "The only question was where to put it on the schedule."

Sunday at seven o'clock was a natural spot, though it's one of the toughest time periods in television. The hour is dominated by "60 Minutes," the CBS ratings giant for fifteen years. FCC regulations require that programming in that time slot be either informational, sports, or aimed toward families and children. "It's very hard to come up with something that is pure entertainment that fits that criterion," says Chad. "Our expectations in terms of ratings were not extraordinarily high. We felt that if we could get good reviews and awards, which we thought it would because it's a quality show, then the audience would be available. By the time everybody saw the show, and saw what its potential was, there was no question in anybody's mind that that was the thing to do."

In May the network ordered thirteen episodes, with production to start in July, just two months away. When Michael called, Chris answered the phone and was thrilled to hear Michael's voice. "He said,

'How're you doing, Chris?' and I said, 'Great!' He said, 'Well, Chris, get ready. The pilot has been picked up for a series!'"

Chris whooped and hugged his parents. "It was so wonderful," he recalls. "It was just unbelievable. My prayers were answered. My dreams came true."

Marian and Frank got caught up in the excitement and pushed away their fears that it would be short-lived. Suddenly there were papers to sign, contracts to negotiate, and scripts to study.

The halls of P.S. 138 buzzed with the news as people who had never dreamed it would happen tried to absorb the shock. Most of them approached Chris with the same half-joking line: "Are you still going to remember me when you're rich and famous?" Chris always assured them that he would.

The reality set in when a local television station came to interview Chris about the show, and twenty people crowded on the elevator so they could be on camera. Newspapers followed, then magazines, until the school bulletin board was filled with clippings about the local celebrity still running the elevator.

That June, Chris and his family gathered for his niece Kara's high school graduation. She was valedictorian of her class, and Chris watched her proudly as she gave a speech to the audience. Minutes later, he started crying so hard that he put on his sunglasses to hide his tears. "It was very rough for me," says Chris. "I knew I was going to be in California doing my show and she was going to be in school at Penn State. I thought, 'How are we going to see each other? How am I going to visit her? It would be hard for me to contact her.' I remembered all the times we spent together. I watched her grow up from when she was a little baby. Now we were going to be so far away from each other."

Kara tried to comfort Chris, but he was inconsolable. "I think I looked so old to him at that point, and he knew everything was changing so fast."

Only three years had passed since Chris' own graduation from Don Guanella. J.R. looked at his brother in amazement, thinking back on how worried the family had been about Chris' future and his obsession with acting. "I spent all that time telling him to forget Hollywood," says J.R. "Now I was his biggest fan."

J.R. was even more than that. Chris, who was about to start earning a six-figure salary, had just hired J.R. as his business manager.

★ ★ ★ ★ ★ ★ ★ ★ ★ ★ ★ ★ ★

I HAVE WANTED to be an actor ever since I was a little munchkin, when I was five years old. That's when I got on the stage at school and everyone clapped. It was a lot of fun. It made me feel good and excited.

I used to look at the pictures that my brother and sisters made when they were models and actors. I said, "I want to do that, too." I wanted to follow in their footsteps. I liked to watch television and imagine that I was a character on the shows. When I told people what I wanted to do, they didn't think it would happen. But I always thought it could. I believed in my dreams.

I have always been in love with show business. I know the names of all the people in *The Wizard of Oz*. I can do some of the scenes and I know all the songs. I have watched it dozens of times. I know a lot about movies and acting. I like to surprise people with what I remember.

I have many favorite actors. I really love Jimmy Stewart, ever since I saw his movie *It's a Wonderful Life*. I like the character he played, George Bailey, and my favorite scene is when he lost everything and his father died and he got out of control in front of his family with Donna Reed, who played his wife Mary. I also like Jimmy Stewart because he didn't go to school to be an actor, and neither did I. My other favorite actor is Sean Connery. He was the original James Bond 007, and I watched all his movies when I was growing up. My favorite actress—really, she is my heroine—is Katharine Hepburn. I would love to work with her some-time. I grew up watching her in a lot of movies, and my real favorite is *On Golden Pond*, where she is Ethel, Henry Fonda's wife. I loved her in *The Philadelphia Story* with Jimmy Stewart and Cary Grant. All of them were wonderful.

This is my friend George Bush, the President. And that's Patricia Neal, a wonderful actress, standing next to me.

Acting is hard work! Here I'm taking a break with my friend Bruce Pasternack, the camera operator.

This is my TV family in the first season. Left to right, Kellie Martin, me, Patti LuPone, Bill Smitrovich, and Monique Lanier.

My friends Joe and John DeMasi are professional musicians. We've been singing together for almost fifteen years, ever since they were my music counselors at summer camp. We've recorded three songs together, and I'm hoping we'll have them out on an album soon. (John DeMasi)

One of my favorite episodes of "Life Goes On" was the one where the Thacher family went to Hawaii. I got to swim with the dolphins! Next to me is Elizabeth Lindsey, who played the dolphin trainer, and behind us are Miki and Kaleo.

When I'm not working on the show, I travel around speaking and raising money for several groups that help people with Down syndrome. This little baby is Casey Bishon Barker, the youngest member of the National Down Syndrome Congress. He has a bright future ahead of him! (Diane and Richard Barker)

I get to meet all my favorite television and movie stars at awards banquets and parties. This is Macaulay Culkin, star of *Home Alone,* at the Fifth Annual Comedy Awards.

In one of my favorite episodes, Corky enters a bike race. (© 1990 Warner
Bros. Inc. All rights reserved.)

PARKING FOR
life goes On
Chris Burke
ONLY

David McFarlane played Arthur, Corky's friend, who is orphaned. They made David's hair gray so he looked old enough for the part. David was on "Quincy, M.E." years and years ago, so he might have been the first actor with Down syndrome on TV.

Quincy Jones is one of my very favorite record producers. I got to meet him when he guest-starred on "Life Goes On." (© 1990 Warner Bros. Inc. All rights reserved.)

My good friend Ashley Johnson is a star on "Growing Pains." I met her in L.A. and now I spend lots of weekends at her house. We like to get on the microphone in her den and sing and dance, pretending like we're giving a concert. (Kendra Dew)

I was voted one of the Ten Outstanding Young Americans for 1991. Mom and Dad were bursting with pride and so was I.

I like the classics, but my all-time favorite movie is *La Bamba* because it's a true story about Ritchie Valens and it inspired me. I also like *The Karate Kid* and *Hamlet* with Mel Gibson and *Dances with Wolves,* but I don't like the sex scenes.

There is no doubt that I wanted to become a big Hollywood star. I also wanted to help handicapped people. I wanted to show everybody that people with handicaps can be responsible. I wanted everyone to see that people with Down syndrome can do a job just like them. We have feelings and interests and we want to do our very best.

When I got my job with "Life Goes On," I just couldn't believe it was true! My prayers were answered. Everything happened so fast. It was exciting to fly out here to California and work with all the people on "Life Goes On." I saw many people I had worked with on "Desperate." Then when the show was picked up for a series, I was in heaven! I was just happy to have the opportunity to do the show. I love Michael Braverman because he is my dream maker.

And now here I am! I love to sit down on Sunday night and watch "Life Goes On" and see my name come on the screen. In "Desperate," it said "Christopher Burke." That's what my parents call me. But now it says "Chris Burke," because that's what I like best.

The best part is that I am doing what I love: acting, like all my heroes. The worst is not so bad. The hours are long and I have a lot of studying to learn my lines. I really thought it would be easy but it's not. But I love it! My family is very proud of me, and that makes me feel good. I'm glad I'm making money so now I can take care of myself and my family. They have always supported me and taken care of me, and now it's my turn.

I like the show because it's about what happens in real life. It's all about this family and Corky, who is this person with a disability who is trying to help his family out. It's good for people to watch and see what Corky faces in his life.

My character, Corky Thacher, is a lot like me. Corky has a caring family just like I do. He likes sports, music, dancing, and going out with friends, just like I do. I'm really happy to be Corky, but I am happy being Chris, too. It's great to be both. But Corky is more innocent. He gets into situations that I would not. Corky is also very serious. I think I have more fun than Corky does. He needs to lighten up! He has every-day problems that I don't have. He gets involved with the personal problems that have been bothering him a lot. That's the biggest reason I'm different from Corky. But in the end, it's all okay because Corky is a good person. Sometimes he says things that I wouldn't say. It's hard playing someone with Down syndrome because, well, I do have Down syndrome, but it's not the same. They want me to just be Chris Burke, but that's not the way I talk. It's difficult to be involved with a character who speaks a certain way because I stutter. People who have Down syndrome do stutter sometimes. James Earl Jones, the actor, used to stutter, too, but he learned a lot. I'm learning too.

Corky can do a lot, but sometimes they treat him like a child and he hates that. He never likes to be embarrassed. He likes to be treated just like any other person who is normal. He doesn't like to be different from other people. Sometimes he has a bad attitude. He likes to do everything his way.

"Life Goes On" is not just my show. There's Bill and Patti and Kellie and Tommy and Tracey, and they all have their stories. I'm just one of many. They're like a second family to me.

Bill Smitrovich plays my dad on the show and he's great. He teaches me a lot about staying in the scene. I've learned so much from him. We throw punches at each other, and we have all these secret handshakes that we do. When I get frustrated, I say to myself, "Just be calm like Bill Smitrovich." Bill is smooth and natural. He knows his character real well.

I love Patti LuPone, who is my mother Libby on the show. She always makes me laugh. She reminds me of Lucille Ball because she does all this crazy stuff on the set. She could be a stand-up comedian, she is that funny. It bothers her when I don't remember my lines, but I'm trying really hard. It's not easy for me to say these lines.

Kellie Martin is my sister on the show and she is like my sister in real life, too. I feel close to Kellie and I feel like I'm a part of her family. We give each other support and love. She helps me with my scenes. I think she's a great actress. I like watching her movies.

Tommy Puett plays my friend on the show, and he's my good friend off the set too. He calls me "Bro," and he mentioned my name on his album. He's a really good musician and I think he's going to make it big. I love going to visit Tommy in his trailer and listening to music and watching TV. We play "dueling remote controls" and flick the channels around.

Monique Lanier was my big sister Paige in the first season and she was nice. She was like a flower child. And now Tracey Needham plays the character of Paige, and she's a flower child, too. I think the world of her.

She brought me a Billie Holiday tape and now I love Billie Holiday. We like to chase each other all over the set. She is so pretty.

Kaley is my dialogue and acting coach, and she's like a big sister to me. She's my mentor, like Pat Morita was in *The Karate Kid,* and I'm like Ralph Macchio. I'm trying to learn about acting, and she's teaching me and training me how to do everything. Sometimes it's tough getting into my character. I have to know what he would say in his own words. Kaley helps me get to know my character. She says, "It's not just saying the lines, it's the way he cares about himself. It's how he feels when it comes out of his system. Don't think about the lines, just think about what the character is trying to say in real life. The thought is you, the character is you." And she always says, "Go steady, Chris." If I forget my line, Kaley feeds it to me and I can do it.

The crew is always just trying to help me out. They're a down-to-earth crew, a wonderful crew. They've taught me a lot about this business. They all love their jobs, and they treat me like a friend, like an actor, not like a celebrity, and that's what counts. I have fun talking to other people and cutting up when we break for lunch, but it's a serious set. I don't think about having fun when I'm working because I'm there to do a job and that's the most important thing. We're a team. We're a family. It's hard work but I'm trying to get used to it.

My favorite scenes are the ones where I show strong emotions. There's one where my father, Drew, says, "Have I told you how proud I am of you?" Another time, Patti LuPone sang "You Are the Wind Beneath My Wings" to me. She's got a great voice. I liked the pilot, where I recited "The Raven." I've loved the shows where I danced, and a show where I rode on the back of a dolphin. And I've had love scenes with pretty girls! That was fun, but those scenes are hard to do and they took lots of takes. One of my favorite shows was when Corky decided to enter a bicycle race. Corky's friend says, "Why try? What if you can't do it?" and Corky answers, "What if I can? When people say I can't do something, it makes me try even harder."

I really liked the one where Corky ran for class president. I gave this speech that went, "I'd like to win. But if I don't, I still have some wishes. I wish the kids who tease handicapped people could stand in our shoes . . . then they would know we have a life, we have dreams, just like you. All we want is a chance to be your friend."

There's one thing I don't like. That's when people write about me and my character Corky and say that we are "victims" of Down syndrome, or say that we are "afflicted with the disease called Down syndrome." Down syndrome isn't a disease; it's a disorder. I was born with Down syndrome. I can't help it. It just gives me different characteristics. Everybody is born different. This is just who I am. Some people treat me differently, but I just want to be treated like anybody else. Maybe someday they'll just describe me as "Chris Burke, the actor."

NINE

★ ★ ★ ★ ★ ★ ★ ★ ★ ★ ★ ★ ★ ★

WARNER BROTHERS STUDIOS is a jumble of beige metal huts and cavernous soundstages housing the sets of a dozen television shows and as many movies. Stern security officers guard the gates leading into the 108-acre lot, keeping out trespassers and sightseers who yearn for a glimpse of their favorite stars. Every day, roughly four thousand people work here: carpenters and designers who build the sets, lighting technicians, camera operators, costumers, producers and directors who bring the sets to life, and the huge population of actors and extras who fill the scenes. The privileged few are sheltered in tiny trailers stacked along the narrow alleys and roads that wind through the lot. Here, among the din, the actors pore over their lines and sit for the makeup and wardrobe experts who will transform them into their characters.

Toward the back of the lot is a patch of woods nicknamed "the Jungle," which in the myopic eye of the camera becomes the deep, dark forest seen in countless television and movie scenes. Nestled along the trees are the outdoor sets: ghostly Western towns, replicas of courthouses, theatres, and office buildings, and a hodgepodge of residential streets. Turn a corner and you may see, sheltered from the perpetual glare of California sun, a London neighborhood, where fog and mist machines blow from the perimeter and actors in trench coats duck under black umbrellas. A few hundred feet away, you may see a vibrant wintry scene straight out of Brooklyn, with plastic chips posing as snow, and derelicts huddling in doorways below neon pizza signs. The next week, with a fresh coat of paint or a heavy wash of mud, the same streets may pass for Mexico, or Chicago, or Anytown, U.S.A. A closer look reveals that the buildings are just empty facades: the sturdy stone and brick are actually painted sheets of plaster of paris hiding cameras and lights. From day to day, the facades, streetlights, doorknobs, and shop windows may be changed to represent any period in time from the eighteenth to the twenty-first century. Even the cement sidewalks can be pulled up, square by square.

It is a surrealistic setting where the hopes and dreams of thousands meet the daily grind of performing: the anguish of repeating lines, hitting the marks, showing the emotion and expression that will someday, maybe, reach millions of people in audiences across the world and make them feel, "Oh, this is it. This is what life means, this is a story or an emotion, or a character I can understand." Then, with luck, a few of the thousands of actors who entered the studio gates in obscurity find themselves awash in the rarefied heat of stardom. This humble lot, which has been rented out to nearly every Hollywood studio for the past seven decades, is where it all began for some of the biggest names in show business: Bette Davis, Humphrey Bogart, Jimmy Cagney, Paul Newman, Jane Fonda, Ronald Reagan, Natalie Wood, Glenn Close, Errol Flynn, Warren Beatty, and Doris Day, to name a few.

Chris had been here twice before, to film the pilot movies, but only as a temporary guest in this world which has seen thousands of people once, twice, then never again. But in July, when he walked onto the set to start the regular episodes, he knew he belonged. His director's chair, emblazoned with his name across the evergreen canvas, sat near the Thacher family's blue shingled suburban house, a thin facade framed by potted trees and Astroturf. The door opens to a warren of rooms, all normal except for an open ceiling filled with lights that stretches fifty feet to the top of the soundstage. Past the entrance hall lies a pleasant middle-class kitchen, a cluttered family room, and a living room decorated with childhood pictures of all the cast, including ones of Chris: as an infant, splashing in a tub, and as a toddler, taking his first steps.

A few blocks away, at the Warner Brothers publicity office, hundreds of more recent professional photos were being stuffed into press kits, along with Chris' brief resume, and sent out to the media. Reporters, intrigued by the novelty of an actor with Down syndrome, began lining up for brief interviews during his spare time. Chris met them in his camper-style trailer parked next to the set. When they were through recording his words on tape and paper, his father would coax Chris to lie down on one of the twin beds for a quick nap.

This was a bizarre world Frank and Chris had entered, made even stranger by the absence of Marian. She had stayed in New York with her job as manager of the stationery show. "We don't want to turn our lives upside down over this," she had said that fall. It was wishful thinking. The three-thousand-mile distance was hard on the couple: it was the longest time Frank and Marian had been separated in the four decades of their marriage. They wrote to each other as they had during the war, but this time they also had telephones and fax machines to fill in between the lines. Chris and Frank faxed cartoons and funny notes to Marian at work; she sent them the office football pool so that Frank could make his bets.

Navigating the phone lines between three time zones was not as easy. Frank and Marian tried to talk every evening, spending long hours catching up on the day's events, and marveling at each new miracle their son had accomplished. But the long hours of Chris' new job made these calls difficult. "Many times, I would get home, thirsting to talk with her," says Frank. "But it would be after nine, which is after midnight in New York. I didn't want to get her out of bed." If anything, the absence had made their love grow. "I think our relationship actually got stronger," says Frank. "But we didn't just miss Marian; we also missed seeing the grandkids and the rest of our family. Chris really didn't understand when I told him, 'I'm giving you the best years of my wife.'"

Beyond that, Frank and Marian rarely talked about the separation, either to Chris or between themselves. "That would just bother us more," Marian said that fall. "I miss them, but it's so worthwhile for Chris. We'll always be behind him. We're just plain and simple folk. We've always had a good life, but this is all very different for us. It's so thrilling for Chris. And I think Frank is enjoying it, too. He had plenty to do in retirement but now he has a whole new career."

Frank moved into his new life as a stage father with typical aplomb. He cooked at night in their furnished two-bedroom apartment, helped Chris study his lines, and chauffeured him to the set calls. At times, a little friction developed between the two. "In a way, we were getting cabin fever," says Frank. "We were so close to each other with nothing to come between us. I don't have the patience Marian has with Chris. I'm more blunt. She is our referee." The squabbles were minor, but they were made larger by the enormous demands of shooting a television series. In New York, Chris had always dressed and prepared breakfast on his own; now his father stepped in to help because time was so limited, but Chris chafed under such close supervision. Sometimes Chris was slow-moving in the mornings; Frank tried to explain how his tardiness would affect dozens of other people on the set. He yelled, he fumed, and finally he threatened to tell Chris' coworkers about his lackadaisical attitude toward work. Other times, Chris preferred to relax when he got home, instead of studying his lines. Or he would sit and watch television rather than eat the dinner Frank had prepared. In time they adjusted, but there was never quite the harmony that the family had when Marian was around to intervene.

Chris immediately fell in love with California, much to his parents' dismay. They were excited about his new career, but they expected that it would be short-lived. After all, the network had only ordered thirteen episodes; the Burkes wanted Chris to be prepared to move back home. But Chris raved about the mild weather, which rarely moves above or below the comfort range, and the beauty of the area. In the evenings, Chris looked out from his apartment window as the setting sun cast its riotous glow on the Hollywood Hills surrounding the valley. The peaks rose solemnly above the clutter of Burbank, resembling a lonely scene from some long-ago Western movie. As nightfall deepened the shadows, coyotes wailed from the brush just outside the apartment, and raccoons and deer scampered in the parking lot.

It was heady stuff for a New Yorker. But Chris had long ago lost his love for that Eastern city when his brother was stabbed in the park, and again when he was hit by a cab right in his own neighborhood. He told some reporters that his hometown was Point Lookout, where, in truth, he had spent more of his later years than New York. And his years in the sheltered suburban campuses had softened him against the grime and hard-knocks rhythm of the city. Here, in L.A., he saw open vistas of opportunity; he felt the complete acceptance and confidence that his coworkers had in his lifelong dreams.

The set, with its millions of dollars of equipment and more than a hundred workers, was a hotbed of activity, one of the most harried places Frank had ever seen. "Everyone in this business works extremely hard," he says. "The hours are long and the pace is very fast." The pilot for "Life Goes On" was set to air in September, just weeks away, and the cast and crew scurried to produce the episodes that would follow. Hourlong television dramas are generally regarded as the most grueling work in show business, much tougher than a half-hour sitcom. "Life Goes On" is no exception. With the pilot, they had three luxurious weeks to film what they needed to fill the hour. Now, each show had to be rehearsed and filmed within eight days, a period slightly above average in an industry where show production schedules range from five to twelve days. They needed extra time not only for Chris, but also for Kellie

Martin: as a minor, she is restricted from working more than nine and a half hours each day, and she must attend school on the set with her tutor for three of those hours.

Each scene of "Life Goes On" is rehearsed, then it may be shot a dozen times, with different takes for lighting, close-ups, and various camera angles. Sometimes there are changes in dialogue or the rhythm with which it is delivered. A long day's work may produce just a few minutes of film used in the final cut of the episode.

Chris works the same hours as other actors, especially when the story line revolves around him. Actually, his hours are often longer: when other actors are relaxing between scenes, Chris is busy trying to learn his lines. Out of roughly fifty-five pages of each week's script, he has sometimes had lines and action in as many as forty-five pages.

Each evening, the actors receive an updated schedule telling them when to report to makeup and wardrobe, then to the set. Some set calls are as early as 6 A.M.; a tough day might run through the night and end at daybreak. Union rules mandate a twelve-hour break before shooting begins again, but that doesn't help much when an episode requires continual night shooting, as did the first episode filmed after the pilot. The story focused on Chris' character Corky getting a job babysitting a six-year-old boy. Late in the evening, Corky must take the boy to safety when the neighborhood is evacuated because of a gas leak. En route, the boy and his puppy slip away down a steep ravine. Corky finds them, calms the boy down by getting him to sing "Three Blind Mice," then devises a rescue line to pull them out of the ravine.

It was a particularly grueling assignment for everyone involved. They filmed through the night in L.A.'s Griffith Park, choking through thick special effects fog that billowed through the ravine. Camera operator Bruce Pasternack was on a crane thirty feet in the air; director Rick Rosenthal and dialogue coach Kaley Hummel were hanging from ropes down the ravine, cueing Chris on his lines.

On the first take, Chris called down to the boy, coaxing him to sing "Three Blind Mice." But then, instead of running back to make the rescue line, Chris immediately chirped his next line, "I'm back!"

"Chris, you haven't left yet!" sighed Rick Rosenthal.

The crew looked at each other with dread in their eyes. "I was thinking, 'This is going to be a long year,'" says Bruce. "That was one of the first times we realized we were not in a normal situation. But that was how his mind worked. He skipped to the next line because that was the next one he had in the script."

When they shot the next scene, in which Chris dragged the tire and rope across the ground and made the rescue line, Chris stood aside while they filmed the hands of a crew member tying the rope to the tree. "I'm sure if we had taken the time, we could have taught Chris to tie the knot," says Bruce. "But we didn't have much time, and maybe it would have taken too long on camera for him to do it."

In the next set of scenes, Chris grabs the rescue line and slides down a steep cliff into the ravine. He takes the puppy in his jacket and instructs the boy to hold on to his back, then pulls them up the rope to safety. The shooting dragged on into the wee hours of the morning while Chris repeated these actions for nine different takes. "He wore a safety wire, but he was actually pulling himself up the rope, hand over hand, with the added weight of the boy and the dog," says Frank. "The first few times, he was in great shape. In each succeeding take, his arms got a little weaker." Chris was also burdened by a sweater and heavy jacket—the episode depicted a chilly Midwestern autumn night—but the combination was sweltering in the July warmth of California. Each night he and Frank returned home, fully exhausted. "There were times I wondered what we were doing here," says Frank.

Chris' new job was physically demanding, but it also challenged him mentally. People with Down syndrome have a shorter attention span and they process information slower, so it was tough for him to comprehend detailed direction. Many times, people talked over his head, using words he didn't understand. Other times, they talked to him as if he were a child, which didn't work, either. "You know about what range Chris is in," says writer Michael Nankin. "But every once in a while, he is much smarter than you think, then every once in a while he doesn't get it." The same held true for his acting: he breezed through scenes that the crew thought would challenge him, and he stumbled on other actions and words for reasons they couldn't understand.

Chris had to learn to listen closely to dozens of different crew members as they took the extra time to explain each scene, each action to him. All actors can be confused by the complicated orders barked their way. Within an hour they might hear: stand here, act natural, speak up, look this way, move your arm, walk slower, emphasize the third word, turn a half inch to your left—no, turn to my left, put more emotion into that line, pick up the glass of water after you say your line . . . the directions can seem endless. Add to this the repetitive nature of the work, in which a scene and a line might be delivered dozens of times, changing slightly each time.

It wasn't easy. Chris had problems before the cameras began to roll, when he struggled to learn his dialogue and understand what was expected of him. Usually the job of explaining the scenes falls on Kaley Hummel, Chris' dialogue coach. Kaley works like a tutor with Chris, drilling him on his lines and finding a way to relate them to him in a way he can understand. She is educated in performing arts and started in show business as an actor, then moved to the production side. This is her most challenging job so far. "I can't say that when Chris reads a script, he has full understanding of everything that's happening," she says. "A script only gives action and dialogue, not the between-the-lines meanings of what is happening. Actors do a kind of homework where they fill in the holes. That is something Chris and I do together." Kaley also makes sure Chris is clear on the intent and dynamics of each scene, which can be confusing, since the show is filmed out of sequence. For example, all scenes shot on location are done together, no matter where they fall in the script. For exterior shots of the Thacher home, the cast and crew move to an identical outdoor facade at "the Ranch" complex of Warner Brothers Studios, a half mile from the main lot. So the final scene of an episode that takes place outside the house may be filmed first, followed by a middle scene, then the opening scene of the show may be filmed days later back at the main set.

Kaley is never far away from Chris on the set. They spend hours together in Chris' trailer, reading and talking about each line he must learn. Then, during the filming, she sits behind the camera, cueing him on his lines. Between takes, she draws him aside to go over the script some more, to keep him focused on his work.

Chris' dialogue is kept short, usually in blocks of no more than three sentences. Certain sounds can trip him, such as repetitive *k* sounds, and *w*'s and *r*'s strung together, as in the Thacher address on "Woodridge Road." Early on, he stumbled on contractions, preferring to say "cannot" rather than "can't." Sometimes it's not easy to determine why Chris is having trouble with a sound. "Once Chris has had problems pronouncing something, he becomes self-conscious about it, and it becomes a hurdle for him," Kaley says.

Despite years of speech therapy, Chris, like most people with Down syndrome, has a slight speech impediment because of a lack of muscle tone in his tongue and the smaller mouth structure. This makes it harder for him to articulate some sounds clearly. He often pauses between lines, or he may stutter or slur words if he does not slow down and think about what he is saying. Occasionally, the writers will change a line or word to make it easier for him to be understood.

Overall, though, Chris does well with his dialogue. "He has such an amazing memory," Kaley says. "There is no limit to the amount he can memorize. But sometimes he can do a scene forty times, then forget his lines just because something distracted him. We always practice right before he goes on." Kaley often greets him on the lot by saying one of the other character's lines, then Chris will respond by reciting his lines. "I try to bring them up out of context as much as I can," she says. "That seems to work best."

At first, Chris had trouble separating real life from the drama taking place in the episode. In the *Babysitter* episode, he was upset when the actors who play his classmates barge into the home where he is babysitting and start jumping on the furniture and spewing soft drink cans at him. He complained about it to Frank, who told Chris that the actors were just doing their jobs and weren't teasing Chris personally. Frank pointed out how, when the scene was over, the boys immediately stopped teasing him; they were more interested in peeling off their jackets in the hot weather. "I told him, 'Chris, this is just to make it a little more entertaining to the people watching the show,'" says Frank. "I had to make a distinction between what was true and what was the drama."

Chris wasn't the only one questioning the scripts. Kellie Martin remembers one line she choked on, where her character Becca looks at Corky messily eating his breakfast cereal and calls him "dribble lips." "I hated that," she recalls. "I told Chris, 'You know this is Becca calling Corky this, it's not me calling you this.' He understood; he didn't care."

As the weeks wore on, the crew learned to make a few changes to accommodate Chris. "It was a whole different set of circumstances than what we were used to working with," Bruce says. "There were definitely times when we were wondering, 'How are we going to get to tomorrow, much less to the next episode?'" For Bruce, the first adjustment was learning to follow Chris with the camera. "He has a different body language than other actors. Other actors will give you physical signs when they're about to move. But with Chris, all of a sudden, he'll turn and go in a different direction. He would move and fake me out, and we'd have to do the scene again because I didn't follow him."

Chris needed more coaching on specifics. For example, he would get up from his chair in a slightly different way each take, something that can pose problems when the film is edited. "It took him a while to realize that what is important for us is the consistency of how he does it each time," says Bruce.

Then there were things he just wouldn't do. One day the crew was shooting a scene in which Chris talked on the phone. "Chris, could you hold the phone in your right hand?" Bruce asked.

"Well, no," Chris answered. "When I talk on the phone I always hold it with my left hand."

"Yes, but just for this shot, can you hold it in your right hand to your right ear so we can see your face?"

Chris shook his head. "No, I can't. I can't hear out of my right ear, so I can't hear someone talking to me on the phone."

Bruce was surprised, since he had never noticed that Chris had a hearing problem. Not that it mattered: the set phone was just a prop. "Chris, no one is talking to you on that phone," he explained. "We're just faking the phone conversation."

That didn't make any difference to Chris. He held firmly onto the phone with his left hand. Bruce finally tired of the argument and changed the camera position. "It was not that he couldn't do it, he just wouldn't do it," says Bruce. "I guess we didn't find the right way to explain it to him." For several months afterward, Bruce thought that Chris really had a hearing problem. But when he mentioned it to Frank, Frank just laughed and told him it wasn't true: Chris could hear perfectly with both ears. Yet to this day, Chris will not hold the phone in his other hand.

In another episode, Chris had to walk down a narrow hallway to the front door. The crew asked him to walk a little closer to the stair banister. "No, I can't do that," Chris told them.

"Why can't you?" Bruce asked.

"Well, the last time I walked down this hallway, Rick told me to walk down the center."

"Rick?" Bruce was confused at first, then he remembered a scene from the month before, when Rick Rosenthal was directing the show. "That one was easy. We just told him, 'Rick's not here now. Kim is the director now, and she needs you to walk near the stairway.'" Chris complied, and Bruce learned a new lesson. "Chris gets programmed into how he's supposed to do something, and that's how he does it every time."

Despite these incidents, Chris is able to tackle almost all of the physical scenes he has in the show. "We've never actually done anything that Chris couldn't do," says Bruce. The show uses a stunt double for Chris only in rare scenes that require more dexterity than he has, or for any action sequences that could injure him. In one early show, Corky takes the wheel in a driver's education car, then rams the car into a trash bin and a tree. In real life, Chris does not drive, and he has no desire to learn, despite his parents' attempts to teach him. Chris prefers to nap while someone else drives, often nodding off within minutes on even a short trip. Michael Braverman noticed that Chris was nervous, even agitated, after reading the script. "Finally I approached him and asked what was wrong. He said he couldn't drive. I said, 'Chris, this is the movies. You don't have to drive. We're just going to make it look like you're driving.' " Chris was relieved, and he enjoyed the filming. In the scenes, he jumped behind the wheel and revved the engine, then a stunt double took his place to crash the car. He climbed back into the wrecked car, and when the cameras rolled again, a close-up showed him rubbing his head with a dazed look in his eyes.

In another episode, Chris worked closely in scenes with a 750-pound pig that Corky had befriended. At first, Chris worked in the scene in which he had to run up a narrow flight of stairs in front of the pig. "That was fun. I wasn't scared of the pig," says Chris. "But my dad and Kaley were worried about me. They thought the pig would run up the stairs on my back." The producers had second thoughts about it too, and they took the safe route, bringing in a stunt double to run the stairs. "Once the pig started up the stairs, there was no stopping it," says Michael Braverman. "It's just 750 pounds of moving pig flesh. It required an instantaneous response. We had to time it perfectly so no one got hurt." Chris wasn't the only one who had a stunt double in the episode. Star pig Sugar did the charming close-ups, while stunt pig Jackie, the climbing expert, took the stairs.

In New York, Marian lost her calm demeanor every time she heard about her son working with animals. She has a morbid fear even of pet dogs. So when Frank called her that fall with news of the latest script, she nearly fainted: Chris had several close scenes with a large white wolf. At first, the producers used a large dog dyed silver to look like a wolf. But the subterfuge didn't translate well to the screen, so the scenes were reshot using a real wolf. In the episode, the wolf is a ghostly guardian of an Indian burial ground where Corky's father is working on a construction project. The wolf appears to Corky repeatedly, then saves him from some Dobermans that are chasing him through the woods. Frank's concerns were less on the wolf, who seemed well behaved, than on the Dobermans, which were the breed the Nazi guards used to patrol Stalag 17. Marian didn't like any of it. Priscilla Rosado, Marian's assistant at work, recalls that Marian was unnerved and scared for the whole week that her son was filming the episode. "No matter how old Chris is, he will always be her baby," says Priscilla. "And here was her baby with animals who can bite people. She was so worried."

Marian's fears spanned far beyond Chris' work with animals and the rigors he was facing in his new job. On the nights she and Frank talked, the questions hung in the air. What if this didn't work out? What if Chris had to come home after the thirteen episodes were filmed? He had had to relinquish his job at P.S. 138. Marian and Frank weren't sure anything else that good would come along again. Chris was certain the show would be a hit, but he must have picked up on their anxiety: he wrote to Pat Mulholland, the school assistant principal, and asked if he could get his job back if the series came to an early end.

The absence was hard on Marian. She worked longer hours during this time. "She didn't like going home to an empty apartment," says Priscilla. "They are such a tight family. She never would really say, 'Oh, I miss them so much. I wish they were here.' She kept it inside, but you could tell she was torn about it, especially on special days like birthdays and anniversaries. I know she missed Friday nights, when she and Frank and Chris had had this ritual of going out to dinner. But I think sometimes she liked her independence."

Marian says her friends rallied around her, inviting her to parties and dinners and weddings on weekends. And not long after Frank and Chris moved to California, her daughter Anne came to stay with her for a few months. Anne's husband Tommy, who worked for the phone company, was on strike for four months, so she left him in New Hampshire with the kids, taking the opportunity to make some extra money by working as a computer operator at Marian's office. Anne and Marian walked to work together, went out to dinner and to movies, and traveled together to a convention at Florida's Walt Disney World. "We had a great time," says Anne. "My mother missed my father desperately, but we made something good out of a situation that could not have been so wonderful. Spending time together like that, just the two of us, is something people are not usually able to do once they're married and have children. We looked on it as something really special."

Out in California, Frank and Chris spent their weekends venturing out into the sprawl of L.A., visiting the beach and tourist spots, but especially the Hollywood attractions Chris found so fascinating. The city, with all its surprises, enchanted Chris in a way he had never known. The pageantry of Disneyland was close by, as were the snowcapped mountains that magically appeared on clear days. In Beverly Hills, the serene palm-lined streets beckoned with elegant restaurants and shops. Chris and Frank took long walks along the coast at Malibu, watching legions of tanned, blond surfers spin elegantly through the deep blue waves.

Of all of L.A., Chris' favorite place was the Warner Brothers Studios lot. Frank had a tough job keeping Chris away even on days he was not working. In any spare moment, Chris loved to walk around the streets looking for his favorite stars, whom he often found eating at the lot café or parking their cars by the sets. He was never at a loss for words; he always ran up to introduce himself, telling the star about his own show that would soon be broadcast. His autograph collection, started at the banquets with visiting celebrities at Don Guanella, grew rapidly.

Chris began looking more like a star himself. He donned sunglasses in the day, and tortoiseshell clear glass spectacles at night. He shook off his preppy wardrobe in a hurry, replacing it with casual shorts, neon-bright T-shirts, and cotton blazers. Frank made no attempt to match the glitz of the city. He drove a modest rental car, then later had the family's 1984 Chevrolet Caprice sedan shipped out from New York.

Within weeks of their arrival, Frank and Chris found a Catholic church to attend. One Sunday, even before the pilot had aired, a woman walked up with an eager grin, thrusting a pen and paper toward Chris. "Aren't you Chris Burke?" she asked excitedly. "I'd like your autograph." Chris was as excited as she was when he scribbled his name and added "Corky, 'Life Goes On.'"

It's not surprising that he signed both his name and Corky's. On the set, the producers were drilling it into Chris' head that they were one and the same. "We want Chris to understand that his personality and the character's personality are inseparable," says director Rick Rosenthal. "I keep encouraging him not to act. I want him to think, 'What would Chris do in this situation? How would Chris respond?'"

Some of the writers also approached Frank and Chris with questions and asked them for ideas. They were surprised to learn that Chris could swim, ride a bike, and babysit for his nieces and nephews. They asked Chris about his hopes and dreams, about situations that had happened in his life, and they patterned the dialogue around the rhythms of his conversations. Chris also provided them with his own story ideas and parts of television scripts he had written. He even created characters for the show, including parts for musicians that he hoped would be played by his friends from the Anchor Program, the DeMasi twins. But the plots and stories were often different shadings of episodes the writers had already written. Still, the writers admired his efforts. "There are not many people who aren't handicapped who are as industrious as Chris," says writer Jule Selbo.

The show's writers and producers also met several times with groups of teenagers with Down syndrome to discuss ways to portray Corky realistically. "We're always surprised how much sharper and savvy the kids are than we anticipated," says writer Michael Nankin. "Their parents were the type who encouraged them from a very early age to take on challenges." Most of the teenagers had been mainstreamed into regular high school classes, just as Corky was on the show, and they had plenty to say about the trials and tribulations they encountered. "Let me be your voice," writer Paul Wolff told them. "Tell me what you want to say."

Mostly, the teenagers wanted people to know how much they could do in their lives, but how often they were stymied by the lack of opportunities to prove themselves. They talked about the constant teasing they encountered in school, and how much it hurt their feelings. They told how they felt they had the right to be in regular school classes, though their teachers weren't always giving them the help they needed.

The writers also met with the parents and siblings of the teenagers to better understand the family dynamics. "They all had stories of when their patience had been tried," says Jule. "But they were very protective and supportive. All of the siblings had been very active in their brothers' and sisters' lives."

"We felt we needed to be very honest to the real feelings and reality of the lives of the families," says Paul. "These meetings changed the way we wanted to write the show. Before, for all of us, people with Down syndrome were those people you would see walking down the street and you avoided their look. After being with Chris and the groups, we began to see how our attitudes were based on fear. When we were doing research on Down syndrome, we found out that hundreds of years ago in Scandinavia, if a child was born with Down syndrome, the family was considered blessed by God, to be worthy of having an angel in their home. Something about that seems right. The rest of us may have more on the ball intellectually, but their understanding of the essence of things is better than ours. So we wrote Chris like we were writing someone very young, with not a lot of intellectual ability, but with great emotional understanding."

Most of Chris' coworkers had never been around anyone with Down syndrome. Looking back on it, many of them say that they babied Chris during the pilot and early episodes because they did not know the full extent of his capabilities. People handled him with kid gloves, taking over small responsibilities on the set that he could have managed himself. If he wanted a glass of water, someone would rush to bring it to him. When he complained about standing too long for a scene, a chair would materialize instantly. "We treated Chris with more care than was necessary," says Patti LuPone. "He got a little cocky, a little 'special.' The director nailed him on it. He needed someone to bring him down to earth, to say, 'It's not just stardom, it's a grind.' He had to carry several shows right at the beginning. It's hard work—dirty, hard work."

Costumer John Linsmeier recalls that Chris was a little afraid of him at first because John was stern with him while others were walking on eggshells. John was not apprehensive: he has a sister who is retarded, and that gave him a better understanding of Chris. "Kids like this are very smart. I know the games they like to play, how they like to get away with certain things. People might feel sorry for them, but they can do a lot. They're always testing you in little ways."

From the start, John was strict with Chris about his wardrobe. If Chris absentmindedly misplaced his jacket, John would make him go find it. "I had to tell him, 'This is work; you have to be neat. The way I put the clothes on you, that's the way you have to stay until every scene is done, so that you match. Wardrobe is what makes the character, along with your acting.'"

Before long, Chris was careful to hang up his clothes before he left at night. He would run over to John before each scene to make sure that his wardrobe was correct. If anyone else tried to change his wardrobe, he would call out for John in a singsong voice, "Continuity, continuity. John's the only one who knows the continuity."

Within the first few weeks, sugared soft drinks were banned from the set's ever present catered food table when the crew noticed that Chris got a "sugar high" from drinking too many of them. But John noticed that Chris was still gaining weight, probably from the cheeseburgers and french fries he was eating nearly every day at lunch. John asked Chris to lay off the burgers; he also hovered around the food table, teasing Chris when he would reach for some calorie-laden goodie. "I want my clothes to fit you," he scolded. Chris retorted, "Oh no, it's just that my blue jeans shrunk." But Chris listened and started watching his diet. He tried walking the one mile to work, but the steep hill along Barham Boulevard proved too much for him. So he started swimming regularly in the apartment pool and doing what he called "the Chris Burke Workout"—dances and exercises to his favorite music. Later on, he sauntered into the wardrobe trailer, pulling up his shirt to show John his new, flatter belly.

Some people thought John was harsh with Chris, but he was only treating him the way he would any other actor, which was the way Chris asked to be treated. Chris wanted to learn how to be a professional, and once the rest of the crew realized this, their attitudes changed. The early hesitation went away, replaced by some fast friendships. One was with Bruce Pasternack; another was with Joe Pennella, director of photography. He and Chris bonded immediately, sharing a love for the New York Giants and John's Pizza Parlor in Greenwich Village. Before long, the two teased each other with nicknames and running jokes about situations on the set.

First assistant director Mark Bashaar lunched with Chris off the set and took him to baseball games at Dodger Stadium. "I found out he wasn't much different from other kids. At twenty-three, he was in many ways like an average teenager. If he's treated as such, he does fine."

Kellie Martin has a hard time comparing Chris to her teenage peers because, she says, in some ways he is more mature, but in other ways he is innocent and naive. "People my age think a lot of negative thoughts. It's a confusing time. But I think Chris has it all figured out. He takes it one day at a time and doesn't worry. He's pretty focused."

In time, Chris' coworkers learned that they could be stern with him when it was necessary. "Chris understands much more than others that you can yell at him and still love him," says Gere LaDue, the second assistant director. "He knows who likes him and who doesn't. If you like him, you can push him around when he needs it and he doesn't take offense." Kaley says Chris never holds grudges. "Chris may get mad just for a minute, then he'll go up and hug the person. Sometimes it catches them off guard, but it's hard for anyone not to respond to him."

Still, as the early excitement and apprehension about working with Chris faded, they were replaced by some very real concerns. As much as he prepared, his limitations were becoming more apparent under the harsh lights of the camera. Mark Bashaar says Chris had a tough time absorbing new directions quickly. "The acting points out a couple of his handicaps more than just meeting him on the street would. There's a lot of memorization, a lot of complicated situations where he has to do three things at once. It took him a little while to get a grasp of that."

Kaley Hummel says that Chris differs from others in that he brings a genuine, heartfelt emotion to the scene. "The best performances are the ones truly felt. No matter how good an actor, you couldn't do what

Chris can do. Chris wouldn't know how to fake the moment if his life depended on it. But on the flip side, when it's six hours later, and we're doing the same scenes, Chris goes from having these brilliant moments to yawning. That's when it's hard." One time, when a scene dragged out to the wee hours of the morning, Chris' eyes grew heavy, then he dropped off to sleep while standing up in the scene. "I saw his eyes go down and then they just didn't go back up. I was laughing so hard," she says.

Bruce Pasternack says he can tell when Chris is fading by the way his eyes start rolling in the wrong direction. "Normally in a close-up, you put the actor he is talking to right next to the camera so his eyes go straight to them. But when Chris is tired, his eyes will go up or sideways or sometimes straight into the camera. We can't use those shots. So I say, 'Chris, you're looking into the camera.' And he says, 'No I'm not.' It doesn't happen often, just when he's really tired."

Working with Chris also takes longer, says Joe Pennella, because Chris takes instruction too literally. For example, the crew marks the set to show the actors where to stand for the proper lighting. But the marks are only an inexact blueprint that often changes. "I would say, 'Chris, you're in a shadow' and he'd say, 'But I'm on my mark.' His mind works in a very linear fashion. He's very conscientious about doing exactly what he is told to do, and sometimes that can get in the way. Sometimes a scene needs to be more organic and less mechanical. But certainly the joys of working with him far outweigh any problems. Overall, he's very easy to work with. There's always a surprise in everything he does. When he gets a scene he's been having a hard time with, he gets ecstatic; he literally jumps up and screams and hollers."

Michael Braverman says Chris puts an enormous effort into his work. "Sometimes he gets it on the first take; sometimes we have to do it twenty times. But even a professional actor with a great deal of experience can't always get it up. He's as good as, if not better than, many actors who have been doing this a long time: at learning his lines, hitting his marks, being ready and cooperative on the set, taking direction and listening. Will he play Hamlet? No. But few actors can.

"There's a certain simplicity to Chris. We know that when he tires, he doesn't work as well. We know he does better work before lunch. Things are a little more magnified in him, a little more obvious. The rest of us are trained to mask it. But Chris has no guile. If he's really tired, he'll sit in your face and yawn. He's not a real stressed guy. He gets frustrated if he doesn't get it. But he doesn't say, 'Oh my God, I blew that scene, they're going to fire me. I'm going to lose my beach house.'"

The other actors admit that Chris' tendency to get distracted makes it tough to do scenes with him. They soon learned to be more prepared and more patient, all while forming relationships with him that mirrored those in the show. From the start, Bill Smitrovich, who plays dad Drew Thacher, had a fatherly relationship with Chris. He counseled Chris on his job responsibilities and attitudes, teaching Chris that all workers on the set—from wardrobe to key grip—were as important as the stars. But just as Chris looks to Bill for advice and direction, he also turns to him for fun. The two often horse around between takes, then Bill will signal when it is time to stop playing and begin working.

Bill also coached Chris on acting techniques and helped him deal with his early frustrations. Chris says, "I learned from Bill, if you miss a line, don't get mad, don't walk away. Just stay calm and do it over."

At first, when Chris flubbed a line, he would drop his head and mutter, "Get it together, Burke!" Eventually, he learned to stay in the scene without moving or talking, while Kaley prompted him by saying his line from behind the camera. It's an important skill; any reaction other than staying with the script can force the crew to shoot another take of the scene.

Patti LuPone remembers that Chris, homesick for his mother, looked to her as sort of a substitute. He wrote Patti long, affectionate letters, which she keeps in a scrapbook. They teased and joked on the set, and between takes they played the card game slapjack.

"Just think of it: only in America can some handicapped kid have his dream come true like this, to be an actor. I've had dreams come true. I've made instinctual decisions that resulted in my dreams coming true. Chris has never wavered, and he's had a whole lot more to overcome. He's a trip, a wonderful, inspirational trip."

Patti was surprised at some of the comments from people outside the set when they heard about the series. "Most people were intrigued by it, and by him. But some people said to me, 'Oh, what a bummer, working with someone like that.' My response was, no, it's harder. It's difficult to play a scene because Chris has a hard time remembering his lines. I don't think that will ever change. But it's definitely not depressing. Chris doesn't have a bummed-out streak in him."

Kellie prepares more for her scenes with Chris because "when he does get it right, I have to get mine right. They can't spend a lot of time with me forgetting a line because they need time for Chris." She has also learned a new acting skill: to remember and repeat the line she said just before the line Chris missed, so that the scene can start over and the take is not ruined. She takes care not to distract Chris too much between takes, when the pressure and tension often break with giggles and jokes, and during scenes, when Chris needs to hone his concentration.

"But it's not a big difference at all," Kellie adds. "I love having scenes with Chris. He shows a different side of my character, Becca. Corky brings out the kid in Becca; he shows her vulnerability in little ways. A lot of times she's trying to be older than she really is, a little more sophisticated than she is. On her own, she would never watch a cartoon on television, but she would watch one with Corky.

"Becca loves her brother, but he embarrasses her and annoys her just like any other sibling would. Sometimes she gets frustrated with him. She doesn't necessarily fight with him; she gets emotional but holds back." The relationship between Becca and Corky is very true to life, as Kellie later learned from fan letters sent by teenage girls who have brothers with Down syndrome. "They say that the writing and the way I play Becca are so realistic. Getting that feedback from someone who knows means a lot to me."

Kellie says Chris has a calming influence on the set. "Sometimes when it gets really tense, I look over at Chris and he's smiling. He's a very calm person, and takes things in stride."

"When there is intense pressure on the set, Chris is the only one who doesn't feel it," says Kaley. "My stomach will be in knots. I'll get nervous, his parents get nervous, the director gets nervous. But the minute the shoot is over, Chris says, 'Let's go! It's over! We're done!' Most actors are so judgmental of themselves, especially if a scene doesn't go well. But he can let it go better than anyone I've ever seen. It's a game to him."

Ordinary tensions roll right off Chris' back, but he is immobilized by arguments between people who are his friends. When tensions flare on the set, Chris stares at the people, dumbfounded, and sometimes goes off to talk to himself. "I don't know what he says. I just let him have the time alone," says Kaley. "Any harsh tones set him off. Sometimes Chris wants to get in there and help, but then I usually try to get him out of there."

Bill says he has learned to hold back rather than argue with someone in front of Chris, because it upsets him so much to watch such conflict. "We've learned not to do that, not to him, not to each other."

Frank rarely stepped in when any conflicts came up. During the weekdays, he usually stayed off the set, preferring to read in Chris' trailer while his son went about his job. The publicity office supplied Frank with the daily New York papers, and even went so far as to put his name on the door to one of the offices where he often dropped in to visit. Occasionally he stepped onto the set, but it was always a strange, intimidating environment. When scenes are shot, total silence is necessary. The soundstage walls are eighteen inches of solid concrete to block the noise outside. Inside, a flashing red light and loud horn go off when the cameras begin to roll, then everyone outside the scene freezes in their tracks, speaking in whispers. Frank is partially deaf in one ear from years of police shooting practice, so he never quite knew what people were whispering to him. "I didn't know if they were congratulating me or cursing me because I had my foot in a scene," he said. "I would just nod my head and agree with them."

One day, Frank walked onto the set, where they were shooting in the kitchen of a small restaurant that the Thacher family had bought. All the booths were taken, so Frank took a chair behind the counter. Suddenly Becca (Kellie Martin) burst out of the kitchen and ran behind the counter, the camera following her right past Frank. The director yelled, "Cut!" then came over and put his arm around him. "Frank, if you had only stopped in makeup and had that shiny nose taken care of, I could've used you in the scene," he said, laughing.

Another time, Frank made himself useful by giving lessons to an actor who was playing a policeman. "Daddy taught him how to arrest people," says Chris. "He turned him around and acted like he was handcuffing him."

Frank and Chris got to be friends with many of the crew members, and sometimes joined them for baseball games or lunch off the set. Frank also contacted some friends who had moved to California from New York and socialized with them on weekends. One friend owned a barbecue restaurant: Chris mentioned the restaurant by name in many of his early interviews, trying to get some free advertising for his friend. One weekend, he worked at the restaurant as a busboy. "He was more excited about that than with what he was doing here," says Kaley Hummel.

As September rolled around, everyone speculated on how the public would react to "Life Goes On." Hundreds of advance reviews praised the show, dozens of them picking the show as the best new fall series. But *TV Guide* headlined its story "Will Viewers Accept a TV Star with Down syndrome?" and criticized the show as "too sentimental." It forecast an early demise for the show, based on advertisers' lack of interest and its deadly CBS competition, "60 Minutes." Pat Mulholland, the P.S. 138 assistant principal, grabbed the issue of *TV Guide* from a store in Point Lookout and ran home, reading it along the way. By the time she reached her home, she was crying. "They gave Chris a bad review!" she wailed to her husband. "How could they do that?" Actually, the article raved about Chris' performance, but Pat was crying too hard to read the fine print. "Any review that wasn't perfect wasn't good enough," says Pat. "They didn't get the miracle of this kid being on ABC opposite '60 Minutes,' of his being a full-fledged actor just as he had always dreamed."

The premiere of "Life Goes On" was set for September 12, following the top-rated "Roseanne" in ABC's Tuesday night lineup. It aired again the following Friday night before settling into its Sunday night slot the next week. The premiere night was an extremely exciting one for the Burkes.

In New York, Marian gathered with close friends. Tears came to her eyes in the opening moments, when Chris came onto the screen, sitting in his television bedroom and smiling sweetly at his television mother. The group cheered as his name flashed onto the television, and again at the end of the show, when Chris finished saying the opening lines of "The Raven."

J.R. mailed postcards to his friends with the date and time of the show. But he had already watched the advance tape, so he set his VCR to record the premiere while he went to a business dinner.

Ellen's family watched it at a friend's house in Vancouver. Anne had a Hollywood-style party in her New Hampshire home for a group of friends, all of whom praised Chris' performance and the quality of the show. One friend was so confident of Chris' future as an actor that she predicted, "Your parents are not going to be living in New York for a long time."

Pat Mulholland remembers a poignant scene where Chris gives Patti LuPone an enormous hug. The next day, everybody at P.S. 138 teased her about it, in light of her strict warnings to Chris about hugging people when he worked there. "They said, 'Chris Burke is telling Pat Mulholland to eat her heart out. He's hugging Patti LuPone on national television, and she loves it!'" During other scenes, Pat cried because she wondered how the tough lines and situations in the script were affecting Chris. "Did anybody talk to Chris about these things when he was with us?" she wailed to her husband.

In contrast, the premiere was a nonevent on the set of "Life Goes On." Most had already seen the tape, so it was just another hectic workday. But a few days later, when the audience ratings came back, the news reverberated through the set. "We made top ten!" The ratings were 17.9, which translates to about 23 million viewers, and a share of 29, which means that 29 percent of all households with their TV sets on during that time were watching the show, more than CBS or NBC drew. It was a higher rating than "thirtysomething," the regular show in that spot, had pulled anytime in the previous season. The Friday night repeat broadcast beat out both NBC and CBS for a 13.4 rating and a 24 share.

Nearly overnight, Chris had become a celebrity. Everywhere he went, people recognized him and wanted to take his picture or get his autograph. Kaley remembers the change that took place so suddenly after the premiere aired. "It was so weird to me when we would go out for lunch to the same places we had been going all summer, and people started approaching him for autographs. I remember when I first came on the show [before the pilot aired], when people would come over to him and say, 'Chris, you're going to be a big star!' I was thinking, 'Why are they saying this to him?' I didn't want his feelings to be hurt. I really didn't think the show would last long. I thought people would think it was depressing, and not watch it. Not just because it dealt with Down syndrome, but it was also this poor family trying to get by. But it really developed; they made it into this great family show."

Hundreds of letters poured in from people all over the United States. Frank and Chris struggled to answer them all personally. "We couldn't just hand it over to a commercial firm. They're of such a sensitive nature that we feel honor-bound to handle it ourselves," says Frank.

Many were from kids like Craig, who wrote, "I love your show. I like Corky's eyes. He reminds me of me." One woman wrote that her baby was born with Down syndrome around the time the show came out. "You're my hero," she told Chris. "I have as many pictures of you around the house as I do my own kids. I'm recording all the episodes so that my son can watch them when he's older." Schoolteachers sent bundles of scrawled notes from their classes. Teenage girls requested autographed photos and asked if he would be visiting their towns. One young woman with a learning disability, who was struggling in college courses, wrote, "I always have a hard time seeing myself succeed. But now, I can see you and your success and you will be my mentor."

Frank and Marian also get their share of fan mail, especially from parents of children with Down syndrome, who recount their experiences with their own children. Other letters are from new parents seeking advice or asking for basic information about Down syndrome. Frank refers these to the National Down Syndrome Congress and other organizations, including local parents' groups. "We're not setting ourselves up as experts," he says.

Some of the mail was misdirected or languished in ABC affiliate offices around the nation, reaching the Burkes months later, or never at all. Robert Neely, Chris' friend and counselor from Don Guanella, wrote twice with no reply. "I knew he was busy, but that just wasn't like Chris," says Robert. A girl in Robert's new school received an autographed photo for her efforts, which piqued Robert so much that he sent a third note, this time directly to the show in California. Frank called him immediately. "We're always hearing about mail that didn't get here," he says. "It's upsetting because we try to answer everything personally." A fan club might help channel the letters, but the Burkes turned down one group that was interested, and they have no plans to authorize any others. "We're not sure that would be a good thing," says Marian. "We're trying to keep this low-key."

The loads of fan mail and the glare of publicity did little to offset the somber mood on the set. Now that the show was in its regular Sunday 7 P.M. slot, the ratings were plummeting. CBS powerhouse "60 Minutes" reigned, often with the number one ratings of all shows for the week. NBC normally lagged behind "Life Goes On" with its "Magical World of Disney," and other substitutes, but on a few Sunday nights it was beating "Life Goes On" for second place. Even the fledgling Fox network was drawing viewers away with various shows and specials. Out of roughly one hundred shows on air, "Life" often ranked in the bottom twenty. Many people on the set worried that the show wouldn't last past the initial thirteen episodes. They knew it was an expensive series to produce, but ad spots were selling at bargain basement prices: a thirty-second commercial during the show cost just $55,000, below ABC's average of $158,000, and significantly less than commercials on the top-rated show "Roseanne," at $375,000.

Yet the ratings game is a confusing mix of numbers. Over at ABC, the executives were happy. They had not expected stellar ratings in the time slot, so they were actually encouraged because the numbers were higher than any other series had drawn in that slot during the previous five years. And networks know that a good show can often rise from the bottom to the top of the list with a little time and publicity. The series "Cheers" moved from dead last to number one over a few seasons; "Hill Street Blues," "Designing Women," "Full House," and many others had beat early low ratings to become stable hits.

Even more important were the demographics, which are statistics detailing the income and education levels of viewers. "Life Goes On" was attracting an audience valuable to advertisers: these viewers were wealthier and more educated than audiences for many other shows, and they included a loyal core audience of families. Women aged eighteen to forty-nine were the largest single group, followed by teenagers and children, who ranked it as their second favorite show on any network. In all, nearly 14 million viewers were tuning into the show each week. Within weeks, major advertisers had jumped on board, and the ad rates began climbing steadily.

Early in October, ABC showed its support for "Life Goes On" by ordering nine more episodes to round out the first season. By this time, it was obvious that Chris had touched a core group of fans very deeply. The shows revolving around his character were some of the most popular and were always followed by a slew of mail.

Rick Rosenthal thinks that part of Chris' appeal to the audience is that he embodies feelings that people have about themselves. "What kid growing up in America really thinks he or she is normal? When Chris is at his best, he lets us in emotionally. He has a wonderfully expressive face. He's able to show the emotions of what so many people feel about being different. Very few actors, very few characters on television can do that."

When writer Michael Nankin came onto the show at midseason, he knew exactly how he wanted to portray Corky. "He's a well-meaning outcast who wants nothing more than to fit in and be accepted and be loved. Everyone can identify with that."

Even though the show wasn't deemed a hit, it was attracting a wave of publicity. Chris and his parents were interviewed by dozens of magazines, newspapers, and television news shows. *People Weekly* said, "America finds a heartbreaker of a hero." *USA Weekend* called Chris "TV's most astonishing newcomer," while *The Atlanta Constitution* described him as "the most likeable new star of fall television. *The New York Times* praised the show as "sensitively written, wonderfully cast and beautifully executed." The *Washington Post* said, " 'Life Goes On' aims at the heartstrings and plucks big." Only *Time* magazine cast a sour note, criticizing it as "sugarcoating the subject of mental retardation" and having "the highest hug-a-minute ratio of any show in TV history."

In late October, a cousin of the Burkes', who is a vice president at a printing company, walked down to check on the November *LIFE* magazine running through the presses. He nearly had a heart attack: there was

Chris on the cover, wrapped in a hug with Patti LuPone. He stood dazed as Chris' face stared up at him from the millions of copies speeding through the presses.

Each new story prompted calls from dozens of the Burkes' friends and relatives, who expressed their surprise and excitement at Chris' success. Still, it was a lonely time for Marian. She could not quite get used to seeing Chris plastered all over magazines and television, but not present at her dinner table, or in the family room watching his favorite shows. She had seen Frank and Chris only once since July, and she looked forward to only another short weekend when they would fly home to New York.

As the season progressed, the Burkes suddenly found themselves in demand for dozens of charity functions around the nation. The jet-setting lifestyle became routine: Frank and Chris would fly into various cities, where they were whisked off in a limo to a hotel and a fund-raising dinner, only to rush back to the airport the next day. "If you ask me what I know about Memphis, or many of the other cities we visited, I would say, 'Well, they have a good airport and the hotel was nice,' " says Frank. "That's all we saw." In later months, Marian joined them at meetings on the East Coast.

At each appearance, Chris would take the podium with flair, urging everyone to reach for their dreams and to help the handicapped reach theirs. Several times he rambled in free association, talking about his favorite movie stars and his friends and family. His parents worried when he strayed off the topic, and they tried to coach him or get him to memorize a speech, but Chris refused. "Chris likes to talk," says Frank. "Before he runs home he'll touch all the bases. He likes to speak from the heart. But he is who he is. I don't know that we want to change that."

Marlene Klotz, the community relations director for KTVK—the Phoenix, Arizona, ABC station—got to know Chris from his public appearances for First Down for Down Syndrome, a charity tied with the Genetic Center of Scottsdale, which sponsors research on Down syndrome. At his first reception with 150 parents, siblings, and people with Down syndrome, Chris amazed her by ad-libbing a speech, then spending time with everyone in the room as they passed by him in a long line for autographs. "He didn't just sit there and scribble out 'Chris Burke,' " she says. "He wrote a personal message to each one. He didn't rush anyone. He spent time with each person, making them feel as if they were the most important person in the room."

The Burkes were amazed at the crowds who sometimes mobbed Chris at his public appearances. "It was like Elvis had walked into the room," says Marian. In larger audiences, security sometimes had to separate him from his admirers, the most fervent of whom were teenage girls with Down syndrome. The Burkes tried to keep the number of appearances down, as Chris' work schedule was hectic enough. But they felt a gratitude to the people and schools and organizations that had helped them in the years Chris was growing up. "They were there when we needed them, so we wanted to be there for them," says Frank. "We didn't look at these as a chore. We looked at it as a commitment we couldn't avoid. We realize Chris is an inspiration to a lot of families. It's time to give something back."

When Paul Wolff accompanied Frank and Chris to a National Down Syndrome Congress convention that fall, he noticed a difference in the type of public response Chris enjoyed from that of other stars he had worked with in show business. "The adulation was not about fame. It was about something beautiful, something meaningful. When Chris went to the podium, he surprised Paul by speaking eloquently about wanting to be a spokesperson for all people with handicaps. He said that he wasn't in this for his own success. He wanted people with Down syndrome to get the respect they deserved. He wanted them to be able to get real jobs, instead of make-do jobs. I knew it was not rehearsed. I was floored. I looked over at Frank, and he was amazed, too. He said, 'I don't know where that came from.'

"This may sound mystical, but it became clear to me that weekend that Chris Burke was prepared for this. He had just the right parents. He was the one who could break through and do this television show, and bring these people the dignity they deserved, the chances they had deserved, and do it brilliantly. It was like all of us were on a train we hooked onto, a train much bigger than ABC or Warner Brothers, or any of us involved. I fully believe it is not just a TV show, it's a sociological event that needed to happen, with all the right cast of characters drawn into it. The ramifications of it are enormous. The world will never be the same."

Paul credits the sweeping power of television, which is most evident when it deals with reality. "But it's Chris' presence that makes it work. Even Dustin Hoffman, when he is portraying someone handicapped (as in the hit movie *Rain Man)*, is not as effective. No matter how good he is, you know it's not real. With Chris, it has tremendous power."

As the year wore on, the writers tapped into that power by giving Chris more dialogue and action. "We kept going to the dailies [the films of the previous day's work sent to editing] and saying, 'Holy mackerel, we didn't think he could do that,'" says Paul. "He can carry his own weight."

Armed with the knowledge of Chris' acting abilities, they began to write even more poignant scenes. The writers often have Corky ask a frank, direct question when the rest of the family is tiptoeing around an issue.

Some of Chris' toughest and most powerful scenes have been with Patti LuPone, who plays his mother. Corky has talked to her about the fact that he will never father a child. He has asked, "Do you wish I had never been born?" then later, "Did you ever have an accident?" When she answered no, he said, "Yes you did. You had me." "He was asking questions true of himself but remaining an actor," says Patti. "He was able to do all this without self-pity. I find that truly remarkable, even miraculous."

The wrenching emotions of such scenes upset some viewers, including Chris' friends and family, who wonder how they are affecting Chris. His niece Kara cries when she watches shows in which Chris, as Corky, anguishes over the fact that he has Down syndrome. "That's not like him at all. Chris is comfortable with himself," she says. "I don't want them to put those ideas in his head."

During long discussions with Chris over these emotional scenes, Kaley has realized that Chris doesn't miss what he does not or may not ever have. Though his character sometimes longs to be "normal" and do "normal" activities, Chris believes fully that he is normal. "He has Down syndrome like I have brown hair," she says. "It's just a fact of who he is. He doesn't whine or mope or feel sorry for himself. And he shouldn't; he has a wonderful life."

Sometimes Chris even jokes about it. Kaley once admonished him because he had chocolate on his chin after eating a candy bar. "That's because I have Down syndrome," he said lightly, wiping his face with a grin.

Chris' coworkers say that he is so normal and comfortable with himself that they often forget there is anything different about him at all. One day a director was instructing him on a scene in which Corky plays footsie under the table with his new girlfriend. "That take was pretty good," he said. "But Chris, next time can you do it a little more surreptitiously?"

The crew started looking around at each other and laughing, says Bruce Pasternack. "'Surreptitiously?' A lot of us didn't know what it meant. Chris just nodded and then did it the same way he wanted to do it anyway."

Chris likes to sprinkle big words into his conversation. When he reads books, he goes through pages with a highlighting pen, marking words he needs to look up in a dictionary. And though he doesn't always understand their meanings, it's not from lack of trying.

"That's about the only time I really notice his handicap, when I use words that are too big," says Kaley. "He doesn't tell you he doesn't get it. I've just learned to stop and ask him, and explain it. The other time I notice it is when he is sick. For example, if he has a cold, he doesn't want you to know it. He's very sensitive about it."

Chris says he actually likes the lines he has that talk about his Down syndrome. But he balked during one episode that showed him in a skit with some special education classmates. In it, the teacher was trying to show them how to deal with insults from insensitive classmates in the regular classes they attended. Chris, as Corky, had to say, "You're not stupid, you're just retarded," to his friend Lisa, played by Karen Rauch, who has cerebral palsy. "I didn't like that. I don't like to call people retarded," says Chris.

Chris generally complains about his lines only when they seem to be hurtful to another character. He had problems with another script, in which Corky argues with his parents and Becca and begins hanging out with a rough group of students.

"At the end of each scene, he was running around apologizing to everyone for talking to them that way," says Paul Wolff, who wrote the episode. "It upset him to think that Corky would be bad and hurt someone's feelings."

Bruce Pasternack says Chris cried on the set before doing the scenes. "I guess Chris has never yelled at his parents. He went through a real emotional upheaval just to do that scene."

Although the situation was not true to Chris, the writers knew it was true to life for other teenagers with Down syndrome. Parents and siblings had made it clear to them that teenagers with Down syndrome don't hesitate to defend themselves when necessary, and often argue with their parents about limitations.

Yet Chris takes his standing as a role model very seriously, and he doesn't want to project any qualities he doesn't condone. He had never liked the troublemakers in his schools; he was upset that Corky would befriend this type of student. His mother advised him that all actors played roles they didn't agree with. "Just pretend you're Jimmy Cagney," she said, knowing that Chris loved Cagney movies. "He played bad guys, but it always turned out right in the end." Chris took the suggestion to heart, putting a swagger in his walk and gravel in his talk.

Relating the scenes to movies and television is something that Kaley does nearly every day. She can usually find another character or action from his vast knowledge of entertainment, then relate it to what he is to do in the show. In his personal life, Chris frequently pantomimes celebrities, from Roseanne Barr to Louis Armstrong and Jimmy Stewart, and can re-create scenes from his favorite movies word for word. He is able to apply that skill to portray his character, with Kaley's help. For example, she described one scene to him simply by saying, "It's like Dorothy looking for Oz." Nearly every episode, Kaley finds she uses *La Bamba* to explain various scenes. "If you give Chris the understanding, he comes up with his own moments," she says. "He's a great mimic."

Gere LaDue, the second assistant director, says it reminds her of a poetry class she took, in which she was having trouble learning to write sonnets. "My professor told me, 'When you learn the form, the poetry will come.' Once Chris is rehearsed and comfortable with a scene, he does that. If you give Chris the form, he'll fill in the poetry.

At a party one night, a man told Kaley that he thought it was sad that the show was using Chris to get higher ratings and publicity. "I told him, 'Hey, he's not a gimmick; they built this show around him. This is his dream come true. How can that be bad?' "

Kellie Martin also fielded some unusual questions. "The first thing people ask me is if Chris really has Down syndrome. They think he's an actor wearing makeup. I guess they can't fathom it because he's so normal. And people ask me if I have to be gentle with him. I guess they think he's going to break."

Just as her character Becca steps in to defend Corky on the show, Kellie has reacted to comments from guest stars and extras about Chris. One day, she heard some extras laughing at him, saying, "He's impossible to work with." Kellie walked over to them and said, "You don't know what you're talking about. You don't even know Chris. How can you say this?"

Kaley says people often ask her what grade level Chris is on. "I say, 'In what department?' You can't say he's like a fourth grader. On certain levels, Chris is every bit as mentally capable as the next person. He reads these big adult books, mostly about music or acting. But there are certain things he's never going to get, like math. I'm glad the writers toned down some of the scenes where he did schoolwork [in regular high school sophomore classes]. A lot of it was way above what Chris could comprehend."

Many real-life parents of kids with Down syndrome criticized certain scenes as unrealistic. The writers wonder, too, if Corky is too much of a "superkid."

"Corky is a little bit higher-functioning than Chris because everything he says has been well thought out in advance, whereas Chris doesn't have that advantage in real life," says writer Michael Nankin. "All our other characters are more eloquent than the actors for the same reason."

Michael Braverman says that originally his philosophy was that Corky would not and could not do things Chris Burke could not do. "On several occasions, we have stretched that. In one of the first episodes, where Corky rescues the boy he is babysitting, Corky was quite heroic, much more than reality would allow. In retrospect, I think that was a mistake. It may have raised the expectations too high for people who are not familiar with Down syndrome. We're watching that now."

Writer Jule Selbo says the portrayals have been, for the most part, realistic. "We've pushed his capabilities in some episodes. But in others, we've lightened it. He doesn't always succeed at what he's doing, but he always tries really hard. In the episode where he runs for class president, he doesn't win. I wrote an episode where he is enamored of a pretty new girl in school. She uses him to go to a party so she can be with another boy. In that episode he failed—he didn't get the girl. He told his grandfather, 'I'm never going to be like normal people. No one's going to love me. I'm never going to have a family.' His grandfather gave him a pep talk, something about how he should never give up."

But a few people think Chris is, in some ways, more capable than Corky. Writer David Wolf remembers one night when an episode's production was completed and Chris jumped up on a chair to give a spontaneous speech to thank everyone for their help and support. "He had ten times more poise than I do. I was thinking, 'Why are we holding him to three lines of dialogue?'"

Bruce Pasternack says he thinks the show may have made a mistake by showing Chris speaking perfectly, without his natural stutter and hesitation. "We've taken a highly talented person with a disability—he's probably in the top five percent of people with Down syndrome—and instead of presenting him as he really is, we've made him in the top millionth percent. We'll do thirty takes to make something perfect when take one or two was really Chris. Chris isn't perfect. It's okay for him to stutter, or have problems with certain lines. But we rarely show him that way.

We make him perfect, which is what we do with the other actors, too. That's just a part of filmmaking. I think he's so phenomenal just normal that we don't need to make him any better. I think it would be nice to show him stuttering once in a while, instead of taking forty-five minutes to get one word out of him perfectly."

One day, a crew member came to work with news of a family friend. The pregnant woman had found out through amniocentesis that her baby had Down syndrome. After watching the show, she made the decision to keep the baby. "It's wonderful, but I don't know if it's fair," Bruce says. "People turn on this show and say, 'Look at this phenomenal kid with Down syndrome.' Well, we've cheated a bit and made him more phenomenal than he really is."

Others on the set think Chris makes a great role model for all kids with disabilities, but they wonder if he is an unfair idol, because he is shown accomplishing so much more than is possible for most.

Craig Safan, the composer for the show who has a young son with Down syndrome, disagrees. "That's like saying that Martin Luther King is an unfair idol because he was able to accomplish so much more than most black people can do. A hero is someone heroic, someone who goes beyond what most people can attain."

Craig, who has written the theme music for "Cheers" and several movies, first got involved with "Life Goes On" because of the subject matter. "When I read in the trade papers that someone was planning a pilot on a family with a kid with Down syndrome, I got so excited that I literally picked up the phone and called Michael Braverman. I didn't know anyone. I didn't go through the normal channels."

Craig says that working on the show and getting to know Chris have helped him step forward from the trauma of having a son with Down syndrome. "All of us expect to have perfect children. This show has tapped into a tremendous hidden well of people who are suffering through having children who are not perfect. And when you're in this world, you realize how many children don't turn out well. This whole group of people has been unrepresented, not knowing that they could come out of the closet and not only express their lives but also do better and expect more for their children. Knowing Chris, seeing Chris on this show has given me and my wife the courage to ask for more for our son."

Yet Craig knows some parents who cannot watch the show because they feel it is too raw. "When you've experienced something in real life, then you see it dramatized, it's difficult. Sometimes I would be sitting in the room, deciding what the music would be, and they'd show me a scene. I'd have tears in my eyes.

"Life Goes On" has more power to change people's perceptions of Down syndrome and mental retardation than any movie or documentary, Craig says. "*Rain Man* was good, but I don't think it affected people's attitudes about mental retardation and autism one bit. Movies just go by. They don't affect people nearly as deeply as a show that's on weekly."

Craig sees the impact of the show in his daily life with his son. They were in a sporting goods store one day when a teenage cashier called out, "Hey, he's just like that little guy Corky on TV!" The teenager then playfully threw Craig's son a ball. "That's because of the TV show," says Craig. "The show made it okay to be friendly with these kids, to interact with them."

When Craig and his family went out to dinner with the Burkes in New York, he was amazed by how many people crowded around, asking for autographs. "In L.A., people see stars all the time and don't say anything. But in New York, everybody recognized him and said something. I never realized Chris was that big a star. To see that kids have that view toward a retarded man is amazing."

Though the Burkes were slowly absorbing the shock of Chris' fame and good fortune, nothing prepared them for what came next: an official invitation to meet with President George Bush at the White House to make a public service announcement to encourage appreciation of the abilities of people with Down syndrome. When Frank called Marian with the news, she was nearly speechless. "It was such an exciting, unbelievable thought," she says. "The people in my office were gaga. It was such a big hit; it made us into celebrities."

Chris and Frank flew to Washington, D.C., along with Rick Rosenthal and his son, and Michael Braverman and his daughter. Marian flew down from New York, while J.R. and Betsy Burke took a train from Philadelphia, meeting everyone at the Hotel Washington. That day, November 9, the television and newspapers were filled with the most astonishing news: East Germany had opened its borders, and thousands were streaming through to a newfound freedom. The Berlin Wall was being torn down, piece by piece, in enormous celebrations that reverberated throughout the world. The Burkes were excited enough to be going to the White House, but now they would be visiting while world history was being made.

The next day, a stretch limousine picked up the group to take them to the southwest gate of the White House. They waited in the West Wing, awed by the elegant artwork and furnishings surrounding them. Then a special events coordinator escorted them through the Rose Garden and through the First Ladies' Hall lined with portraits of all the presidents' wives. Chris went to have makeup applied for the public service announcement. The rest of the group was led to the Diplomatic Reception Room, where foreign diplomats and ambassadors are greeted by the President. The oval-shaped room was painted with historical scenes; in the adjoining room, they admired glass cases of presidential china, from George Washington's humble blue and white plates to the Reagans' elaborate red and gold Lenox. The windows framed a stunning view of the south lawn of the White House, and in the distance, the Washington Monument and Jefferson Memorial.

The family took it all in with awe—except for Frank, who talked with the security men, one of whom remembered when Frank worked in police security, escorting presidents who visited New York.

Within the hour, the group was hustled into the hallway to meet the President. The White House photographer, the Secret Service, and a bevy of aides buzzed about, apologizing for the wait, which they blamed on the historic events taking place in Germany. Then Chris, Frank, and Marian walked outside with the President to be interviewed by reporters for "Entertainment Tonight." Afterward, the President talked with people outside the White House fence, then suddenly gave a loud whoop. In a flash, his dogs came tearing through the Rose Garden. As the group petted the dogs, Marian mentioned to the President how much she admired his wife Barbara. "Well, you'll have to come up and meet her," said President Bush casually. Marian answered that she would love that, but to herself, she thought it was unlikely, since it was not scheduled on the agenda. They were escorted back inside, and Chris and the President went off to film the public service announcement.

"I was quite honored to meet the President," says Chris. "I liked him. He was down to earth. I told him I thought it would be great if we did a show where the Thachers go to the White House to visit him. He said, 'Well, [British prime minister] Margaret Thatcher is coming next week.'"

After Chris and the President finished, Bush walked Chris to the First Lady's dressing room. Barbara had just returned from swimming, and she was having her hair done. "Oh, don't tell anyone I have a hairdresser!" she teased him. "This will be our secret, Chris."

Then the President took Chris into his private office, where they swapped photos and autographs. "It was really interesting because I love country music and so does President Bush," says Chris. "We talked a lot about that. And I asked him about his job. It sounds interesting."

When Marian, Frank, J.R., and Betsy were escorted into the room, Chris was still chatting amiably with Bush. J.R. remembers that Chris was calling the President "George," but Chris denies that. "I'd never do that to a guy like that. You're supposed to say 'Mr. President' or 'Mr. Bush.' And I didn't call his wife 'Babs,' even though Patti LuPone does."

The private tour continued down to the Lincoln Bedroom and across to the Queens' Bedroom, where visiting royalty have stayed, and then to a sitting room with an enormous needlepoint rug that Barbara Bush had made. As they were admiring the rug, Barbara entered the room, followed by her son Marvin.

"We were in awe the whole time we were with them," says Marian. "But Chris took it all so naturally, like he met the President every day. They were both charming, and made us feel comfortable. They're such regular people, and they are very comfortable around young people." Barbara chatted with Marian about mutual acquaintances: Dan Burke, the CEO of ABC, and his wife Bunny, who is Barbara's tennis partner. Marian and Frank had met them at network meetings. Barbara said her friends had sent her a tape of the pilot, which she and the President had thoroughly enjoyed.

Then the group walked out to the White House lawn to watch the Bushes board a helicopter for Dallas. "I got a big kiss from Barbara," says Chris.

Afterward, the group lunched in a private dining room. Chris asked for, and was given, one of the pewter presidential serving plates. Then they were taken on a full tour of the White House. After more than five hours, it was time to go, but the Burkes were still walking on air. "The whole thing was so amazing," says Marian. "We have gone from the depths of despair, when Chris was born, to heights of unbelievable experiences like this. Chris has opened doors for us that we would never have gone through. We know we would have never gotten up to those doors, never mind walk through them. Chris takes it all in stride. We're the ones in awe."

Within a day, the Burke family was again separated by three thousand miles. When Frank and Chris returned to California, they looked forward to Thanksgiving in Vancouver with Ellen's family and Christmas in New York and New Hampshire with J.R. and Anne. Chris always loved seeing Manhattan at the peak of its Christmas beauty, with its festive window displays, the gigantic tree in Rockefeller Center, and the holiday show at Radio City Music Hall. This Christmas, they hoped, would be as normal as all the holidays before, when the family gathered in New York for their traditional Christmas Eve mass and dinner and caroling at a neighborhood restaurant.

But this year, it didn't happen. The show was running behind schedule, so they only had a three-day break over the weekend. Frank tried to make the best of it. He and Chris went shopping for gifts and holiday decorations, but the balmy California weather did little to put them into the spirit. "It was very strange, having to put on sun block before shopping for a Christmas tree," says Frank. When Marian arrived, they again flew up to Vancouver to be with Ellen and her family. On Christmas Day, they ate a big breakfast, then rushed to catch a plane back to Los Angeles. "We had Christmas dinner on the plane," says Marian. "It was horrible, but we were together. You have to make a number of sacrifices in the world of show business. It's easier for people who live in California. But we have deep roots in New York."

Frank and Marian were proud of Chris, but they still had problems thinking of their son as a professional actor. So it was with some surprise that they heard, in early January, that Chris had been nominated by the Hollywood Foreign Press Association for a Golden Globe Award as best supporting actor in a dramatic television series. Marian told her coworkers, who immediately asked her what she was going to wear to the glitzy awards show. "Why, I haven't thought about it," she answered.

"We were hysterical," says her assistant Priscilla. "We told her she should buy something new, like a designer gown. But Marian was so cool about it. She wore something she already had. When she came back, she had met all these celebrities, and we were asking her all these questions about them. We had to pull it out of her. It was so wild because she was the last person on earth you'd expect to be hobnobbing with these Hollywood stars. But by then, Marian was like the celebrity of the office."

More awards followed. The Academy of Family Films and Family Television picked Chris as best television actor. He was honored all over the United States by various organizations—winning, among others, the 1989 Youth in Film "Inspiration to Youth Award" and the 1990 St. Genesius Medal, given to a person in the entertainment business for outstanding achievement. Faces International picked him as one of the top ten new faces in the public eye. Later, he was recognized by the U.S. Junior Chamber of Commerce as one of ten outstanding young Americans aged twenty-one to thirty-nine. And Chris became the spokesman for both the National Down Syndrome Congress and the McDonald's McJobs program.

But Chris and the show were conspicuously absent from the Emmy Awards (television's equivalent of the Academy Awards), although guest star Viveca Lindfors won the best supporting actress award for her portrayal of an aging ballet teacher in one episode.

Composer Craig Safan says the industry thinks of "Life Goes On" as a kids' show. But he says that it has been more revolutionary, more ground-breaking, than many other touted shows. For example, "Twin Peaks" had caught the lion's share of attention when it premiered in 1990, but it had failed by the next season. "They were being different for the sake of being different," says Craig. Another show, "Cop Rock," was later hailed as merging music and drama, but Craig says "Life Goes On" has done that more realistically by using the talents of Patti LuPone and visiting musicians.

Still, "Life Goes On" was nominated for favorite new television series in the 1989–90 People's Choice Awards; it won best television series in the Academy of Family Films and Family Television Awards; and it was recognized by the 1989 National Telemedia Council for its "positive approach in working towards a Media Wise Society." And *Scholastic Magazine* readers in schools across America voted it the best new television series of the season.

Such honors were welcome, but they did little to calm the anxieties on the set. Few people thought the show would be back for a second season. The ratings were still low, and the long hours were not only taking their toll on the cast and crew but also wreaking havoc with the show's budget, putting the show in a less favorable light at the Warner Brothers offices. It was an itchy time for people trying to schedule their personal lives, unsure if they should buy that new car or bigger home, since they might be unemployed once production was finished in April.

Michael Braverman was not as anxious. Before the series aired, a high-ranking ABC executive had told him "just get me a teen"—meaning that he wanted an audience share in the double digits. Now, "Life Goes On" was attracting 14, 15, 16 percent of the viewers watching television in that time period—the highest share in several years.

Then in April, the news finally came. ABC had renewed the show for a full twenty-two episodes for the 1990–91 season. It was a surprise decision, because "Life Goes On" finished the season ranked 98th of 124 regular series; its ratings were far below many of the shows that had been canceled. Of the 26 new network shows that had debuted that fall 1989 season, only 7 returned for the next year.

The cast and crew looked forward to the eight-week hiatus, when they could finally relax and take vacations. But Chris didn't want to leave, and he didn't want to hear others talking about it.

At the close of the season, Chris and Kellie Martin were invited to appear on "The Arsenio Hall Show." This was the ultimate for Kellie, who laughs when she recalls how much she talked. She answered a few questions for Chris, who later teased her about it. Chris was a crowd pleaser, waving his arm and whooping the way Arsenio does to stir up a crowd, but he was strangely silent for most of the interview.

After the Arsenio show was over, Chris flew back to New York for a fund-raiser. He traveled alone, since he was being met at the airport in Newark. "This was the first time he had traveled without me, and it was the first time I had been separated from him for more than a year," says Frank. "When I put him on that plane, I was one sad person. I felt lost."

Chris wasn't bothered by it. All the years commuting from school had made him comfortable traveling alone. And he knew he was seeing his dad two days later, when he flew back to attend the show's wrap party.

At the party, Chris acted like a host, greeting guests at the door and making a short speech about how much he had enjoyed working with everyone through the year. Then Michael Braverman showed the "Life Goes On" gag reel, made up of funny takes from various episodes. One was of Chris, during the pig episode, walking in the door just as the pig began relieving itself. Another was Chris flubbing his line and shaking his head violently in frustration.

As the cast and crew looked back on the year's work, they realized how much Chris had grown, both as an actor and as a person, during that time.

"I find that Chris understands what it means to be an actor, to exhibit emotions or behavior and comment on it," says Bill Smitrovich. "When he's good, it's absolutely magical. Sometimes my wife and I watch the show and say, 'Did he get that? Does he understand?' It's hard to know. He does have that innate talent. Like any other actor, he needs to be nurtured, but in a special way. He really has grown, has become an actor. He has the desire. He is highly motivated."

After the party, Chris and Frank flew home to New York. Early the next day, Chris was out the door before his parents awoke. He walked the three blocks up to P.S. 138 and rode his old elevator to the class-rooms above. There was a new operator, a young retarded man the school had hired to replace him. When Chris walked down the familiar hallway, his former coworkers surrounded him, hugging him and praising him for his work on the show. Chris greeted everyone by name and asked about their children and spouses. He was glad to see them, but they were not the main reason he was there. Within minutes, he pulled away from the group and walked into the classroom where he had first volunteered.

There were new children in the room, ones Chris had not met. Like the previous students, they were severely retarded. They didn't know they were looking at a TV star; they knew nothing of the fame and fortune he had found. But he got down on his knees, hugging and playing with them for the next few hours. "It was really touching to see him so concerned about them," says Tom Roeder, the classroom teacher. "He really showed his heart was still here with the kids."

Pat Mulholland gave Chris a big hug and reminded him of something she had said when she first asked him if he wanted to be the elevator operator. "I had told him, 'Chris, I want you to be my Helen Keller.' Because of Helen Keller, the American Foundation for the Blind has so much power, and it is the most endowed of all the organizations for people with handicapping conditions. She put a face on the condition; she made people understand about her handicap. And you can always use the story of Helen Keller as something to strive for. But we didn't have anyone like that, until Chris. Our kids are unable to advocate for themselves, and now we finally had someone to cheerlead for us. I told him, 'Chris, you've really and truly done it. You are my Helen Keller.'"

Chris stayed close to his former coworkers during his hiatus, volunteering at the school and appearing at special events in the citywide program. He handed out class rings at a special school graduation, where the girls swooned and screamed at him. "Do you have a girlfriend?" one of them asked. "You're all my girlfriends," he answered.

One day, Tom and Chris met at lunch for their favorite meal, scrambled eggs and french fries at a nearby diner. But this time, people recognized Chris and crowded around him in the small space, pushing and shoving to get an autograph. Chris still remembers it with a shudder. "It scared me very much because I thought about John Lennon, and how he was killed by one of his fans in New York. I like meeting my fans, but not when it's scary."

Tom was amazed by the fans' reactions, but he had seen the groundswell throughout the first season, when he went around to regular parochial and public schools in New York City, talking with students about the community integration programs in which they would share activities with his handicapped students. "When I ask the kids if they watch Corky on 'Life Goes On,' they all raise their hands. We discuss Chris, how he is limited in certain ways—in how much he can learn or how quickly he can learn it—but he is still capable of learning, and being a good actor. Chris has become someone that children can look to in understanding the differences but also in respecting the abilities that every child has, whether they have disabilities or not."

When describing Chris, Tom likes to quote William Butler Yeats: "No lasting achievement is possible without a vision. No dream can become reality without action and responsibility."

Chris stayed busy during his hiatus, going on a whirlwind tour for the McDonald's McJobs program. In several cities around the United States, he gave talk show interviews and delivered speeches at rallies and banquets. Then, at a dinner in Washington, he again met President George Bush. When Chris spotted the President entering the room, he rushed over to shake his hand. The Secret Service entourage reacted by quickly surrounding Bush, but the President stopped them. "It's okay," he said, waving them off with his hand. "This is my friend Chris Burke."

TEN

★ ★ ★ ★ ★ ★ ★ ★ ★ ★ ★ ★ ★ ★

AS THE EIGHT-WEEK HIATUS drew to an end, the Burkes packed their bags for Hawaii, where the first two episodes of the new season were to be filmed. It was an exciting time, not only because it was their first trip to Hawaii, but also because Marian had just retired and would be joining Frank and Chris in their show business world. "We had realized we could not go through another season apart," says Frank. "Time is too precious. No one has a contract with God for how much time they have. And we knew we didn't want to be separated like that again." Frank and Marian went sightseeing and relaxed by the beautiful pool, where Marian got to know the cast and crew she had only met briefly before. Other times, they dined in their luxurious suite, staring out at the panoramic view of Waikiki Beach and the skyline of Honolulu.

From the start, the trip wasn't much of a vacation for Chris. He had nearly a hundred pages of action and dialogue to master, and he also had to prepare for scenes in which he would surf and swim with the dolphins. The story line started with Corky winning a raffle prize for this trip to Hawaii, Libby and Drew's dream vacation. But Hawaii turns into a nightmare soon enough for the Thacher family. Their luggage is lost, their hotel is a decrepit, lizard-filled horror, and their free dining and entertainment coupons, provided by the raffle, have expired. Within hours, the disgruntled family decides to return home. Then famed entertainer Don Ho hears of their plight and sets them up in a luxury hotel, introducing them to luaus and a range of vacation adventures. Corky learns to surf, and he is asked to help care for the dolphins at an ocean theme park.

The Thachers' paradise is tarnished once again when Becca meets

Kimo, a handsome young man who suddenly loses interest in her after meeting Corky. When Kimo admits to Becca how he is not comfortable around someone who is "different," Becca gives him a piece of her mind.

All was not bliss in the real-life paradise, either. Hoards of tourists and locals crowded the areas around the production, straining against barricades and ropes to watch the action. Chris was unsettled working in front of an audience. Kaley coached Chris to ignore the circus atmosphere, telling him, "This is like theatre. Just pretend you're an actor on the stage." The advice didn't work. As the hours stretched long and Chris tired, he grew more and more distracted, flubbing his lines and losing his concentration.

Chris still made time to sign autographs and pose for photos. Early one morning, as he prepared for work, a group of kids and their parents walked by and spotted him. They walked by again, staring at Chris, then summoned up enough courage to slowly approach him. "Chris was sitting there, jet-lagged and tired, but when they walked up, he just turned it on," says writer Jule Selbo. "He talked with them and handled the situation very well. He was very aware that he wanted to be available to people."

The crowds weren't always admiring. In one scene, Chris rode in a car with another actor while the camera recorded their conversation and Kaley cued their lines from the back seat. Crowds strained against the ropes lining the streets, waving and calling to Chris as he rode by with his window open. Chris couldn't respond because he was working, but some in the crowd didn't seem to understand. One man in the crowd yelled out, "Hey, that retard is really stuck up!" When Chris heard it, he looked back to Kaley and rolled his eyes. "He blew it off right away," says Kaley. "I think it hurt me more than it did him."

The episode was the most physically challenging Chris has ever had; it called for Chris to swim and surf and run on the beach. During Chris' teenage years, J.R. had tried to get him to surf, but Chris had always been too scared to join him. But the producers hired an island surfing legend as his coach, so Chris gave it a try. On his first attempt, he stood up shakily, then waved his arms and fell in. A few tries later, he spilled into shallow water onto a patch of coral, and was scraped and cut by the sharp edges. By the end of the day, his neck and back had reddened into a painful sunburn. The next day, the producers hired an attendant versed in first aid to make sure Chris didn't get exhausted or sunburned. By the time the scenes were filmed, Chris was cutting through the waves expertly, though he vowed never to get on a surfboard again after the filming was over.

Swimming with the dolphins was more pleasant. In the show, Corky is asked to help feed and care for dolphins at a water park, because their trainer thinks they will find him interesting. The show was based partly on reality: dolphin experts say that captive dolphins are naturally attracted to and respond more to any person with physical differences because they make interesting subjects for the dolphins' sonar "vision." Dolphins have shown a particular interest in people with Down syndrome; some dolphins in Florida have been used in special education programs, to motivate young children with Down syndrome to learn to read and talk.

Chris had looked forward to swimming with the dolphins for months, ever since he heard the story line. In the script, Corky enters the water hesitantly, but in reality, Chris jumped right in with gusto. "He was fearless," says Jule. "The minute we got to the dolphin area, he tore off his sneakers and ran right down there. He couldn't wait to get in with them."

"The dolphins, Miki and Kaleo, liked me," says Chris. "They were really friendly. I learned how to pat the water, and then they'd come up to me and I'd grab their fin real fast and hold on tight and they'd take me around. They swim really fast. I loved riding them. I'd like to do it again."

Chris was in the water with the dolphins for hours, along with guest star Elizabeth Lindsey, a former Miss Hawaii who played the dolphins' trainer. Because of some technical problems, the shooting dragged on longer than expected. "I was amazed at Chris' stamina," she says. "I swam competitively for years, but it was exhausting for me. I know it was tougher for Chris. We were under tremendous time restraints, so they had to push him really hard. Sometimes they snapped at him. My nerves were fried, but he never complained. He just kept trying."

Elizabeth says she had certain preconceived notions about Chris before working with him. "I thought he would be childlike and innocent, which he is, but he is, in addition, a fun, flirtatious young man." In her first scene with Chris, they delivered their lines while squeezing through a narrow stairwell on a boat. When the first take was over, Chris looked up at her, his face close to hers, and joked, "Hey, baby, wanna make out?"

Elizabeth says Chris is enormously talented as an actor, conveying the right mix of emotions for the right tone in his dialogue. In one scene,

Corky talks about how he feels a kinship with the captive dolphins because they're different from their fellow dolphins living in the wild. "He understood that intuitively," says Elizabeth. "He was talking about how he is different, too. Chris wasn't upset by the lines at all."

After a few weeks of Hawaiian adventures, the cast and crew settled back into their routine at the Warner Brothers Studios lot. Now that they were away from the distractions of the Hawaii crowds, it was apparent that Chris was a different person from the kid who had stepped onto the set just one year before. He had matured, both physically and mentally, and seemed more comfortable with the technical end of filmmaking. During the hiatus, he had made a solemn vow not to get frustrated with himself when he encountered problems on the set. "I said to myself, 'I'm not going to freak out when I miss a line,'" he says. "'I'm going to stay calm and work hard to learn my lines. I'll be the new improved Chris Burke.'"

Michael Braverman says that Chris has grown exponentially as an actor and a person. "During 'Desperate' and the first year of the series, I don't think he had a full grasp of the process: which way to look for the camera, how to modulate your voice, how to be cognizant of the camera and deal with other actors in a scene. The concentration it requires, the discipline it requires, the focus it requires—he has grown in all those areas."

Kellie Martin says Chris has learned to observe and listen closely to direction. "He has relaxed and developed the freedom to improvise. That's very hard. It took me five years to pick that up." In one scene, Chris was packing a trophy in his suitcase, which Kellie kept pulling out. "He kept putting it back in, more times than was in the script. He slapped my hand—that wasn't in the script. But it was great; we ended up using everything in that scene. I said, 'Chris, you stole that scene!' and he said, 'Good!'"

Director Rick Rosenthal credits the fast-paced, stimulating environment of the set for the dramatic changes in Chris. "I think the rigors of the show have pushed his ability to read, to learn, to memorize. He's forced to think more. His verbal abilities have improved dramatically, and I think he's much more self-assured. He's been exposed to vast numbers of people with drive and determination, people he wouldn't have met otherwise. He feeds off these relationships in a very positive way."

Others credit some of the change in Chris to the fact that Marian is nearby, instead of three thousand miles away. "He's different now that his mother is here," says Patti. "Frank is too. They felt very lonely without their wife and mother. This business is so hard when it separates families."

Marian made the transition from high-powered executive to full-time mom with relative ease. She grew to like California, though not with the same passion as her son. "It's very easy to relocate here even though we miss our friends and family," she says. "It is hardest when we miss something because we can't get back to the East Coast. It's a bit of a social sacrifice for us, but it's so worthwhile."

At the start of the season, some crew members worried that Marian would baby her son on the set, as she sometimes had when she visited during the first season. "Frank would say, 'Get in there and do it, you can do it,'" says Bruce. "But when Marian came to visit, Chris would sometimes hide underneath her arms and she'd say, 'Oh, he's tired. Leave him alone.' But now that's not a problem."

At first, it was hard for Marian to be on the set when Chris was working. She stayed out of his eyesight so she wouldn't distract him. But even in the far corners of the set, she tensed each time Chris said his lines, and cringed if she heard any stutter or misspoken word. She couldn't bear to listen to the barking, sometimes harsh tones certain directors had for her son, though she bit her tongue unless she felt the criticism was unwarranted or too stinging. Before long, Marian preferred to stay back at the apartment or in the trailer with Frank unless she had reason to believe someone was treating Chris unfairly.

"His parents are not there to really look out for him, but just to make sure he's on the right track," says Tommy Puett, who plays Corky's friend Tyler Benchfield on the show. "They know what he's capable of and they know his limitations."

Kellie says the Burkes are now on the set even less than Frank was in the first season. "Chris knows everybody now. He's pretty comfortable. If something goes wrong, if he's having a bad day and people are getting tense, Frank and Marian would be there immediately. He slipped and fell once, and they were there within minutes."

The second season also brought changes in the show's casting. Monique Lanier, who played Chris' older sister Paige in the first season, had left the show to have a baby. She was replaced by Tracey Needham, a tall blond actress from Dallas. Patti LuPone also became pregnant in real life, so the same situation was quickly written for her character Libby. To help fill the episodes that Patti would take off on maternity leave, new characters Gina (played by Mary Page Keller) and nine-year-old Zoe (Leigh Ann Orsi) were added as Libby's carefree younger sister and niece, who would come to help out in the Thacher household while Libby was confined to her bed with pregnancy complications.

The pregnancy spawned a whole new set of tough scenes for Chris. One episode showed Libby and Drew worrying that the baby will be born with Down syndrome. Corky is upset by their concern, so Libby asks him, "Would you want the baby to have Down syndrome?" He has no answer.

"Nobody's giving him a break; nobody's soft-soaping anything," says Patti. "He just delivered his lines and understood the full effect."

Later, Corky overhears Becca and Libby excitedly talking about the results of an amniocentesis, which showed the baby was normal. He runs out of the house crying, while Libby follows after him. When he trips and sprawls on the ground, Libby rushes to comfort him. On the set, the scene was a problem, but not because Chris was upset about the lines. "He kept laughing," says writer Michael Nankin, who directed the episode. "I think he was embarrassed by the raw emotion. Patti LuPone was having a lot of trouble doing her part with him grinning up at her during this emotional scene. After a few takes, she grabbed his cheeks to keep him from smiling. On film, it looked like she was trying to connect with him. The scene was electrifying. That's one of those happy accidents you always hope for."

Chris says he likes the scenes in which his character is mad or upset. But Michael says Chris sometimes shies away from such strong emotions, especially anger. "I've also found that with other Down syndrome actors [guests on the show]. They've lived a life of trying to deflect strong emotions, and over the years they've developed a mechanism to avoid it. They laugh about it, or go in a different direction. It can be difficult to get them, as actors, to jump into those strong emotional moments."

But Michael Nankin says Chris' responses to other poignant scenes are fascinating. "You never know quite what you're going to get. Sometimes he brings a whole different color to a scene, a tone you never anticipated." In the same episode where the amnio is discussed, Corky has his nineteenth birthday, which he doesn't want to celebrate because he is upset that he is still in freshman English class at high school. But his family wakes him up at midnight with a birthday cake, then they sit and talk about the day he was born, and how much he means to them. The scene was lit by the light of the cake's candles. "This magic happened," says Michael. "Chris turned into this wonderful little angel. It was totally unexpected. Nobody told him to do anything; he just brought it to the table. Those are the moments you pray for."

Bruce Pasternack says such moments are not so much acting as something that comes from deep within Chris' soul. "He has two kinds of smiles. One is a kind of fake acting smile. And he has another smile that comes from his soul. Kaley can sometimes get him to do it when she's standing near the camera. It's just magic. He brings a lot of magic moments to the show. He is quite charming on camera, just by being himself."

Kellie Martin says that special smile depends on who the director is that week. "I can tell from watching the episode when Chris likes a director," she says. "A director he likes can get certain things out of him you'd never expect, like his quirky little smile. He puts more passion in his lines and he smiles more."

Each week, a new director comes to the show, bringing a different style and expectations. This rotation allows the director seven days to study an approach to the script, mapping out locations and set schedules for the most efficient filming.

The directorial shift can be difficult for all the actors, but especially for Chris, who is often given explicit acting instructions one week, then told "not to act" the next week. Chris prefers the detailed direction, and he works better with some directors than with others. He has had a stormy relationship with Rick Rosenthal, the co–executive producer who directs many of the episodes. More than any other director, Rick pushes Chris hard. Some of the cast and crew say Rick gets the best performances out of Chris, while others criticize him for browbeating Chris to the point that he cries and can't perform until he calms down.

Rick realizes he's regarded as being strict, but he says it is because his expectations of Chris are higher than those of most people. "I've seen what he can do, but it's not always easy to get, because sometimes it's locked up inside of him. He has the ability to create lovely insightful moments, which is the essence of acting, to illuminate the human condition. He does that with surprising regularity. There is a very fine line between Chris when he's magical and Chris when he's not. When Chris is magical is what we try to capture. That's what audiences really respond to."

When new directors come to the set, Chris invariably tests them just to see how strict they will be, much as students push the boundaries with a substitute teacher. Writer Michael Nankin experienced this the first time he tried his hand at directing an episode. "Chris just horsed around," says Michael. "He'd stop a scene and say, 'Oh, I want a drink of water,' or 'I'm not comfortable standing here.' He pushed to the point where I had to say, 'Chris, you can't fool around anymore. The sooner you do this scene, the sooner we'll be done.' He wants to see at what point you'll step in."

Some directors are uncomfortable working with Chris, and they never really stand up to him. At these times, Kaley has learned to step in to make Chris toe the line. "Sometimes they look at me and I know they're thinking, 'Gee, she's harsh with him.' It's just because I'm being firm. I try not to be. I try to give him space until we need to work. But people hand-hold him too much. I wouldn't do that with any other actor I work with, so I don't do that with Chris."

Chris' level of comprehension still mystifies his coworkers. Rick has tried to determine how deeply Chris understands what he is doing. "I asked him if he could tell the difference between a bad show and a good show, and he said no. We talked about good acting and bad acting, and he said he doesn't know the difference. If we ask him to act scared, sometimes he'll do a lot with his arms and expressions. We say, 'No, that's bad acting because you can see the acting. When you want to show that you're scared, do it with your eyes. That's good acting.' Sometimes, he'll say, 'Okay, I see.' But I don't know if he sees it for the moment or if it becomes part of his intellectual heritage."

As much as Chris has improved, those unpredictable difficulties continue to puzzle his coworkers. They often discuss it, hoping to find some pattern so that they can understand and work with him better. A few crew and cast members who watch Chris tire on excruciatingly long shoots think his hours should be limited, maybe to a minor's restriction of nine and a half hours. Chris disagrees. "I'm as much an adult as Bill and Patti," he says. "I can work the same hours."

Kaley agrees with Chris. "I don't think minor's hours are the answer. He just needs to know when to rest. He would always rather be socializing. When he's tired, it's hard to predict how he'll perform."

"On days when Chris works twelve hours, the last few hours we don't get much," says Bruce. "It's pretty pointless to continue when he's that tired." But Chris' stamina is only one part of the problem. Sometimes the day gets off to a bad start, and everyone tenses, thinking Chris will require a dozen takes to do a scene. Then he'll surprise them by getting it right and continuing smoothly. Other times, he is fresh and ready, and knows all of his lines, then suddenly he goes into what the crew calls "meltdown," where it may take forty-five minutes to film one word or action from him.

That happened one day when Chris had a scene in which he had to walk up a staircase, turn his head, and say his line at a certain point. Every time, he said it before he was in the range of the camera. The crew coached him and pleaded with him, to no avail. Finally, the director suggested that Chris switch places with Bruce Pasternack behind the camera. So Chris, after much more coaxing, looked into the lens while Bruce walked through the scene. "Do you see me now, Chris?" Bruce asked at the point where Chris had been saying his line.

"No," said Chris.

"Well, see, that's because it's too soon." Bruce kept walking up the stairs. "How about now?"

"Yes," Chris answered, looking closely at the spot.

When Bruce went back to the camera, the crew was making bets on whether the trick would work. "I said, 'Nah, he won't get it.' But sure enough, on the first take, Chris did it perfectly. The only problem was, for the next week, he wanted to look at every single shot through the camera."

What Chris doesn't enjoy are the close-up shots in which he is off camera, saying his lines to the actor having his or her close-up coverage. "He is always trying," says Kaley. "But if it's a long scene, it can get too frustrating for him and everyone else. It isn't as much fun and he gets bored. It's not that he's lazy. He is a very good team player. He just stops listening and thinking about what he's saying, and he misses his timing."

Those limitations cause problems, but not as much for the crew as for the other actors, says Bruce. "Everyone likes Chris, but everyone gets frustrated once in a while. The other actors get more frustrated than the crew. They're the ones who have the toughest time working with Chris. It's not a question of not being able to tolerate him; it's just that working opposite Chris can be a wonderful experience, but it can also be very difficult."

By the second season, the honeymoon was over between Chris and some of his coworkers. "This is the most difficult job I have ever had," says Patti LuPone. "Chris is very hard to work with because he doesn't always know his lines."

When Patti has her coverage—when the camera is trained on her in a close-up that will be edited into the master scene—she often asks Kaley to sit in for Chris and read his lines for him. She doesn't like to depend on Chris to provide the rhythms for the scene, which have to be consistent in all the shots. Normally every actor in the scene stays on the set, off camera, delivering their lines and acting their parts to help the actor in the close-up re-create the reactions and emotions. Some of the other actors also ask Kaley to step in as a substitute if Chris is tired, or if he is flubbing the rhythm, consistency, or diction of his lines or actions.

The timing of a scene is one of the most crucial parts of acting, says Bill. "My favorite quote is 'All art aspires to music.' That is particularly true for acting. A scene is broken down into beats, rhythms, crescendoes, allegros . . . it's all different. The way you speak a line goes up and down in a tempo. Sometimes with Chris, it's like you have a symphony and the cymbals have to come in at a certain time. Cymbals are loud and important and make a big impact. But when the cymbals aren't hit when they should be, it screws up the music. We're all instruments; we all blend in. You have to have that rhythm, and if Chris is not there on your coverage, you need someone to read the lines for him."

Chris occasionally gets upset when Kaley is asked to take his place, but other times he's happy to be relieved of the responsibility. But his absence makes work tougher for the other actors. "Chris has limitations, and that's part of it," says Bill. "Sometimes the limitations are caused by his malady; other times, he's just not working as hard as he should. It all depends on his attention and concentration. When Chris is right there, he provides his notes for that rhythm and his delivery helps the pace of the scene as a whole. But there are times he's just not there."

Chris is not the only actor who misses off-camera work. Patti was sometimes excused during pregnancy and, later in the season, when she was feeding her baby. Kellie was sometimes restricted by minors' hours or by having to attend school. Even Bill missed a few scenes in Hawaii. But Chris is the only actor who is asked to step aside.

Bill says it is most important for Chris to be looking at him from behind the camera when the close-up scene is emotional. "When I speak my lines, I'm looking into his eyes and feeling those rhythms. It's hard to project the same emotions when there's someone else there saying his lines. Imagine looking through a window and painting a field of red poppies. Then someone closes the window and you can't see them anymore. You close your eyes and try to imagine them, but it will never be the same."

Chris has improved dramatically in his ability to help the other actors, but sometimes he levels off, says Bill. "There are times he knows instinctively what his reactions should be. He's not a walking robot, but he needs strong direction and guidance. He's not always prepared, as far as knowing his lines."

Marian and Frank are acutely aware of the occasional friction on the set between Chris and some of his coworkers. "You would think people would be understanding," says Marian. "However, this is a high-pressure workplace. Tensions and personality conflicts are inevitable. But when Chris senses the tension, it is harder for him to work. He has difficulty concentrating. It confuses him because he is trying so hard to do what is expected of him. And he respects his coworkers so much that he wants to rise and meet their demands."

A few times, when the Burkes have heard of or witnessed insensitive treatment of Chris, they have wondered if the fame and fortune are worth the price.

"We are willing to abide with it because we know how much good Chris is doing for so many people," says Marian. "But if the friction ever built to the point where we felt it was harmful to Chris, we would walk away from it all. And if Chris ever decided he was no longer happy with this job, we would be more than happy to return to New York. Really, I think that is unlikely. Nearly everyone involved with the show treats Chris with respect and understanding."

Some of them go so far as to credit Chris for their jobs. "It's simple. Without Chris, 'Life Goes On' doesn't exist," says Bruce. "Chris is what makes this show special. Everyone understands that except maybe some of the other actors. All of us are replaceable, all the actors are replaceable except for Chris. When Patti got pregnant and left the show for three months, we missed her a lot but the show kept going."

Tommy says he has heard the dissenting talk, and he knows that some of the cast and crew don't like to be around Chris. "Whether they want to know it or not, Chris is the star of the show. We wouldn't be here without Chris. And that's what everybody needed to realize two years ago when we first started. Some of them haven't realized that yet."

Tommy steps in when he hears people making negative comments to Chris or criticizing him. "I try to do it away from Chris because he doesn't need to see that part of me, or that part of them. I tell them, 'If you put more stress on him, the more confused he's going to get, and the longer we'll all be here. If you don't shut your mouth and just deal with it and try to be more professional, we'll be here on this scene till tomorrow.' People just don't want to accept that. They don't want to have to deal with someone else's problems."

Tommy says not many people on the set seem to understand what

Chris' capabilities are. "The people who do understand will push him to an extreme to make him do everything he is capable of doing. Such as me. When I ask him a question, I want a full answer. Michael Braverman has high expectations of Chris, and he expects Chris to fulfill them because he knows he can. His parents are the same way. They're the ones who ground out this path for him."

Rick says that before Chris came on the show, he had fulfilled and exceeded any expectations his family had for him when he was born. "But when you enter a whole other world as part of a TV show, there is a whole new set of expectations. The network expects that the show will be what it was at the start. The studio expects the show to continue to be produced in a timely and economic manner. The executive producers want Chris to be exactly who he was when he first started acting. It wouldn't surprise me to see a certain amount of burnout. We see it sporadically, especially when Chris is tired. It's tough for him to lift up, get back into the show. He's a kid who in many ways has been pushed, but in other ways, expectations of him were exactly what his abilities were or sometimes below. Clearly, he has abilities no one thought he had."

Tommy says Down syndrome has affected Chris more physically than mentally. "He's got great brain capacity. His main problem is the disfigurement of his mouth. He knows what he wants to say, but sometimes he gets a mental block or gets tongue-tied on a word, so he can't get out what he wants to say. It makes him seem incapable of talking like everybody else, but sometimes I have the same thing, when I want to say something, but I can't get it out. It's just more noticeable with him, because with his obvious differences, people are more aware of what he's saying."

After two years of "studying" Chris, Tommy says he's found that many of the things Chris doesn't understand are based on miscommunications from his schooling or experiences in life that haven't been fully explained to him. "His parents have done phenomenal things with him, but I think he has the capacity for so much more. The more information he is given, the better he understands the big picture. If you just give him a short answer to a question, it will breeze right past him. But if you go in-depth and give him a large amount of information, he sucks it all in and he'll remember everything you've said. The more information he has to work with, the more the circle is brought together."

The best example of this, says Tommy, is with the size of parts Chris has on the show. "When he has just a small part in an episode, he is unfocused and has no direction. He's frantic, he doesn't know where he's going, and those are the scenes that go twenty takes. But on the episodes where he has a big part, he becomes focused immediately because he's excited about it. He analyzes and dissects each part of it, and he knows exactly what Corky's doing at every turn. If they give him a fat monologue or a lot of dialogue, unless he gets tongue-tied, he can do it in one or two takes."

The producers try to balance the episodes so that they revolve around all the main characters. Bruce thinks Chris works best when he has about a third of the show—enough to keep him interested, but not so much that he is overwhelmed.

Marian and Frank are comfortable with the differences between Corky and Chris. "They've shown both sides of a person with Down syndrome, a person who is not necessarily Chris," says Marian. "It is entertainment first. We have to remember that. They have to do what's going to be salable, yet intertwine it with the abilities people with Down syndrome have. They've shown the things he is not able to accomplish. It's like the way Corky is taking regular classes in a regular high school. Maybe it's not always realistic, but it brings mainstreaming more into the realm so that people can understand it."

Chris' toughest episode in the second season was one titled *Corky's Travels,* where Corky was lost and wandering around Chicago during a rainstorm. Chris reported to work each night for eight days, spending many hours shivering in the torrential special-effects rain.

Chris says that his least favorite scenes, initially, were the ones with a kindhearted young hooker who takes him home. Corky has his first sexual experience with her, though the show is vague about whether it proceeds past just some long kisses. The prostitute asks Corky if he has ever gone beyond kissing anyone and he says no. She asks him if he thinks about it, and he says, "All the time." Then he tells her softly, "I'm scared I'll never find out what comes after kissing." The hooker looks at him for a moment, then reaches back and turns off the light.

When Kaley practiced the lines with Chris in his trailer, he was doing them so perfectly that she stopped after a few times. "He had just the right mix of innocence and wonder," says Kaley. They went to the set, and during rehearsals, Chris blushed as he said his lines to the pretty young actress beside him on the couch. The crew teased Chris, accusing him of flubbing a line so that he'd have to do it over another time. So for the first few takes, Chris was still blushing, but several hours later, when they were still shooting the scene, he had become more jaded to the experience. "Unfortunately, his coverage [for close-ups] was last," says Kaley. "If they could have gotten those first few takes in a close-up, he would have won an Emmy hands down. Kissing is very hard for actors, because after the first hundred times, it becomes forced. It was funny watching him kiss, because he was very good, very practiced and natural. And no matter what he says, he enjoyed every take. Every time he was smiling and saying, 'Okay, let's do it again!' "

"It was scary and embarrassing for Chris. But he played it very gently, very sweetly," says Rick, who directed the episode. "It's poignant, not salacious. It may make some viewers uncomfortable. But this isn't just a kids' show. If we're dealing with a subject that's too serious for kids, we handle it in a way that kids won't be upset by it. An eight-year-old seeing this will think Corky is just kissing a girl. But Chris is twenty-five, and playing a nineteen-year-old."

"To me, it's interesting about these people we regard as childlike, but other parts of them work on the same levels as everyone else," says David Wolf, the writer of that episode. "A normal teenage boy is widely preoccupied with sex. It's something we barely touch on in the show. It's a very human side of him that can get lost. It's another way in which his emotions are not far from those we all experience."

Still, David knew that to portray Corky in a sexual light might cause problems. "We anticipated trouble with the network, and maybe some concern from Chris' parents, but everyone's been enthusiastic about it."

Marian says when she first read the script, she felt queasy. "I took it in to Frank and said, 'Oh my God, what do we do about this?' The main thing was the part with the hooker. And that line, 'I'm scared I'll never find out what comes after kissing.' That was a little rough for us. We discussed it, and we felt that it was something that could happen in real life. We said, 'Is it better that parents know this is something else they really and truly have to prepare their children for? Is it better for it to be out in the open?' "

When Marian and Frank talked to Chris about the script, he said he didn't object to it and thought it was okay. "I never asked him if he knew what it was about," says Marian. "I think it would be a little embarrassing for me to ask him about things like that at this point in his life." Chris may have been shy talking about it with his mom, but he picked up on the innuendo and joked about it with the crew members, greeting them with a cheery "Hey, did you hear I'm getting laid?"

When Marian and Frank saw the finished result, they liked it much better than they thought they would. Guest star Leon Redbone sang five original songs that Craig Safan had composed especially for the show, all tying into the theme of how life is sweeter when it includes challenges and new experiences. And the Burkes were proud to see that Chris was stretching his acting talent throughout the episodes, showing sides of himself as an adult that many people would not ascribe to someone with Down syndrome.

Chris' coworkers see some of those sides of Chris even more than his parents. A few even describe him as a "ladies' man" for his constant flirting and the crushes he develops on the set. "Chris is the first person to recognize a pretty girl," says Kaley. "And then he's off flirting with her."

He has a strong affection for Teresa Austin, his makeup artist. "He has told me that he loves me, and he has said that he wants to marry me," she says. "It's not that I don't take him seriously. There have been other girls he's been in love with, and right now, it's me. In a few months, it will be someone else. It all depends on how people treat him. I'm close to him, I'm touching him every day, and I think that's what he's responding to. He knows the reality of the situation; he knows that I have a boyfriend. I try to play it down. I know a girl with Down syndrome, and I'll say, 'Chris, you should go out with her. She's really cute.'"

In recent months, Chris has turned his attention to Karen Rauch, an actress with cerebral palsy who has played his girlfriend on the show. They date infrequently but talk on the phone fairly often.

He also likes to call Tommy Puett's girlfriend and flirt with her while Tommy listens. "He'll pick up the phone and call her and say, 'You really want to go out with me, don't you? You don't want to go with Tommy anymore.' She'll say, 'Yeah, Chris, you're right.' Then he'll turn to me and laugh and say, 'Oh, Tommy, you know I wouldn't take your lady away from you.'"

Costar Tracey Needham had to set Chris straight when he patted her lovingly on the rump while she was wearing a short waitress uniform on the set. "I had to sit him down and have a little talk with him," she says. "There were some other kids on the set and it wasn't a good situation. But he quit right away. Usually I just chase him. We have this little thing where I'll tap him on the back or he'll tap me, then we chase each other all around the set."

Teresa says Chris never really gets obnoxious because he so quickly pulls back if he thinks he's offending or hurting anyone. "This crew adores him. When he's not working, he's usually sitting in his director's chair reading his lines or talking with someone. He's not a hot dog type. He's a real gentleman."

The writers say that the impetus for the love scene in *Corky's Travels* came partly from knowing Chris and partly from the meetings they have a few times each season with teenagers with Down syndrome and their parents. The parents reminded the writers that their sons and daughters dealt with issues of sexuality just like any other teenagers.

"They're young adults," says writer Brad Markowitz. "If you think that because they have Down syndrome, they are any less boy-crazy or girl-crazy, then you should have seen how these girls reacted when Chris made an unexpected appearance. They jumped out of their chairs and went wild. They mobbed him like a rock star. The guys sat there, going, 'Oh, geez.' "

The main criticism parents had for the show was that it did not show enough of the daily struggles they encounter. "They said it looks too easy," says Brad. "They say it's really like quicksand, that their heads are above it, but they're always pulling up. Not that they were complaining, or saying it wasn't worth it. But every single day, being a parent never stops."

The teenagers, all of whom attend regular public school classes in the Los Angeles area, had one primary complaint: Corky does not endure the constant teasing from classmates that they do in real life. "The teenagers said the others are either teasing them or being condescending, or acting like they're not even there," says Brad. "They take a lot of abuse; kids can be really cruel. Corky has an awful lot of sympathetic, friendly people around him and not much in the way of aggravation. We don't deal with that issue much on the show, because we emphasize the friendships Corky has, to show he's accepted."

Still, as the writers have become more aware of the teasing through their meetings with the teenagers, they have added more of those situations when it is germane to the overall story.

Often, Corky's nemesis is Brian Russo, an insensitive football player who gives him a hard time at every opportunity. "The actor who plays Brian is Eric Welch, and he's really a very nice person," says Chris. "He told me that he does have concerns about what his character is doing to Corky. He doesn't like playing a jerk because he doesn't agree with what he is doing. But it's important because he's showing viewers how it's wrong to do those things. But I want Corky to learn that he has to stick up for himself. I want Corky to tell Brian what he really feels, that he doesn't like the way Brian has been treating him."

Michael Braverman says Corky is portrayed realistically in his relationships at school. "Corky doesn't really have a best friend, or any close friends for that matter. You can go through all forty-four episodes, and you'd be hard put to come up with one single name. It's perhaps Tyler Benchfield, but even that is through his sister Becca."

On the set, Chris' best friend is probably Tommy Puett, who plays Tyler. At twenty, Tommy is closer to Chris' age than most of the cast and crew, and they share a love for music and movies. They became friends immediately during the pilot and first season, and they grew closer during the second season as Tommy's role in the show was expanded.

"Chris and I have a different kind of relationship than he and his father have," says Tommy. "I have such an offsetting beat from his normal family lifestyle. It gives him the idea that there's more out there than just sitting around the house watching TV and going to an occasional movie. He can have a life for himself."

Chris amazes Tommy with his memory for anything related to entertainment. "It's remarkable. He can watch a movie, then four years later remember everything about it, the dialogue and the names in the credits. One of the guys who's a grip on 'Life Goes On' worked on a movie five years ago. He was in the last-end credits. Now there are 155 people working on this set, and Chris walks up to this guy and said, 'Hey, you did that movie. I saw your name in the credits.' The guy sat there in awe. He said, 'Nobody saw that credit, not even my wife.'"

On the set, the two often sit in Tommy's trailer, listening to music or watching reruns of their favorite sitcom, "Three's Company." Chris also likes to watch Eddie Murphy concert films. "He understands probably 87 percent of the jokes," says Tommy. "He catches most of the blunt, open jokes and he laughs." Off the set, Tommy has introduced Chris to his family and many of his friends, and tries to get together with him on the rare weekends the two both have free time. Tommy has his hands full promoting his hit rock album, titled *Life Goes On.* He also manages and produces a rock group called Mirror Image, and he hosts "America's Top Ten," Casey Kasem's rock music television show. "Chris is really excited about the show," says Tommy. "I get him copies of it before it airs."

Tommy says he and Chris often talk for hours about their "outrageous goals" in life. "You've got to set big goals but be realistic. If you take everything in stride and know what you're capable of doing with the talent you have and the drive you have, you can make it. And I think Chris will probably do most of what he wants to do. He would love to see himself where I'm at, doing what I'm doing. Those goals help him work harder. He admires a lot about me, and he sees himself as sort of following in my footsteps, like I'm his big brother. It's important to have someone who inspires you. He's always had this dream of being a recording artist. I think that's great to have so many goals, having a disability like he does. That's what brings people out of their disabilities—striving harder and working harder."

Just as Chris emulates Tommy, Tommy says he is inspired by Chris. "If I had Chris' drive and determination and his memory for everything in entertainment, I'd be double what I am now in life. I'd be the Doogie Howser of the 1990s, with a doctorate degree and everything. I look up to Chris because I know how hard he works at what he's doing. I feel fortunate being how I am, but I know he works doubly as hard as I do to get where he's at."

Aside from Tommy, Chris has several close friendships on the set, with Kaley and Kellie Martin and several of the crew. But Teresa Austin says Chris doesn't always make friendships immediately. "He's extremely polite with people he doesn't know well. The longer he knows you, the more he opens up, the more he lets his guard down. When I first started working on the show in the second season, people told me that Chris is real affectionate, but he won't be until he knows you. Chris does not trust people at first meeting. He's been burned and abused by people in the past—not on the show, but in school. The only incident I know about is when the boy attacked him with the pine branch. I think that made him not trust people as much. It was extremely traumatic for him. He likes to see himself as strong and capable, like his hero, 'The Flash,' and not as a victim."

Chris has also learned how fame can attract false friendships, she says. "When you're a television star, no matter if you have Down syndrome, people will try to take advantage of you. Everyone wants something from you, so you develop a thick skin regarding it. We're his family; he sees me and the rest of the crew every day. We take care of him, and he trusts us and knows we don't want anything from him. We just help him get through his day. Any change throws him off. If he has to work with another makeup artist, it upsets him, even if he knows them. He becomes attached to people. As his makeup artist, I am his mirror. I make sure he looks great so he can go do his lines and not worry about how he looks. Any actor you work with becomes attached, but it's a little more obvious in Chris. That sense of routine is very important to him."

Chris' innocence sometimes combines with his childlike honesty to create some uncomfortable situations. Once, just after a hairdresser had been fired, Chris walked into the makeup trailer, noticed the hairdresser's absence, and asked where she was. The person who had asked for her dismissal—and that of several others before her—was in the trailer, so everyone was walking on eggshells, not daring to discuss it. "Usually a person will look around and see the situation and be quiet," says Teresa. "But Chris wouldn't let it go. We tried to get him off of it and talk to him about other things. Until we answered him, he was going to keep asking. Finally we just said, 'Oh, she took another job.'"

Another time, a 350-pound extra sat in Teresa's chair, and the fabric started to rip. "The whole trailer was silent, then Chris blurted out, 'What's that sound?' We all knew it was fabric ripping. We were trying so hard not to laugh. The poor actor was embarrassed and he made a joke about it. He said, 'Oh, I guess I'm ripping the chair.' And Chris said, 'You're ripping the chair?' It was just out there, and everybody was dying. He has absolutely no tact. But that's just Chris. That's why I think of him as a twelve-year-old. How many times when you were twelve did you put your foot in your mouth and say, 'Oh my God, how could I have said that?' It's just the subtleties he misses."

And Chris doesn't always think ahead to what his character needs for a scene, Teresa says. Once he had to fall to his knees on the floor, an action that would be repeated for each take. Most actors would read the script and think, "Oh, I'm going to fall in this scene; I'll need pads in my pants." But in Chris' case, the costumer anticipated it for him. In a scene where a character is shown painting, another actor would think to tell the hairdresser to put some paint in his hair. "That's something we do for him," says Teresa. "Seeing the future of an event—he doesn't always understand that completely. He's dependent on people to think of these things for him and take care of those needs."

Teresa has also seen how Chris tests people to see what he can get away with. She once had a photo of the cast members taped to her mirror, and Chris wanted to pull it down to look at it more closely. Teresa said no, but Chris reached for it anyway. "I just gave him a look and that stopped him immediately. He wants to see if you're the type of person he could boss around. You have to set guidelines. Not that he would be abusive. Emotionally, he's about twelve years old. Most of the time, it's just funny. He comes over and whispers, 'Don't tell anyone, but I'm going to "The Flash" set.' He doesn't seem to realize that there's a whole core of people on radios monitoring where he goes. He thinks he's getting away with it."

Second assistant director Michael Scott is one of those people whose job is to monitor the actors' whereabouts at all times, to make sure they are available when they are needed on the set. "Chris has a coy way of trying to get rid of me when we're shooting on stage 19 [at Warner Brothers Studios]. On breaks, he dashes off. I turn the corner and see him running as fast as he can to the set of 'The Flash.'" The CBS show about the cartoon-based superhero, which ran against NBC's "The Cosby Show" on Thursday nights during the 1990–91 season, was Chris' favorite. Chris' curiosity got the better of him if he thought he had a chance to talk to the cast or crew of the show. When Michael ran after Chris to "The Flash" set to bring him back to his own set, Chris always apologized when caught. "He's like a big kid on a long leash," says Michael. "He's a pretty good kid, but I often have to reel him in."

Kaley remembers a day when Chris crashed another set on the Warner Brothers lot, where comedian Dan Ackroyd was having photos made for an upcoming movie. "He walked in and said 'Hi, Dan!' and Dan said, 'Oh, come here, you work with my friend Patti LuPone [who costarred with Dan in the movie *Driving Miss Daisy,* in which she played his social-climbing wife].' Dan brought Chris into the photo session, and then Chris said, 'Can my dialogue coach be in the pictures, too?'"

Chris has always been enamored with those celebrities he watches in movies and on television, but now he feels a kinship with them. Kellie Martin remembers an awards ceremony where John Travolta and Kirstie Alley entered the room together. Chris pulled them over to Kellie and started telling the couple what a great actress she was. "I nearly died. He always introduces me to people I want to meet but am too shy to approach. He's never embarrassed. He always has something to say. If he doesn't want their autograph, he always gets it for a cousin or friend who will appreciate it."

The tables are turned when Chris goes out in public. One weekend, when Chris, Kaley, and Kellie were leaving a Janet Jackson concert, someone recognized Chris and called out "Hey, Corky!" Suddenly, the whole crowd started rushing toward him. "He got mobbed," says Kaley. "People went nuts. It was scary."

When the crowd got out of hand, Chris and the others turned to run from them. Kellie says she freaked out. "I gave Chris my hat and pulled it over his eyes so people wouldn't recognize him. He took it off and was waving it at everyone. I said, 'Chris, oh my God, let's run to the car!' He handled it so well. He was really enjoying it. It is amazing how people recognize him everywhere. I think it's also because people are staring at him anyway, because he looks different, then they realize who he is."

As Chris' fame grew throughout the second season, the demand for him to do public appearances exploded, not only from the numerous organizations devoted to people with handicaps, but also from business conferences who wanted to hear his upbeat speeches on his personal drive and determination.

Marlene Klotz, the community relations director for the Phoenix ABC affiliate, has noticed that at benefits for the Genetic Center of Scottsdale, Chris usually turns the focus from himself to the message he wants to convey. "It's not to put Chris Burke on stage and spotlight him. It's to spotlight what any person with a disability can do if given the chance. He enjoys being the model for that type of opportunity, and he does it so well. He speaks with humor and warmth and compassion; he is entertaining and quick-witted. He never wants to take any kind of credit for the show. He's always insistent upon it being a family show— it's not just Chris and 'Life Goes On,' it's Corky and Becca and his mom and dad. He's real careful about that."

Marlene was reminded of the mission Chris sees for himself when she took a camera crew to the set of "Life Goes On" to do a segment on Chris at work. "He didn't know I was coming, but when I got to the set, the first thing he said was 'Let's go shoot a PSA for hiring the handi-capped.' He was ready to drop everything he was doing just for that. I said, 'Chris, I'm not here to shoot a PSA. I'm here to do a story on Chris Burke.' And he said, 'No, Marlene, that's not the most important thing.' He took my arm and led me behind the counter [of the set's Glen Brook Grill, the restaurant the Thacher family owns] and said, 'I want to stand here.' Then he picked up a pancake turner and recited just what he wanted to say, right off the top of his head, something about how people should hire the handicapped and give them a chance. His heart is so much into the general public hiring the handicapped. It's another dimension of his compassion, not only for people with Down syndrome, but for any other person with a handicap or misfortune."

But as the season progressed, the Burkes struggled to fit the engage-ments into Chris' schedules. Sometimes, they planned to attend a benefit or awards dinner, thinking that since Chris had a light workweek he would be free to leave on Friday. Then the shooting schedule would change, and Chris would have to work late Friday night. Too many weekends, they found themselves rushing to the airport early on Satur-day, dropping into an event for a few hours, then returning home, completely exhausted for the next workweek. Chris does the speeches gratis and is only reimbursed for his and his parents' expenses, though his agent Harry Abrams is trying to change that. But the Burkes resist charging a fee because they wanted to be available to the groups they feel are helping people through difficult situations.

The charity work has prompted some grumbling from Chris' coworkers, who think it is interfering with his full-time job. "It can be a detriment to his work because he doesn't have time to prepare or he loses the focus," says Bill Smitrovich. "It's physically debilitating, and his senses are keen. I wouldn't dream of jumping on a plane to the East Coast to play Mr. Big at some fund-raiser, then taking a red-eye to get back before work."

"Chris gets very positive feedback in his role as a spokesman," says Rick Rosenthal. "But sometimes I think it's more fun for Chris to be a celebrity than to be an actor. When he's good and rested, then he loves acting. But if there's a limo waiting, sometimes the lure of those distractions is more powerful than facing the concentration of the moment."

After a few months of particularly grueling weekends and workweeks, the Burkes decided to curtail the number of appearances and try to schedule them into the eight-week summer hiatus. Chris was relieved. "I like going to speak to the groups, but it's very hard to fit it in," he says. "My work comes first."

One thing Chris wasn't worried about was the show's ratings. "A lot of people watch the show and like the show, and that's what's important," he says. "I think 'Life Goes On' will go on and on and on."

His optimism wasn't shared by everyone. Throughout the fall of 1990 and the winter of 1991, the "Life Goes On" ratings were climbing a little from the first season, but the show faced even stiffer competition from "60 Minutes" as public concern grew over the conflict in the Persian Gulf. Still, "Life Goes On" came in second in the time slot every week in the 1990–91 season, soundly beating NBC and Fox, and drawing an average of 14 million viewers each week.

Michael says part of the problem is that "Life Goes On" is preempted every few weeks by ABC specials that the network has contracted. The producers noticed that the ratings rose steadily when new episodes aired several weeks straight, but fell on the weeks just after the substitutions. Advertising that promoted specific episodes of the show also increased the ratings, though ABC reserves most of its promotional time for its higher-rated shows. Still, it was often outdrawing shows that were considered household names: "thirtysomething," "Twin Peaks," "China Beach," and "Real Life with Jane Pauley," among others.

"One problem we still fight with is that people don't know enough about this show," says Rick Rosenthal. "Our research groups tell us that it's perceived as a Down syndrome show. It could have been, if it didn't have a strong family cast. If it was about Down syndrome only, it wouldn't have the scope and appeal that it has. But really, the message of the show is that just about every family in America has some degree of handicap. Any family with divorce, abuse, alcoholism, or addiction has a certain handicap. This is a show that goes beyond a family who has a son handicapped by Down syndrome. Becca, who redefines teenage angst, is an overachiever. Paige has an inability to hold a job. The parents have their own sets of handicaps. This show is at its best when it is most honest in dealing with all of these tensions."

Toward the middle of the second season, the set was again abuzz with speculation about the chances for another season. The third season is of ultimate importance for any television series, because it means that a show will reach that magic number of episodes—66—that makes it eligible for syndication to individual television stations throughout the United States. Domestic syndication can be the thick icing on the profits of any television show, split between the studio and anyone who owns a piece of the show.

The producers were cautiously optimistic that "Life Goes On" would survive to the third season and prosper in syndication, despite skepticism by many industry analysts. "We've done everything they said we couldn't," says Rick. "At the start, we were told, 'Gee, that's a nice pilot, but it will never sell as a series.' Then they said, 'Yeah, it's a nice series, but it will never sell in syndication overseas.' Well, we've done quite well all over the world. We were told it will never sell in domestic syndication because the market for hour-long dramas is soft. But it's the perfect show. It has the seal of parental approval."

Once again, the show that Michael Braverman describes as "the little engine that could" won out against the odds. By early spring, ABC had ordered four scripts for the third season of "Life Goes On." And a few months later, the show was one of only four dramas that the network renewed for the 1991-92 season.

The producers and writers aren't yet sure what situations the Thacher family will encounter in the third season. But toward the end of the second season, an episode addressed Corky's future. In the show, Corky is frustrated in school because he is flunking a math class. Becca is studying for college entrance exams, and that only compounds Corky's frustrations and fears that he will never graduate. Then he meets Arthur, an older man with Down syndrome who has never attended school and lives comfortably with his mother, working when he pleases in an electronics store.

Corky idolizes Arthur and longs for a life free of the challenges he is facing. But then Arthur's mother dies, and Corky watches Arthur crumble. Since Arthur has never been challenged, he is immobilized when his support system is gone, and he cannot adapt to the changes in his life. Corky drops his plans to quit school, and instead he concentrates harder on making his way toward a more self-sufficient future.

"Corky learns it's the hard work and challenges that pay off," says Michael Nankin, who wrote and directed the show. But the show's writers and producers also gained a lesson from the episode. "What we learned, when we were casting the part of Arthur, is how unique Chris really is," says Michael. "We were looking for a man forty-five years old with Down syndrome who could act. We did a very thorough search, all around the country. There's been such a shift in the past twenty years in the way they've been raised. All the men who were raised to have these opportunities were much younger, in their twenties. Just because they're high-functioning doesn't mean they could act. We were asking them to come in as a guest star on a network TV show and be up to the level of everyone else. It was impossible. Every time a guy came in, we appreciated Chris even more."

Eventually, they hired Canadian actor David McFarlane, who worked briefly many years ago with Michael Braverman on a "Quincy, M.E." episode. Since David is in his thirties, he was cosmetically aged for the part. Everyone, including the Burkes, was surprised at the vast difference in the personalities of the two young men. David is older and more mature, but he is also quiet and more introspective about his life. Chris and David worked well together, though the crew noticed that Chris was a little out of sorts at first. "Chris felt the competition of David on the set, and he reacted to it the way a child would," says Bruce. "He was a little jealous, and afraid of competing. He took a step backward and started having more trouble with his lines."

The issues raised in this episode will likely come up again, as Corky grows older and more independent. The producers say Corky may try living away from his family.

As for Chris, he would like more scenes in which he is dancing, singing, or telling jokes. And he wants more story lines built around Corky's friend, Lisa, played by Chris' real-life friend Karen Rauch. Whatever happens, everyone expects Chris will grow and learn even more as the series continues. "When I started doing this show, I thought of Chris as a kid with Down syndrome who wanted to be an actor," says Bill. "Now I think of him as an actor who just happens to have Down syndrome. He does have that innate talent. He really has grown and matured. He has become a professional actor."

"I've seen him grow as an actor and a human being," says Patti. "This gives him confidence. If you're confident in something like this, it would really reinforce your entire life. He can keep up with the pace because he wants it so much. He has a great appreciation of the fact that he's having a dream come true."

His coworkers have also felt profound changes in themselves from the time they've spent with Chris. "Chris is a constant reminder to me that life is precious," says Kellie. "He doesn't take anything for granted."

Tracey Needham, who plays Corky's older sister Paige, hopes the series will teach people not to have prejudices. "When people watch someone with a handicap on this show, and they can see he's normal, it will make them let their guard down so they can relate to it. It becomes more familiar, then it's not so scary. You can put yourself in that situation. Everyone has had some battle, something they've had to work against, that they can relate it to."

Michael Braverman thinks the series may help open doors for other actors with handicaps. "I think it's incumbent on directors to at least read a handicapped actor for a handicapped part. But just because someone is handicapped does not necessarily make them the best actor for the role. It's wrong to cast someone just because they're handicapped; you just cast the best actor for the part."

The impact of the show has spread far beyond the United States. Today, around the world, you can turn on a television and see Chris facing challenges and changing attitudes in a variety of languages. "Life Goes On" is syndicated to television stations in Australia, Bermuda, Bolivia, Bophuthatswana, Brunei, Canada, Chile, Colombia, Costa Rica, Finland, Germany, Greece, Holland, Indonesia, Ireland, Italy, Japan, Kenya, Kuwait, Luxembourg, Malaysia, Malta, Mexico, Namibia, New Zealand, Panama, Peru, the Philippines, Portugal, Puerto Rico, South Africa, Spain, Taiwan, Thailand, Turkey, the United Kingdom, Venezuela, and Zimbabwe, and at U.S. military bases throughout the world. More countries are being added each month.

" 'Life Goes On' and Chris have changed the public's perceptions of developmentally disabled people," says Michael. "That's not the goal we started out with. It's something I never thought of or planned—I never knew it would have such an impact. But we're seeing this groundswell. Maybe now people won't turn away from someone who has some type of disability. Maybe they will approach someone, actually accept them as a human being."

★ ★ ★ ★ ★ ★ ★ ★ ★ ★ ★ ★ ★

MY FAMILY thinks that I have gone Hollywood, but to me I haven't gone Hollywood. I'm the same Chris. I'm just working for a living at a regular job, and I want a house here in California, but now I call it L.A., not Hollywood.

I do feel like a star to my fans, and they look up to me, and I feel like a role model to them. I think it's great to meet your favorite star, like I am a star of "Life Goes On." I always wanted to meet the actors in person instead of watching them on their shows. When I go visit schools and places, people start screaming, "Corky! There's Corky!" They get all excited. I just can't believe it myself.

I did not expect to be a star. I feel that I have a job and they expect me to listen and be a willing worker. I want to work hard at becoming an actor, and that is what is important to me. I want everybody to know that I can work hard enough and do a good job. I want everybody to learn to watch me on "Life Goes On," to see my character Corky and the way he feels about his family and what he has inside of him. It's great that they see a person with a disability and see what he has to face in his life, so people can learn that Corky can do lots of things.

Lots of people watch "Life Goes On" and love the show. They've never seen a show like it. It's not just the ratings that are important, but I'd love to see the show go into the top ten. I like making money, but I don't really want to be rich. Just having a job and doing my job and taking care of my family, that's all that counts.

The most important thing is that the show really helps a lot of people in their real lives. I've always been interested in helping people who are handicapped. I love doing that. I don't know when I knew that was what

I wanted to do. I've just always had friends who were severely handi-capped, at Camp Anchor and Don Guanella and P.S. 138. Some of them didn't have families. Some of them did, like Erin, Jim Gillis' daughter. I love her very much. She is severely handicapped and she is a wonderful, beautiful little girl. When I found out about Nora, it made me want to help even more. She is really special to me.

I never feel uncomfortable around people who are severely handi-capped. I like to work and help them do things and make them laugh. I feel like in the "We Are the World" video when Michael Jackson and everybody got together to help the people in Ethiopia. They were artists helping people who needed help.

It is so important to help handicapped people. They're the ones suffer-ing. They need your help. You can't just stand there and say, "Should I help? What should I do?" You just do it. I can't just stand there and do nothing. I can't be that way. I care about them and I want to help, so I do. I have a saying: think of others, then yourself. These are people who need more help than I do. I say to myself, "I care. I'm going to help." Sometimes it takes patience but I enjoy helping people. I'd like to look for another job out here, something where I can try and help other people, like maybe I could be a Big Brother to somebody.

I also want to continue with my music career. I'm learning how to play the fiddle. My friend Joe DeMasi showed me how to do the short strokes, so now I can play "Rocky Top." I've been writing and recording songs with Joe and John DeMasi, and now we have three good ones. I have this great idea for a music video for our song "My Forever Girl." It's about a teenager who wants to be out in the world, but he really misses his girlfriend. He wants her to go on the road with him. There's love in the air for him and his girlfriend. I would show him running on the beach, thinking about his girlfriend, and then she is running toward him. It would help a lot because all the people could look at the video and they can see that in spite of his handicap he can fall in love with a person he really likes a lot.

Back in the old-time movies, they never had a person with a disability. They never had a person who was handicapped in show business. Today I have seen lots of actors with disabilities on TV. I want to see more of that. And I want to go and do more things besides "Life Goes On." It would be good for people to see me on different shows, so they can see that I can act and I'm not just Corky Thacher.

One thing that has happened is that I am a spokesperson for the McDonald's McJobs program. I have a business card that says "Chris

Burke, Ambassador." I get to go around the country and talk to people about how they should hire people with handicaps. I think that is what is very important. We need to be out there in the community. We need to have our voices heard. When I have a job, I do my job and I like to work. Everyone should have that chance. I say to people, "Give them a chance! Make their dreams come true!"

ELEVEN

★ ★ ★ ★ ★ ★ ★ ★ ★ ★ ★ ★ ★

WHEN CHRIS BURKE was born in 1965, the doctor summed up his future with "He'll probably never walk or talk. He won't amount to anything." Even the most optimistic person couldn't have predicted television stardom for Chris or anyone else with Down syndrome.

Now Chris, who earns roughly $250,000 a year, may soon reach a whole new level of achievement if the series continues its course, then sells well in domestic syndication.

Chris Burke will be a millionaire—a self-made millionaire—before the age of thirty.

His father finds this amusing. "If you told him that and then handed him five $20 bills, it would mean more to him that what you just said," says Frank. "Chris has no concept of money, and he's not concerned with it. Not that we try to shelter him from it. Even when I try to show him, 'This is what's in your checking account and in savings,' he's not interested."

Although Chris excelled in basic math classes in his early school years, he focused more on practical math, such as paying the correct amount in a store and getting the right change back. Today he's also careful to always get the bill. Chris now has his own American Express card, and he won't go to a restaurant without motioning to the waiter to bring him the check. He even picked up the tab at a breakfast meeting when a large group of public relations executives were courting him to be one of their clients. "It's funny: he gives the waiter the card, and he thinks that's it, it's all paid, that's the end of that bill," says Frank. Not that he's a spendthrift: the only kind of spending sprees Chris enjoys are at the local malls, where he picks up new California-style clothes and his favorite music on compact discs. That is not much different from the days before he was a star. "He's always had everything he wanted," says Frank. "There was no lack. And he doesn't ask for much."

There is only one big-ticket item Chris has requested, and it is the one thing that the Burkes have not let him buy: a house in California. Chris envisions a dream mansion, set on a hill near the studio, with a pool and a great view. His desire grew stronger after watching *La Bamba,* the life story of Ritchie Valens, in which, after reaching stardom, Ritchie buys his mother a big new house.

When he first mentioned the dream house to Frank early in the first season, Frank explained that it was not practical. Later, when Frank won $100 in a football pool at Marian's office, Chris was unusually excited. "Great, Dad!" he said. "Now we can put it toward buying a house out here!"

A hundred dollars wouldn't go far. A modest bungalow, sans view and pool, in a good neighborhood near Burbank would set the Burkes back about half a million dollars. For now, they've decided that their furnished two-bedroom apartment up the hill from the studio would be hard to beat for convenience. They can get Chris to the set within minutes, without a drive through horrendous traffic or the thick fog that envelops the valley. And the Burkes feel safe in the large gated complex, with a security force monitoring the grounds. A house would also mean ongoing maintenance, which would crimp their jet-set weekend lifestyle. "We go away so frequently," says Frank. "As it is, we pack and leave and don't give a thought to the apartment. It's comforting. When you have a house, you're always wondering how safe it is."

Chris has not wavered in his desire. "I hate living in an apartment," he says. "That's why I want a house, because it's peaceful and quiet." Marian and Frank are showing signs of giving in; they've looked at a few rental houses in the area. Marian is even considering moving some of their furniture from New York for the third season. But a purchase is still out of the question. They don't want to give up their apartment in New York, or their summer home in Point Lookout. "We already have two abodes," says Frank. "Why buy another?"

More importantly, Frank and Marian don't want to spend any money unnecessarily, because they want it to last Chris for the rest of his life. "It all boils down to, we don't want to take Chris' money and put it in a house," says Frank. "Our purpose is to get Christopher in a financially secure arrangement. For him to buy the house would be depleting that."

Marian and Frank also hesitate to set down roots in California because they don't know what the future holds. They miss the close group of New York friends and relatives they've shared their lives with for the past forty years. "Whether Chris' future is here or not is hard to say. We'll be here as long as 'Life Goes On' lasts," says Marian. "We'll have to wait and see. If there's something out here for him, we'll work around that."

Marian says Chris has always been adaptable, whether he was going back to school or going to visit someone. "He's always ready to go on to the next thing. He still loves all those people he worked with at P.S. 138. Even though he thinks he wants to stay here, if we did wind up back in New York, I think it would be okay. We are banking on that."

Yet Chris is adamant about wanting to continue his acting career. "Going back to New York doesn't solve anything," he says. "This is my job. This is the business I'm in. My life is here now."

"Life Goes On" is probably good for a few more seasons, but after that, what happens? Will Chris become like Norma Desmond in the classic Hollywood movie *Sunset Boulevard,* growing old and desperate waiting for new acting work that never comes?

Not likely, says executive producer Michael Braverman. "He's gone this far. I don't think anyone with good sense would say how much further he can go or not go. He is a very specialized actor. If there are roles requiring his specific persona, he will continue to work. It's doubtful there will be another series that could use him regularly, because it's been done. But it is quite possible that people will write roles for him."

Chris' brother J.R. agrees. "He's carved out a niche for himself. There's certainly nobody with his experience, if they want that type of person. Hopefully it will be based on his abilities rather than his disability. It seems to me that his career will continue, but the acting profession is such a fickle business."

Some people who know Chris think he would have trouble adjusting back to a regular lifestyle if "Life Goes On" were canceled. Makeup artist Teresa Austin says it's difficult for any actor when the limelight suddenly goes dim, and they're caught in that limbo insiders call "the Island of Lost Actors."

"I've worked with people who have been famous and then they're not," she says. "They have such a hard time when it's not there. Right now, Chris has a hundred friends here and millions of people watching him. He sees a future outside the show, but you just don't know. It concerns me, but then again, it concerns me about all the actors."

Tom Roeder of P.S. 138 says he doubts Chris would harbor the disappointment for long. "What he's done now could stand on its own for the rest of his life. It's wonderful how he's used his fame and success to help other people. There's nothing at all prideful about it. The real beauty of it is the way he and his family are using this TV show, this life, to influence other people. It's not the money he is making and the fact that everyone knows him. He's representative of all those people in the world who have disabilities. I don't know how many actors feel that sense of responsibility that Chris feels. He's doing more than any single person out there in affecting people's attitudes about people with disabilities. He's alleviating fears and misconceptions about people with disabilities, and he has created awareness in society of the need to involve handi-capped people in the community. I see that as what Chris is truly accom-plishing, rather than an individual achievement. His family has him so involved in recognizing that gift and enjoying it."

Tom says that attitude gives Chris a better perspective about his fame. "There is a quality Chris possesses that stems from the kinds of things his mom and dad have lived through. He has faith. He appreciates life too much to ever be caught up in a life that makes or breaks him. He's not living through this in an unnatural way. Chris has as much enjoyment being with people [from P.S. 138] as he does being in Hollywood and being with the stars. My daughter [in the fifth grade] wrote an opinion paper about him that said, 'Even though Chris is a star, he never forgets his family and friends.' To me it was a real insight. Here is my daughter recognizing that Chris is still a good friend and still cares about his parents. He never loses that sense of family and friends."

J.R. says his family has talked with Chris about the fleeting nature of fame. "We'd be kidding ourselves to say there wouldn't be an adjustment. But I don't know that he would miss being in the limelight. As it is, I think he's a little tired of it. The weekend charity things, the public appearances—I think he's had his fill of that. At this point, what really interests him is the acting."

Chris has ambitious plans for himself in show business. "I want to have my own show, a talk show called 'Let's Meet the Stars' where I would interview celebrities and ask them about how they got started," he says. He has also written letters to the producers of several of his favorite television shows, telling them of his interest to appear as a guest star and suggesting roles he might play. On "Full House," for example, he would like to play a long-lost uncle to the children. Currently, other shows' shooting schedules might interfere with his job on "Life Goes On," but there's a chance he might be able to work it in during future seasons with some advance planning.

Chris' agent Harry Abrams says Chris will likely work in show business even after the show's demise. "He has become a star in his own right; he's reached stardom the same way that Meryl Streep and Jack Nicholson have. His career is made, as far as I'm concerned. The longer the show stays on air, the longer that fame will last and the stronger it will be. I think it shocked a lot of people that he could hold up to the rigors of the show. The TV creative public will remember him for years to come." Abrams says Chris could make the jump to feature films, if the roles are right for him, but sees more promise in made-for-television movies. "If a case developed about a disabled person Chris' age, and it caught the nation's attention for a week or two, chances are that some creative person would write a TV movie about it. And they would probably turn to Chris to play that role."

Already, at least one movie production company has contacted Abrams about a role for Chris in a two-hour TV drama based on the real-life story of Phillip Becker, a boy with Down syndrome whose parents refused permission for surgery to correct his life-threatening heart condition. Abrams warns that though a network is interested, projects can often fall apart or take years to get off the ground.

Emily Perl Kingsley, who first recommended Chris for the acting job in "Desperate," is betting that other offers will follow, as the entertainment business realizes it is neglecting a very large audience, the millions of people with disabilities. "It's slowly getting better. Screen Actors Guild now has a performers with disabilities committee. But the number of roles is not nearly in proportion to the number of people with disabilities in the general population. The disabled represent America's largest minority group: it's larger than any of the various pressure groups you can imagine. Think of all the effort put into integrating shows racially and by gender. But for the largest group, those with disabilities, the parts available are still only crumbs. I'm not even talking about a leading part like Chris has, which is obviously a tremendous step forward. I'm talking about integration of extras and supporting parts, where the story doesn't revolve around the disability. It's all positive, all headed in the right direction, but there's still a lot of prejudice out there."

Emily says Chris has laid some important groundwork. Now that people can see that someone with Down syndrome can hold down an acting career, they are more likely to create similar roles, and parents are more likely to support their children's ambitions. When Emily's teenage son Jason, who has Down syndrome, auditioned in New York for a small part in a TV series called "True Blue," Emily was surprised at the number of young men with Down syndrome who responded—many more than she had seen at similar auditions in years past. (Jason got the small role, which was to expand to a major role in the second season, but the series was canceled.)

Chris is confident there will be enough steady parts to keep him busy. But just in case, he has alternative plans. He wants to pursue a music career as a record producer, like his idol Quincy Jones. At the very least, Chris would like some sort of singing career, despite J.R.'s warnings that he, like many of the Burkes, is tone-deaf. That didn't stop him from recording three songs with Joe and John DeMasi, his friends from Anchor Program. One is a rap song called "Make Your Dreams Come True"; the others are soft love ballads titled "My Special One" and "My Forever Girl." In all three, he chants the chorus while the twins sing back up. Joe says Chris helped write the lyrics, then the three put the music together in a professional recording studio. "John and I felt, if Chris can be an actor, there's no reason why he can't have a record out. Now we just have to convince the record companies." One executive has already expressed an interest in the songs; they may be included with others in a "Life Goes On" soundtrack.

If his show business career wanes, and his singing career never materializes, Chris says he might return to school to take acting or music classes. But he is not at all interested in pursuing a college education. "Some people with Down syndrome go to college, and some don't," he says. "I don't have any desire to go." He also doesn't rule out working in a school again, though he says he enjoys his new career more than he did the ups and downs of his elevator operator job.

Tom Roeder says Chris would be welcome back at P.S. 138, though he doubts Chris would go back to his elevator job. "I don't think that elevator would have contained him for long, anyway. He is probably capable of taking on a position with more responsibility and judgment. But I don't think he'll ever give up on acting. But if there was a period of time in which he wasn't working as an actor, he would certainly find something where he was around children."

Chris, who misses working with children, has already thought of that. "I want to start a babysitting service, to make more money," he says. His experience with his nine nieces and nephews, he says, makes him a natural. "I love babies. I even like to change diapers," he says, then laughs. "Well, kind of. But babysitting is hard work. You cannot take your eyes off the child and you have to be very aware of the child. When they don't behave, I never spank them. I just send them to their room and let them learn their lesson."

J.R. thinks it's more likely that Chris would expand his role as an advocate for the handicapped, maybe in a salaried position doing community relations for a school or a company. After just two years on television, Chris is already more experienced at that type of work than most actors. He has starred in commercials for hiring the handicapped and against drug abuse ("I'm too smart for that," he says in one). Besides serving as a volunteer spokesman for the National Down Syndrome Congress and the National Down Syndrome Society, he is also the spokesman for First Down for Down Syndrome, a program through the Genetic Center of Scottsdale, Arizona, and is an experienced fundraiser for the three private schools he attended. And The McDonald's Corporation pays him a salary to serve as its first and only spokesman for the McJobs program. Pat Brophy, national special employment manager for McDonald's, says Chris is a role model for all children, whether or not they have disabilities. "Chris has been a real asset to us. Here is a young man who had a dream and made up his mind he was going to fulfill it. He didn't let anything stand in his way in order to do that.

"At McDonald's we have a saying: the power of believing is almost unbelievable. Chris has that same perspective. He'll do what he wants to do," says Pat. And though Chris is on a year-to-year contract with McDonald's, he might still hold the job after "Life Goes On" runs its course. "I don't know, but like Chris, I'm forever optimistic. I see his show going on and on for years. I'm sure that with Chris, no matter what happens, there will always be opportunities for him because people make their own opportunities."

Through the McJobs program, Chris preaches his favorite message: "Hire people with handicaps. Give us a chance to prove we can do a good job." Now, with the recent passage of the Americans with Disabilities Act, corporations will be required to heed this advice. Though the federal law doesn't specify Down syndrome, or even persons with mental disabilities, it prohibits employers from discriminating against anyone with disabilities, and it requires "reasonable accommodation" so that these people can fulfill jobs for which they are qualified.

McDonald's McJobs program, in place since 1981, has hired more than nine thousand people with various disabilities in thirty-two states. The corporation trains them for eight weeks, then holds a graduation ceremony with caps and gowns and, sometimes, class rings. The graduates are placed, usually in groups of four, in a McDonald's restaurant, with a job coach who supervises them one on one until they can work on their own. Then the coach moves on to another restaurant, coming back to check on them weekly. "If you put them in the right situation, they can be successful," says Pat Brophy. "They are some of our best employees. They're loyal, dedicated, and they really appreciate having the job." Eighty-seven percent of McJobs graduates stay on for at least one year. Their job stability is remarkable in the fast food industry, where overall employee turnover averages 140 percent within a year.

Futurists expect that employment for people with handicaps will increase dramatically in the decades ahead, as part-time and supported employment become more common. And the new generation of people with Down syndrome entering the work force will have the benefits of early intervention, mainstreaming in regular school classes, and specialized job-training programs. The generation Chris' age and older was not really expected to work; many were coddled in unchallenging special education classes or raised in institutions where job training was nonexistent. The majority of these older adults are unemployed, though many work in sheltered workshops, where they are paid 20 percent of minimum wage for simple manual labor. But the focus on employment is definitely moving away from the workshop to supported employment in the communities, or as advocates call it, "real jobs with real pay."

Fast food is not the only source of "real jobs" for people with Down syndrome. Other businesses hire people with Down syndrome to assemble bicycles and medical braces, computer equipment and electronics. They work in laundry rooms and kitchens of hotels, sort checks at bank branches, and tend to plants in nurseries. There are people with Down syndrome working as assistants in dental offices, and some who work as interoffice delivery or maintenance personnel. Many have found employment as teachers and assistants in day-care centers and nursery schools. A special school in Florida trains its higher-functioning students to help feed and care for its more severely affected students, then places them in jobs as aides in nursing homes.

The arts can be fertile ground for hobbies and, sometimes, employment for people with Down syndrome. One young man has proven himself as a professional artist, with paintings shown in California galleries. A Canadian woman weaves intricate tapestries that sell throughout North America. Another works as an understudy in a traveling puppet show. Some have shown talent in music, and several people with Down syndrome perform in a modern dance troupe that travels throughout the United States. A few youngsters are finding work as models in print ads, including ones for the Target department stores. McDonald's and Ivory soap have produced TV commercials starring people with Down syndrome. Recently a young man who had trouble finding steady acting work after appearing briefly in one movie put his knowledge of music to good use as a clerk in a music store.

Employment for people with Down syndrome means more than money: often it is their ticket to independence. Hundreds are now making the decision to live on their own away from their families, in group homes and supervised apartment settings where they are among their peers. The demand for such residences is so great that, in many cities, it has outstripped the supply of units available.

Chris' sister Ellen thinks such an arrangement would be ideal for Chris. "Right now, he's pretty content with my parents. But in the far-off future, I would like to see Chris in one of the apartment situations, where he's living independently but with supervision. I think that would be great for him, for my parents, and for all of us. As he continues to grow and mature, he'll come up with ideas on how he wants to live. Then it will be up to us to arrange it, so he can be as independent as possible. We would all welcome him," said Ellen. "He's definitely not a problem. But I don't think that's the best way to handle it. I would like to see him independent, but still close to us. He's a very independent type, and wants to do what he wants to do when he wants to do it."

Chris toyed with the idea of living on his own when he worked at P.S. 138. He wrote down, on his long list of goals, that he wanted his own apartment by age twenty-five. He planned to live in Peter Cooper Village in the same building as his parents. He also wanted to build a cabin on a vacant lot next to Anne's house, out in the countryside of Connecticut, where her family lived before moving to New Hampshire.

Now that Chris lives with his parents in California and depends on them for help in meeting the demands of his career, he says he's happy with the arrangement. "I like living with my parents," he says. "I like my family around me. That's important to me. I don't want to move now."

Marian thinks Chris would be lonesome living on his own. "He likes his privacy, but he likes to know someone's there, too. He likes having us close by, which makes us feel good. He likes to write his letters, watch movies, and play his music. Right now he's been writing songs. I don't ever worry about Chris making friends or finding things to do. He's always managed to do that. When he's home by himself, he keeps himself well occupied and he's very self-sufficient."

Marian says Chris could do well sharing a room with someone or living in a lightly supervised setting. "He can wash clothes and cook simple things. He's good at cleaning." Chris even surprises his parents by sneaking in and making their bed when they're in other parts of the apartment. Throughout his life, Chris has enjoyed pitching in and helping around the house. Stardom hasn't changed that. When he visits Anne and her family, he still works with her husband Tommy in the yard and cleaning out the garage, and he even takes on odd jobs for the neighbors. "He likes to be given things to do," says Anne. "He loves to feel like he is needed. He's still the same Chris as before."

Marian says Chris could fit into any one of their families. "They all have a very nice camaraderie. Naturally, that's our preference. We feel it's better to be with family. It would make us feel better if he were with any of them. I know that no matter who he went with, he'd be happy." Chris would probably choose to live with J.R., a decision that would go over big with Dewey, Michael, and Brendan, his three nephews. When Chris visits, the boys follow him around the house and cry when he leaves.

The talk of Chris' future is mostly centered on what would happen to him should Marian and Frank die or not be able to care for him anymore. The issue seems far away, since both Marian and Frank are just in their sixties and enjoy good health. For years, Marian and Frank tried to talk with Chris about what might happen when they die, but he always turned a deaf ear to them. "We want him to gradually face it. It hurts him very much when any of our friends or close relatives passes away," says Frank. Chris also grieved deeply a year ago, when one of his friends from school, just twenty-four years old, died from heart failure. "Every now and then we mention how we won't be here forever," says Frank. "He can't visualize it, but then again, neither can we."

Chris' lack of interest took a sudden turn late in the second season, when he studied the script where Corky meets Arthur, an older man with Down syndrome who is suddenly orphaned. "Corky walks in and Arthur's mother is dead and he can't wake her up," Chris says. "Arthur is very scared and doesn't know what to do. His family didn't want him to live on his own." Chris was also bothered by a scene where Corky wonders what will happen to him when Drew and Libby die. "It was very tough for me to do this episode. It bothered me a lot. I had this nightmare that something happened to my parents. They died. I went in their room and tried to wake them up and I couldn't get them to wake up. I don't know exactly how I was taking it. I was thinking, 'What would happen to me if I lost my parents?' I know that we'll all die someday.

We're in God's hands. But if it happens to my family, I don't know what Chris Burke would do.

"I do want to have my career on my own. But what would happen to my career? I wouldn't want to leave California because my career is here. I want my family around me. But they have their own families. J.R. and Betsy are happy in Philadelphia. They have a nice home, and I don't think they'd want to move here, away from their friends. Maybe another family would adopt me and I could be like a son or a big brother to them."

Chris mentioned his fears to some of his close friends in California, who told him he would be welcome to live with them if the need ever arose. And while Marian is not altogether comfortable with that thought, she is glad that Chris has made such strong friendships. These relationships, with coworkers from "Life Goes On" as well as with other actors he has met, are the basis for an active social life that does not always include his parents. Chris' newfound independence has taken some adjustment for them. "We used to joke about being the Three Musketeers, because we did everything together," says Marian. "We have always had so much fun together. Going out with Chris gives our lives that extra umph. But now, more and more, he is wanting to make plans on his own. This experience with the show has made him desire more independence. He wants friends on his own without Frank and I being around. He wants to make his own decisions about how he spends his leisure time. I feel that now, at twenty-five, he is going through this sort of rebellious stage that we usually associate with teenagers. I hope it doesn't cause any problems. We keep talking about it. He is aware that Frank and I are paramount in his life."

Chris frequently goes out to parties and dances, but because he cannot drive, he is still dependent on someone to chauffeur him. His parents have urged him to learn to drive for almost ten years, but he has always steadfastly refused. "I know he would be capable of learning to drive," says Marian. "We may not want him on the freeways out here—they're tough for anyone. But he is just not interested, and Chris has to be interested in something to pursue it."

Chris' lack of mobility hasn't stopped him from forging some casual romantic relationships. In the past year, he has dated a young actress who has guest-starred in some "Life Goes On" episodes, and another young woman with Down syndrome who lives close by. He also enjoys several platonic relationships with some young actresses he has met at the apartment complex. "I think I have more in common with women who are involved in show business, because they understand about the long hours," he says. "I'm really busy on my job, and that comes first. So it's not always easy."

His parents encourage him to date several women instead of having exclusive relationships. "We try to keep it at a low level," says Marian. "We think it's great he goes out, and we encourage him to see as many people as possible, because it's more fun. My feeling is that it will always just be dating. He enjoys being with people. He enjoys being with anybody and everybody, no matter what level of relationship. He truly has a good time, no matter whom he's with. So I don't think it will ever go beyond that. I think it would be difficult with him and anyone else if it got beyond just dating."

The question hangs in the air: will Chris every marry? Dozens of people have asked Marian and Frank about it, and they're never quite sure how to answer. Many adults with Down syndrome do fall in love and marry, though they are usually supervised in their homes by social workers and/or their families. And although the move toward independent living in group homes and apartments has increased the number of these marriages, the law is still hazy on the issue. There are still unresolved questions as to whether a person with Down syndrome is competent to enter into a marriage contract. And marriage is under the jurisdiction of state law, which can vary widely. Many states still have laws prohibiting marriages of people with mental disabilities, though they are often not enforced.

Legality aside, Marian and Frank have a number of concerns about marriage when it pertains to their youngest son. The issue was first raised several years ago, when one of Chris' girlfriends wanted to get engaged. At the time, Chris was not interested, but the Burkes realize that could change. "I don't think it's the ideal situation," says Marian. "People say, 'They can do so many other things; why can't they be married?' But no matter what, you're not going to remove that one thing, that level of responsibility you must have in order to be married. Marriage is not to be looked at lightly. We've explained that to Chris and talked to him about it."

Chris can have problems understanding priorities, which could cause trouble in a long-term relationship, says Frank. "Christopher can pretty much take care of himself, but I don't know if he could handle someone else as well. And we'd always be concerned that somebody would take advantage of both of them in just plain everyday things. Overall, a marriage might result in more unhappiness than happiness for Chris."

A marriage for Chris might add considerably to his parents' responsibilities, something they don't welcome now that they are retired. "It would probably wind up being, instead of us having just Chris, we would have Chris and somebody else to handle," says Marian. "There is so much that we give of ourselves to Chris, and to our children and grandchildren. I don't know if it would be that easy for us to take on someone else. I think it would wind up being a huge, tremendous responsibility for us if there was marriage in the offing. He gets so much joy from his nieces and nephews. I think you can substitute, and that this is what you should work toward, more than working toward normalizing that part of their life."

Chris agrees that his role as uncle is a fulfilling one. But he is intrigued at the thought of falling in love and having a wife. "I don't know what will happen," he says. "I think about it all the time. I feel like that Frank Sinatra song," he says, then starts singing, "Love and marriage go together . . ." He pauses for a serious moment, his brow furrowing. "I know that it used to be against the law. I don't want anyone to say things like 'These two shouldn't get married because they're handicapped.' People with Down syndrome can get married: I've met a couple out here who have Down syndrome and they got married. Someday, maybe I will get married, maybe I won't. Maybe I'll just stay with my career, because that means a lot to my happiness. Marriage might get in the way. To get married, I'd have to really, really love someone a whole lot.

"I think of it like in the movie *The Little Mermaid*. There are lots of mermaids in the sea! I want someone I will love and trust and cherish. And to me that is not just someone with Down syndrome or a disability."

Kaley Hummel thinks that eventually Chris will find someone he loves and want to get married. But she agrees that it will have to be an almost perfect relationship to take his heart away from his first love, acting. "Chris is more focused on entertainment and music than any person I've ever known. His passion is entertainment; he was born to be an entertainer. And his family comes first. Everything else in his life is secondary."

Chris' brother J.R. is also open to the possibility of a wife for Chris. "Yes, I see him at some point getting married, but living in a supervised setting. I think he would love that. He has said to me, 'Someday I'd like to be married.' He emulates what the rest of us have, and since we are all married, he thinks he should be, too. But the judgment would have to be made on the reality of the relationship."

His sisters disagree. "I can't see him married," says Ellen. "Chris just seems so content with the way things are going. He seems to like having a girlfriend, but marriage is a very different kind of relationship, and I'm not sure he realizes that. I think he would need some type of counseling. I just can't see that scenario working out. He seems to have so many interests to keep him going that I don't get the feeling he's yearning for a relationship like that at this point in time. I could be very wrong."

Anne also wonders if Chris could sustain a lifelong romantic commitment. "I know how difficult it is for normal people to get along and raise a family, and handle all the responsibilities. I'm not one of these advocates for retarded people getting married and having children. I just don't think it's meant to be."

Even if Chris does eventually marry, it is highly unlikely he will ever father a child. Scientific information is limited, but there is only one reported case of a man with Down syndrome having impregnated a woman.

In contrast, women with Down syndrome are usually fertile. Yet there have been fewer than one hundred cases in which females with Down syndrome have given birth (none of the fathers had Down syndrome), though this number will probably rise in the coming years because of intimate relationships that develop in group homes and apartments. One reason there have been so few births is that up until the past few decades, women with mental disabilities were routinely sterilized by parents and institutions. The surgery was required by law after a mandate by the U.S. Supreme Court in the 1920s. Today, the pendulum has swung in the opposite direction. Even if a mentally disabled woman wants to be sterilized, she often has to navigate a maze of red tape to show she is competent enough to make such a decision. Many hospitals and doctors refuse to perform the surgery, fearing lawsuits if the woman changes her mind and blames them for allowing it.

Children born to women with Down syndrome have about a fifty-fifty chance of having Down syndrome. But the whole issue of mentally disabled parents brings up another sticky tangle of legal questions that vary state by state, case by case. A few mothers are allowed to raise their children themselves, with close supervision by family and social workers. Others must immediately give up their children for adoption or placement in foster homes. Again, the legal trend is shifting. Now most courts place the burden on the state to prove that the mentally disabled parent is unfit to provide adequate care. And in some recent cases, women with Down syndrome have proven that they are fit to meet the responsibilities of parenthood.

This may surprise people who assume that any person with Down syndrome is mentally retarded. But in some cases, that assumption is not true. A few have average intelligence, and a handful have tested above one hundred, the average IQ for the general population. Most of these people have had the rare mosaic form of Down syndrome, in which the extra chromosome is found in only some of the person's body cells. But even trisomy 21, the form of Down syndrome Chris has, doesn't mean a clear case of retardation. Even if a person's test scores fall below seventy, "retardation" is a combination label that includes consideration of how well the person can adapt to his or her environment. Chris, for example, does not fit the criteria of many experts because he is socially adept.

But one aspect of intelligence is harder for people with Down syndrome: judgment. People with Down syndrome are often more trusting, and they may miss subtle cues that they are in danger. This lack of judgment can make them susceptible to sexual or physical abuse. Most schools and community programs now offer education to combat this, teaching appropriate physical boundaries and responses to situations in which abuse might occur.

Many of these issues are fairly new and will continue to increase in significance as the Down syndrome population moves into a greater role in regular public schools, in the work force, and in the community. Today there are about 250,000 people with Down syndrome living in the United States, with another 5,000 being born each year. Life span has increased dramatically in the past few decades: today, nearly 80 percent of adults with Down syndrome will reach age fifty-five, and some will live through their seventies.

Word travels slowly. When the Burkes set up an insurance policy for Chris with Lloyd's of London, the agents were surprised at his brief medical history. One man called to ask for more details because, he said, Chris had lived beyond his life expectancy. "You're living in the Dark Ages," retorted J.R. "People with Down syndrome always used to be institutionalized. If you had been put in an institution at birth, you'd probably be dead, too."

Now that people with Down syndrome are expected to outlive their parents, a whole new set of concerns crops up. There are extremely few geriatric facilities for people who are mentally retarded, and scientists have only recently discovered the differences that will require special care. People with Down syndrome have a greater risk of developing Alzheimer's-type dementia, personality changes, and memory loss, and the conditions sometimes appear as early as thirty years of age. The link between Alzheimer's and Down syndrome is not clear, but scientists are searching for clues on the twenty-first chromosome.

Leukemia is also more prevalent. One rare form of leukemia occurs four hundred times more often in children with Down syndrome than in the normal population.

The greatest medical complications occur before birth. Four out of five pregnancies involving Down syndrome are believed to end in miscarriage. Some scientists believe that as many as one in two hundred conceptions is of a fetus with some chromosomal defect, the majority of which are Down syndrome. About 15 percent of women who are pregnant will miscarry; more than 50 percent of those miscarriages are believed to be caused by Down syndrome or another chromosomal abnormality.

These medical complications remain a mystery, but they may hold the key to cures and treatments, not just for people with Down syndrome but for the entire population. Each person with Down syndrome inherits an individual set of genes on the extra twenty-first chromosome that may affect the degree of handicap they will have. Scientists are trying to find which specific genes cause the mental retardation and health problems associated with Down syndrome.

In recent years, with advances in molecular genetics technology, the study of chromosome 21 has intensified. In an international science effort, chromosome 21 is the first to be "mapped," a process that identifies each of more than one thousand genes present on the chromosome. Once the genes are mapped and their functions are better understood, scientists may be able to intercede, in utero during the pregnancy, with proteins that would inhibit the development of leukemia, Alzheimer's, and possibly even the mental retardation of Down syndrome. Some scientists have even introduced the genes into laboratory mice, producing Down syndrome–type conditions that will provide a model for testing treatments.

"Cures" of various sorts have been heralded throughout the history of Down syndrome, though none have stood the test of further research. What haven't been discounted are the results of early intervention. The stimulating programs start as early as two weeks after birth and can boost a range of physical and mental abilities. Older students are showing similar progress from the use of computers that bridge the gaps in their communications and learning processes. Even toddlers work with special computer "tutors"; sometimes they can communicate via keyboard even before they begin to talk. Integration in public school classes has also helped many young students with Down syndrome reach aptitudes beyond what special education had offered.

This is clearly an era of great hope for people with Down syndrome. With the new treatments and medical discoveries on the horizon, combined with the lessening of stigma in society and the recognition of legal and educational rights, the generation of children born with Down syndrome today have a brighter future than ever before. No one knows what achievements they will be able to reach.

Yet the long-term future of Down syndrome in our society is hard to predict. Some experts think that the numbers of babies born with Down syndrome will increase, since more women now delay childbearing till later years. Others expect a huge decline in the numbers of babies born with Down syndrome, due to new pregnancy screening. Today, the vast majority of pregnant women over thirty-five, fearful of giving birth to a baby with Down syndrome or other genetic disorders, will undergo amniocentesis or chorionic villus sampling, both of which can induce miscarriage in about 1 percent of those tested. Doctors don't recommend these tests for women under thirty-five years of age, because the risk of testing is greater than the risk of Down syndrome. Yet 80 percent of babies with Down syndrome are born to women younger than thirty-five, because of higher overall birth rates. This may change with the widespread use of new screening procedures developed in recent years that carry no risk of miscarriage. One is alpha-fetoprotein (AFP), which can assess the risk for Down syndrome by measuring levels of hormones in a sample of the mother's blood. California law now requires doctors to offer AFP to all pregnant women, to check for a variety of prenatal conditions. But there is also advanced ultrasound, which has been used to detect Down syndrome by measuring the length of the fetus' leg bones.

According to *The New York Times,* the majority of pregnant women faced with a diagnosis for Down syndrome will choose to abort. There are no true statistics for the numbers who make this private decision, but several studies estimate that the newer, widespread testing will reduce Down syndrome births by 60 to 90 percent. So instead of about five thousand babies born with Down syndrome in the United States each year, there would be five hundred to two thousand.

In many cases, the pregnant women have access to genetic counselors and parents' groups who can give them a better picture of the situation they might face. But most only talk with their obstetrician or family physician, who might see only one or two cases of Down syndrome in an entire career. Sometimes the picture they paint is not much different from what Marian Burke heard from her doctor when Chris was born: that the baby will be severely retarded, possibly never walking or talking, and fraught with medical problems.

In the late 1970s, the choice was not always allowed; a few clinics that offered amnio required that any woman with a positive test for major genetic disorders have an abortion. Several doctors even advocated state-mandated amniocentesis for all women over thirty-five, followed by free abortions for those testing positive. One doctor justified such a program by comparing its estimated $63 million expense to the costs of full-time residential care for the "defective offspring," which he thought would be more than $2 billion.

That debate has faded in the light of medical advances and better understanding of the potential of people with Down syndrome. Only a small fraction will be severely retarded, and fewer than 10 percent born today will be placed in institutions. And another choice has surfaced for women who have babies with Down syndrome but don't feel that they can care for them. Several adoption agencies now specialize in placing babies with disabilities; some even have waiting lists for people seeking to adopt babies with Down syndrome.

Amnio was not yet available when Marian was pregnant with Chris, and she says she is glad she never had to face such a decision. "No matter when you hear the diagnosis, it is devastating. There is no easy answer for people facing this issue. I wouldn't dare tell someone what they have to do, except that if they have this child, to give them every opportunity to develop. I can say, it's not all that bad. They do bring you a lot of joy. And with all the education and treatment available now, it's not going to be as hard for these kids, or for their parents, as it has been in the past. I was never thrilled that Chris had Down syndrome. I always wanted only the best for my children. I always wished he was normal. We just made the best of it. I cannot imagine not having been given the challenge of Chris, and now being able to feel the pride that I do. I can't imagine life without Chris. He has added so much to our lives; I have a much, much richer life because of him. It is sad to think that because people have a choice, they may not make the right decision."

The controversy doesn't always end when a baby with Down syn-drome is born. Up until recent years, at hospitals all over the United

States, medical treatment was routinely withheld from babies with handicaps when they were born with additional medical complications. An early death was considered preferable by parents and doctors who thought the baby would never enjoy any discernible quality of life. For example, Yale-New Haven Hospital reported forty-three deaths of infants with Down syndrome, spina bifida, and other disorders due to medical nontreatment from 1970 to 1972.

Then in 1979, the case of Phillip Becker, a twelve-year-old with Down syndrome, galvanized opposition to medical nontreatment. Phillip had a life-threatening heart condition that surgery could correct. But his parents, who had placed Phillip in an institution, refused to permit the operation, citing the futility of extending a life "devoid of those qualities which give it human dignity." When a California juvenile agency sought a court order for the operation over the parents' objections, the California courts and the U.S. Supreme Court all upheld the parents' decision. But a coalition of advocacy groups pursued the issue, and in 1981, a couple who had volunteered in Phillip's institution was granted custody and authorized his surgery.

Then in 1982, Baby Doe, a boy with Down syndrome, was born with an incomplete esophagus that kept him from absorbing any nutrition. The parents decided not to allow a simple operation that would have corrected the condition. Several organizations intervened, taking the parents to court to either force them into allowing the surgery or relinquishing their custody to someone who would. Hundreds of people offered to adopt Baby Doe and pay for the surgery, but the Indiana Supreme Court ruled in favor of the parents. After several days, the boy starved to death, unable to absorb any nutrition. His parents had not even allowed intravenous feeding.

A 1983 national poll found that 43 percent sided with the parents' decision, while 40 percent did not. Columnist George Will condemned the court decision, writing, "There is no reason to doubt that if the baby had not had Down's syndrome the operation would have been ordered without hesitation by the parents or, if not by them, the courts. Therefore the baby was killed because he was retarded."

The controversy raged for the next several years. On one side were the associations such as the National Down Syndrome Congress. They were aided by President Reagan, who asked the Department of Health and Human Services to enforce treatment for all newborns. But medical and hospital associations fought Reagan's new regulations, and the U.S. Supreme Court agreed with them, striking down the new rules. Then Congress jumped into the fray, strengthening child abuse laws with measures to protect children with disabilities and requiring states to develop safeguards for their care. So now, each state determines when it will intervene in what is considered a private doctor-patient relationship.

Most hospitals now have ethics committees that review infant care cases, sometimes with input from parents of children with Down syndrome and other disabilities. In general, treatment is withheld only when the baby suffers a terminal, inoperable condition. But medical nontreatment of babies and children with Down syndrome—still common in nations around the world—may not have been stopped altogether in the United States. In 1989, the U.S. Commission on Civil Rights reported that infants born with disabilities and additional medical complications continued to be denied adequate medical treatment. Even today, there may be dozens of other Baby Does around the nation, who are left to die quietly, without medical treatment or publicity about their plight.

At the core of each situation is the question "What kind of quality of life can a person with Down syndrome enjoy?" Following Baby Doe's death, the lawyer for the parents praised his clients for their courage in letting their child die. "There would have been horrific trauma," he said. "Trauma to the child who would never have enjoyed a quality of life of any sort, trauma to the family, trauma to society."

Not every child with Down syndrome will grow up to be as bright and as capable as Chris Burke. It's safe to say that few will ever star on a television series or earn a million dollars in their lifetimes. But Frank and Marian wonder how anyone in this day and age could not see the value in the life of people who, like Chris, are born with an extra chromosome. "When a baby is born, there is no guarantee for anyone that he or she will have a happy and productive life," says Frank. "But many, many persons with Down syndrome have very full lives, much more so than such a large proportion of our society, especially the victims of drug abuse and the whole array of social ills. Chris far exceeded what we ever thought he would be capable of doing. Look at what he's accomplished. You get out of life what you put into it. And he has put in so much more than most people."

Marian thinks back to the days after Chris was born, when she met a woman in the hospital whose son was in a coma. He had been in a severe motorcycle accident as a result of drug abuse. "That boy was born a perfectly normal child, but he grew up to give such heartache. I was heartbroken then, about Chris, but Chris grew up to give us so much

246 · *Chris Burke and Jo Beth McDaniel*

joy. He has never done anything that would hurt us, or make us ashamed."

J.R. agrees. "Chris has never been a problem. You have heartaches with any child, whether they're handicapped or not. I don't think we've had any more heartaches in our family with Chris than we could've had, had he not had Down syndrome. Our situation may be an exception, but I strongly believe that the only thing we did differently with Chris as a family is that we didn't treat him differently. He was just a regular member of our family. We never put limitations on him, and we never listened to those people who wanted to put limitations on him. That's made a big difference in maximizing his potential. I get so mad at people who tell me that Chris is highly unusual. We know numerous, numerous people with Down syndrome who are every bit as capable and have as much potential as Chris, and are realizing their potential—just not as visibly as Chris."

Marian agrees that Chris is in some ways an exception. "We feel Chris is outstanding. I realize that many other children will never reach the heights he has. But they all have something in them that is worthwhile. They just have to find that something. People think they have no ups and downs, or interesting things that happen in their lives. But Chris has always had a very full and interesting life, even before he got this job. He is a sensitive and caring person, with a lot of love for the world. He is a perfect joy."

Chris does not understand why anyone would think he is less of a person just because he has Down syndrome. "I have a wonderful life," he says. "I have a great family. I have a great career. I have great friends." And though he has far surpassed the expectations anyone ever had for a person with Down syndrome, he is only twenty-six years old, with plenty of hopes and dreams left to fulfill. "I think I have a great future," he says. "I have big plans and lots more things I want to do. I want all my dreams to come true."

★ ★ ★ ★ ★ ★ ★ ★ ★ ★ ★ ★ ★

MY MOTHER always calls me her angel. I love when she says that. "Chris is my angel." It sounds nice and makes me feel great. Sometimes I'm really her devil! No, I'm just joking. I know I'll always be her angel because I love her and she loves me and she's loved me since I was a little baby. I'll always be my mom's special one and that means a lot to me. I'm writing a very nice Mother's Day song for her right now and I think she'll like it.

I'd like to say to my parents, "You are the best parents in the world. You amaze me. You taught me so much through the years and gave me love and support. I've learned so much from you. If it wasn't for you two, I wouldn't be Chris Burke. I wouldn't be the same person at all. I wouldn't be on television. You taught me the true meaning of life, which is thinking of others, taking care of yourself, and being happy. I owe everything to you." They went through so much when I was born. Now I just want to work and take care of them, just like they have taken care of me my whole life. And I'm going to take care of myself.

My brother J.R. and sisters Ellen and Anne are the greatest, too, because they have loved me and supported me and treated me just like a brother, and not just like someone who has Down syndrome. They taught me to not give up, to keep trying. My brother gave me a picture frame. It says, "Obstacles are what you see when you take your eyes off the goal." I've learned from my family to never take my eyes off the goal. I hate the word "can't." "Can't" is like a disease that keeps you from doing things. I have an extra chromosome, but I can do lots of things. I'm happy for myself. I've had my dreams come true, and that's what's important.

So many great things have happened because I'm on "Life Goes On." They named a school after me in New York! The Christopher Burke School! I was so honored, I was speechless. I didn't expect it at all. I went to visit the school and met all the students, and I danced with them and helped teach them. It was really great. I knew some of the students because they went to the school where I used to work, P.S. 138. They have a big bulletin board with pictures of me from the show put up everywhere. They gave me presents and flowers and I said to them, "I feel like Sylvester Stallone's character Rocky when the people of Philadelphia made a statue that honored Rocky, and he didn't know what to say. I don't know what to say." It's great that the school is for handicapped students because I always wanted to work with children who have handicaps, so it was a really big honor to be able to work for them. They are an inspiration to me. The principal said I was an inspiration to them. I think I am.

Then there's another big honor. This woman named her little boy after me, Chris Burke. I'm glad she didn't name him Paul Newman or Tom Cruise! She adopted him and she also adopted two other little boys, and they all have Down syndrome. That makes me so proud, I don't know what to say. It makes me feel like a hero. I'd love to meet little Chris Burke someday. I just hope all his dreams come true.

Maybe me being on the show might help little Chris when he grows up. I can be his role model. Maybe people will see what I can do and they'll look at his abilities and not his disabilities.

And that is the best thing about "Life Goes On" to me. I think that I am helping thousands of people all over the country to have better lives. That makes me very, very excited. I want to keep doing that the rest of my life, even if I am not acting. Everyone needs to know that we are people, too. We have dreams and hopes and ambitions. We laugh and have fun, and we can be serious and do a good job. We can do lots of things if people give us the chance. And the show has opened doors for lots of families who have a son or daughter with Down syndrome or other disabilities. It gives them hope in their private lives, and lets them know that life must go on.

READERS who would like more information on Down syndrome may contact the following organizations:

The National Down Syndrome Society
666 Broadway
New York, NY 10012
1-800-221-4602

The National Down Syndrome Congress
1800 Dempster St.
Park Ridge, IL 60068-1146
1-800-232-6372

Association for Retarded Citizens
P.O. Box 1047
Arlington, TX 76004
817-261-6003